The Language Poets Use

WINIFRED NOWOTTNY

The Language Poets Use

THE ATHLONE PRESS
London & Atlantic Highlands

Published by
The Athlone Press Ltd,
1 Park Drive,
London NW11 7SG
and
165 First Avenue,
Atlantic Highlands, NJ 07716

First edition 1962
Second impression with corrections 1965
Fifth impression 1975
Reprinted 1981, 1984, 1991

0 485 12009 7

Reprinted and bound in Great Britain by
Short Run Press Ltd, Exeter

TO MY MOTHER

AND THE MEMORY OF

MY FATHER

Preface

THE matter of this book first took shape in a course of inter-collegiate lectures to students of English in the University of London. Presentation in print demanded the recasting of passages too obviously designed to meet the needs of oral delivery, and the alteration of divisions of the matter originally determined more by the ticking of the lecture-room clock than by any real fissure between topics. In attempting to remove some features, tolerable in a lecture, from which the reader of the printed word might well be expected to recoil, I hoped not to have to do anything which might obscure the simplicity of my original purpose, which was to draw attention to the operation and interaction, in poetry, of various forms of meaning-fulness, ranging from the neglected obvious to forms whose complexity makes it difficult to find terms and methods with which to bring them within the scope of critical commentary. But I found that it is hardly possible to recast lectures into a printable form without succumbing to the urge to reconsider and rewrite, especially in passages where a reader would expect to find an argument closer than the lecture-room permits. I have tried however to keep to the principle which first determined the order in which topics were to be treated: that is, in an ascending order of difficulty of formulation. If in some places the examples chosen to illustrate theoretical points seem to be hand-picked for the purpose of special pleading, I hope this may find some justification in their fitness for the purpose of making one particular aspect of a large issue particularly clear. And since the strategy of the lectures was to burrow my way into an organic whole, it will (I hope) be found that though in the earlier stages there are passages of apparent indifference to the real structure of a problem, these will find some redress later on, when what was blandly passed off without comment recurs as a bitter brew of multiple problems interrelated.

The book begins with a rapid review of the workings in poetry of staple components of language and it attempts to suggest something of the diversity of the interaction between the corporeality of words (as systematized in poems) and the meanings they bear. The second chapter tries to dismantle the hurdle of 'poetic diction' by arguing that we cannot, in speaking of poetry, use 'language' and 'vocabulary' as interchangeable terms; attempts to interchange them are more manifestly unsuccessful in commenting on poetic language than in commenting on the non-poetic, because poets are at liberty to select from and to re-make the various stereotypes of the common tongue and to manipulate the context of their occurrence so as to alter their implications and effect. In devising the original course of lectures I soon realized that my task was turning out to be not so much one of systematization as of dodging, shouldering aside or poking through those obstacles which some critical pre-occupations interpose between the student and the poem (as well as those other obstacles interposed between the critic and his audience by 'common-sense' versions of the nature of any linguistic system of meaning), and if the greatest of all these obstacles is the notion of a 'poetic diction' differing primarily in its vocabulary from the usages of ordinary life, the next in order of obfuscating power is preoccupation with metaphor; accordingly, the next chapter [III] starts from a position as far removed as possible from veneration of metaphor as the major repository of poetic power and vision; it examines in a deliberately cold-blooded way the linguistic mechanisms of some common forms of comparison, arguing that these mechan-isms are of evident technical importance to the poet because they vastly extend the vocabulary at his disposal for treating any given subject. The main aim of Chapter III is to show reason for regard-ing metaphor as being at least as much a solution of certain general problems of vocabulary as it is the oracular mouth of the poet passing judgment on the nature of reality, but it may prove that this chapter gives back with one hand what it takes away with the other, by stressing the complexity of even the commonest figures of speech. In the fourth chapter the complexity of metaphor receives further discussion, in relation to the concept of the 'structure' of a poem. The fifth chapter, pursuing the topic of the concealed complexities which may inhere in structures using a 'simple' vocabulary, dis-cusses the operation, in a poem as a whole, of structuring at levels not overtly determining the diction; that is, at the level of metrics, stanzaic form, lineation and the like. In the sixth chapter the concept of a structure of meanings is discussed in connexion with poetry whose diction is overtly stylized into verbal patterns and it is argued that these, so far from being necessarily merely decorative, mannered, or superficial, can contribute decisively to the idiosyncrasy of poetic structures of meaning. In Chapter VII the question of 'ambiguity' (skirted in preceding chapters) is brought into the open and an attempt is made to relate the humdrum ambiguities of language at large to the execution of some poetic purposes. Chapter VIII suggests that some of the considerations put forward in Chapter VII may be useful when we are dealing with poems whose originality, embodied in ways for which it has become customary to use the word 'symbolism', sets them at such a remove from the language of common life that is has sometimes been questioned whether there may not be some peculiar discontinuity between that language and theirs, and whether methods of interpretation applicable to poems less 'obscure' have to be abandoned when we deal with these. If in hurling myself against the bastions of symbolism and obscurity I have, after all, made no appreciable dents in them, I shall be content if I have in the process at least made a few dents in the 'common-sense' objections to such uses of language, and a few dents too in the emplacements of those critics who treat 'symbolism' as a means of levitating out of the sphere of language and transcending linguistic forms of meaning. For this chapter particularly, but also for the book as a whole, the only defence of theories gone astray must be—to use the words of I. A. Richards—that 'in this subject it is better to make a mistake that can be exposed than to do nothing, better to have any account . . . than to have none'.[1]

For all that has gone astray the responsibility is mine. I am indebted to Professor Geoffrey Tillotson, Professor James R. Sutherland and Professor A. H. Smith for their encouragement and forwarding of the project of bringing out the book, and to many friends in the English department and other departments of University College, London, for information, suggestions and advice. To Mr D. G. Mowatt and Dr B. A. Rowley, who read the manuscript and made illuminating criticisms of the tenor and presentation of the argument, my debt is particularly great, and I must also thank my husband for sustained help in this as in all my work.

While I was writing the book, the kindness of Biddy, John and Gio Fiori was an inexhaustible resource.

University College London   W.N.

[1] I. A. Richards, *The Philosophy of Rhetoric*, Mary Flexner Lectures on the Humanities, III (New York, 1936), p. 115.

Acknowledgements

THE author and publishers make grateful acknowledgements to the undermentioned for permission to quote from copyright material as specified here and in detail in the relevant footnotes:

Faber & Faber Ltd and Random House Inc: *Collected Shorter Poems, 1930–1944* by W. H. Auden

Faber & Faber Ltd and Harcourt, Brace & World Inc: *Selected Poems, 1923–1958* by E. E. Cummings

Faber & Faber Ltd and Harcourt, Brace & World Inc: *Collected Poems, 1909–1935* and *Four Quartets* by T. S. Eliot

Faber & Faber Ltd and The Macmillan Company: *Collected Poems* by Marianne Moore

Jonathan Cape Ltd and Harcourt, Brace & World Inc: *A Map of Verona* by Henry Reed

Faber & Faber Ltd and Alfred A. Knopf Inc: *Collected Poems* by Wallace Stevens

J. M. Dent & Sons Ltd and New Directions: *Collected Poems, 1934–1952* by Dylan Thomas

New Directions: *Collected Earlier Poems* by William Carlos Williams

Macmillan & Co, Ltd and The Macmillan Company: *Collected Poems* by W. B. Yeats parakettes

Contents

A Note on References

IN quotations from Shakespeare's works the text used is, for convenience of reference, that of the *Globe* edition. In the apparatus of documentation, data of publication and distribution are generalized under the first place named in the imprint.

I

Elements of Poetic Language

IN considering the language of poetry it is prudent to begin with what is 'there' in the poem—'there' in the sense that it can be described and referred to as unarguably given by the words. For, as R. A. Sayce remarks,

The critic's first and most important task must be to discover, as far as he is able, the objective characteristics of the work under consideration. Even if he does no more than this he will have put the reader in a position to see for himself the merits and defects of the work.[1]

This kind of approach is much practised by modern French critics, whose principles and methods are described in a useful summary by H. A. Hatzfeld:

The best means of recognizing the art of a literary work, according to a generally accepted method in France, is the so-called *explication de texte*. . . . The books with this title explain a given text by means of a close analysis of its lexicological and syntactical features, including the so-called figures of speech and rhythmical elements . . . . they try to transpose the artistic procedures found in the text to a theoretical, communicable, analytical, quasi-grammatical language of the critic. . . . If they probe deeply enough and proceed systematically, preferably on a comparative basis, they cannot fail to reach the goal of a kind of objective criticism.[2]

One may, indeed, wonder how far a goal so methodically arrived at will correspond to the artist's real score; Hatzfeld himself points out elsewhere that after such analyses have been carried out there still remains the further problem of how to deal with what he calls 'the symbolic meaning, overtones and subconscious elements which are so important in poetry'.[3] But the value of examining objective

[1] R. A. Sayce, *Style in French Prose: A Method of Analysis* (Oxford, 1953), p. 126.

[2] Helmut A. Hatzfeld, *A Critical Bibliography of the New Stylistics Applied to the Romance Literatures, 1900–1952*, University of North Carolina Studies in Comparative Literature, No. 5 (Chapel Hill, 1953), p. 1.

[3] Helmut [A.] Hatzfeld, 'Methods of Stylistic Investigation', in *Literature and Science*, International Federation for Modern Languages and Literatures, Proceedings of the Sixth Triennial Congress, Oxford, 1954 (Oxford, 1955), p. 46.

characteristics carefully, before talking at large about the imaginative constructs reared on the foundation of words, is that this results, at least, in a recognition of the part played by the corporeality of words, and by the structures which connect them, not only in determining lesser poetic effects but also in directing the larger mental and imaginative processes activated by the poem; it may well lead, further, to a recognition of the fact that the various elements of poetic language interpenetrate one another with an intimacy which is of first importance in any consideration of how poetry 'works'.

Some poets, in weighing words, are consciously as vigilant of the effects which may be produced by use of their corporeal characteristics as they are of their conceptual meanings. Valéry for instance thinks of the poet's scrutiny of words as one which focuses first on such things as gender, syllabic structure, sound values and metrical possibilities—and, after these, on their meaning and tone:

> Je cherche un mot (*dit le poète*) un mot qui soit:
> féminin,
> de deux syllabes,
> contenant P ou F,
> terminé par une muette,
> et synonyme de brisure, désagrégation;
> et pas savant, pas rare.
> Six conditions—au moins![1]

Valéry's archetypal poet, looking for one word which has to satisfy at least six conditions, may suggest an approach to the problem of defining the criteria by which we classify a work as a 'literary' work. A contemporary critic declares that 'we have no real standards to distinguish a verbal structure that is literary from one that is not'.[2] A criterion we might provisionally adopt is this: that a verbal structure is literary if it presents its topic at more than one level of presentation at the same time—or, alternatively, if one and the same utterance has more than one function in the structure of meaning in which it occurs.

A simple instance is the presentation of an object not only through

[1] Paul Valéry, *Autres Rhumbs* (Paris, 1934), pp. 143–4.
[2] Northrop Frye, *Anatomy of Criticism* (Princeton, N.J., 1957), p. 13.

the meanings of the words which deal with it but also through their sound, as when Pope, in his translation of a passage of the *Iliad* describing chariots racketing down a hillside, tries to put Homer's description into English words that shall not only correspond in meaning to the meaning of Homer's words but shall also repeat, in a different metrical structure and in the sound-system of English, the marked onomatopoeia of the original:

> First march the heavy Mules, securely slow,
> O'er Hills, o'er Dales, o'er Crags, o'er Rocks, they go
> (XXIII, 138–9)

and having thus represented the steady plod of the mules by a steadily-repeated grammatical construction, Pope goes on to represent by a metrical dislocation the jolting of the chariots (an effect heightened by its contrast with the plod of the previous line):

> Jumping high o'er the Shrubs of the rough Ground,
> Rattle the clatt'ring Cars, and the shockt Axles bound.
> (ll. 140–1)

(In the second of these lines the clutter of consonants serves to represent the noise which goes with the jolts.) A few lines later, translating the passage describing trees crashing down, he hurls the adverb into the first foot of line 146 to represent the force with which, in line 145, 'the Forest hurles her Oaks':

> Loud sounds the Axe, redoubling Strokes on Strokes;
> On all sides round the Forest hurles her Oaks
> Headlong. Deep-echoing groan the Thickets brown;
> Then rustling, crackling, crashing, thunder down.
> (ll. 144–7)

Knight, citing this passage as one of the best examples of Pope's interest in 'style of sound', remarks that 'the precise way in which something is done has the most important kind of effect on what it is that is ultimately done'.[1]

What is ultimately done here may, from one point of view, be said to rank no higher than mimicry, or rather a succession of mimicries

[1] Douglas Knight, *Pope and the Heroic Tradition: A Critical Study of His 'Iliad'*, Yale Studies in English, 117 (New Haven, 1951), p. 18.

of successively-stated attributes of the scene the poet is describing Though it is true that the corporeality of words is used here to give the conceptual senses of the words a renewed contact with perceptual experience, yet, none the less, if the mimicries were removed (as some at least could be by rearranging the same words into an order not significant in relation to metrics and lineation) the conceptual meaning of the statement would survive unimpaired. This chapter is not the place to discuss the relevance and adequacy of this view but it is the place to point out that no simplistic view of a 'style of sound' is possible, for several reasons. One is that the systems capable of mimicry are themselves various (as Pope's lines clearly show) and we might find, if we set about relating the variety of mimicking systems to the variety of attributes it is possible to mimic, that the interest of the diverse kinds of relation between the mimicking and the mimicked might vary enormously from one case to another, even if only in respect of the distance between the medium and what it mediates. The phrase 'Rattle the clatt'ring Cars', where consonantclutter stands for car-clatter, might well raise issues different from those involved in considering, say, the opening lines of Tennyson's *Œnone*:

> There lies a vale in Ida, lovelier
> Than all the valleys of Ionian hills.

The word 'lovelier' has an equivalent, more distant than sound for sound, in the sinuosity of the lines; moreover, the equivalence is more complex than a simple one-for-one relation, for it is clear that the 'music' of consonants and vowels is not easily extricable from the teasing relation in sense between 'a vale' and 'all the valleys'. Another reason why we cannot dismiss even a mere mimicry as trivial or freakish is this: as soon as we ask why the consonants in Pope's line are construed as clattering, we encounter theoretical problems as yet uninvestigated and too formidable to permit of easy verdicts on any instance in which they are involved. A third reason for suspending judgment on the status of effects such as these is that it is not easy to say where mimicry ends and other purposes take over. Pope's lines show how corporeality can be ordered so as to permit some representation of the perceptual quality appropriate to the concepts involved in the sense of the line at statement-level. But corporeality may be ordered in what looks like the reverse direction: that is, so as to focus attention on the most important conceptual relations involved in a statement. Features of sound and spelling can emphasize meaning, as when Shakespeare, remarking in *Henry V* (IV, ii, 43) that the exhausted and ill-equipped army on the eve of Agincourt is a travesty of the well-found army that set out, writes,

> Big Mars seems bankrupt in their beggar'd host

—calling in alliteration's aid and that of a sound-change through the alliterating words to make emphasis fall on the contrast between 'Big' and 'beggar'd', a contrast which adds to the impact and meaning of 'bankrupt'. One relation of sound-effect and meaning has been briefly but clearly characterized by Empson: 'I think myself its most important mode of action is to connect two words by similarity of sound so that you are made to think of their possible connections'.[1] '*Made* to think' describes what happens in the case of this alliterative line of Shakespeare's. The sound-effect focuses attention on the meaningful connection of 'Big' with 'bankrupt' and 'beggar'd', and makes the reader or hearer apprehend them in a grouping whose intellectual point cannot, therefore, be missed; the line 'reads itself' because a certain area of it is spotlighted. In such a case sound is a device of persuasion; the sound of the words and the meaning of the words are inseparable critical issues. On looking more closely still one sees the involvement of the prosody with the alliteration (and so with the emphatic meaning): all three alliterating words are stressed and the first of them is doubly emphatic by virtue of the fact that the strong stress on it is irregular. Normal speech patterns determine the stress 'Bíg Márs', which checks the regular flow of the blank verse pattern, making 'Big' stand out.

In this example, effects at lower levels are used to reinforce the usual meanings of words. But reinforcement of meaning is not the only possibility open to the poet in his patterning of the corporeal form of words. He may use it as a source of sustained ironic com-

[1] William Empson, *Seven Types of Ambiguity*, 2nd edn. (London, 1947), p. 12.

5

mentary, as in Berowne's speech on Dan Cupid in *Love's Labour's Lost* (III, i, 176–90):

> And I, forsooth, in love! I, that have been love's whip;
> A very beadle to a humorous sigh;
> A critic, nay, a night-watch constable;
> A domineering pedant o'er the boy;
> Than whom no mortal so magnificent!
> This whimpled, whining, purblind, wayward boy;
> This senior-junior, giant-dwarf, Dan Cupid;
> Regent of love-rhymes, lord of folded arms,
> The anointed sovereign of sighs and groans,
> Liege of all loiterers and malcontents,
> Dread prince of plackets, king of codpieces,
> Sole imperator and great general
> Of trotting paritors:—O my little heart!—
> And I to be a corporal of his field,
> And wear his colours like a tumbler's hoop!

Here, while the words describe Cupid as being both powerful and petty, the pattern of alliteration 'says' in addition, or more precisely, that love is *as* powerful *as* it is ridiculous; this is said by making each term of power link alliteratively with a term of ridicule: 'Regent of . . . rhymes', 'sovereign of sighs', 'Liege of . . . loiterers', 'prince of plackets', 'king of codpieces'. To be more exact, this is said not only by alliteration but also by the assonance in 'imperator'/ 'paritors' and by the oxymoron in 'senior-junior'[1] and in 'giant-dwarf'; all these devices are pressed into service in order to sustain throughout the description of Cupid a diction that allows no compliment to exist except in strict relation to a contrary term of detraction. The function of the devices is to make the relation between the contrary terms strike our attention as forcibly as possible.

It would seem that there may well be a sliding scale of relations between ordered corporeality on the one hand and meaning at statement-level on the other, and though the construction of such a

[1] The *Globe*'s 'senior-junior' is an emendation; the early texts have 'signior *Iunios*'. Richard David, pointing out in his *Arden* edition (1951) that there is a pun on *senior/ signor*, cites passages in support of his decision that, since the editor's choice of either word must necessarily leave the other element of the pun unrepresented, *signor* is the better choice.

scale and the determination of the place upon it of any particular poetic effect would be a formidable task, a criticism indifferent to the whole problem must labour under heavy disabilities. The critic commenting on the way something has been done must carefully consider, before he condemns the manner, the exact nature of the matter in the poet's hands; otherwise he may fall into the error of condemning those very features most intimately related to the poet's intention, as when Leigh Hunt criticized Pope's versification on the score of its alleged monotony in the placing of the caesura and (perhaps at a loss for examples?) gave prominence in his indictment to the following passage from *The Rape of the Lock* (ii, 1–18):

> Not with more Glories, in th'Etherial Plain,
> The Sun first rises o'er the purpled Main,
> Than issuing forth, the Rival of his Beams
> Lanch'd on the Bosom of the Silver *Thames*.
> Fair Nymphs, and well-drest Youths around her shone,
> But ev'ry Eye was fix'd on her alone.
> On her white Breast a sparkling *Cross* she wore,
> Which *Jews* might kiss, and Infidels adore.
> Her lively Looks a sprightly Mind disclose,
> Quick as her Eyes, and as unfix'd as those:
> Favours to none, to all she Smiles extends,
> Oft she rejects, but never once offends.
> Bright as the Sun, her Eyes the Gazers strike,
> And, like the Sun, they shine on all alike.
> Yet graceful Ease, and Sweetness void of Pride,
> Might hide her Faults, if *Belles* had Faults to hide:
> If to her share some Female Errors fall,
> Look on her Face, and you'll forget 'em all.

He complains:

Out of eighteen lines, we have no less than *thirteen* in *succession* which pause at the fourth syllable,—to say nothing of the four *ies* and the six *os* which fall together in the rhymes; and . . . the ear has an additional monotony humming about it,—

> Quick as her eyes,
> Favours to none,
> 'Oft she rejects,
> Bright as the sun

7

and he sums up his case against Pope's versification with the words, 'this kind of sing-song'.[1] The sing-song effect (if this is indeed a proper description of the effect of having a marked pause after the fourth syllable of the line in each successive line) is confined to the group of lines beginning with 'On her white Breast . . .' and ending at '. . . you'll forget 'em all'; the six lines which in Hunt's quotation precede these, do not in fact show the same feature, and after '. . . you'll forget 'em all' the placing of the pause is again varied. It is, certainly, striking to find a solid block of lines displaying no variation in the placing of the caesura; more striking that these lines constitute one unit (the description of Belinda's person and demeanour), before and after which there is no comparable monotony of caesura: more striking still that this unit displays 'an additional monotony', the inversion in four contiguous lines of the first foot of the line. It would almost seem that the poet had gone out of his way to be repetitious in his versification, and it is possible to see in the nature of his subject-matter a good reason why he should have done so, for the sense itself invites us to infer that beneath the outward animation of Belinda's looks there lies a level imperviousness, the even-handed indifference of the enthroned beauty to her rout of admirers; the critic may then conclude that the monotonies of this passage (in diction so animated) are contrived, and are intended to be a metrical equivalent to Belinda's indifference. If this seems a speculation too generous to Pope, we must at least admit that he himself devises as the climax of this ironically animated passage a line which explicitly says that, glorious as Belinda is, her condescension is perhaps as meaningless as it is universal:

> [Bright as the Sun, her Eyes the Gazers strike,]
> And, like the Sun, they shine on all alike

—a line whose diction seems to aim at an ultimate in banality. Not content with the explicit 'all alike', Pope selects a banal simile ('Sun' for favour) and has the sun do the least original thing possible (it does not beam, blaze, or glow—it merely shines), and to complete the obviousness the last word of the line ('alike') chimes with the second

[1] For fuller quotation of Hunt's attack, and discussion of it, see Geoffrey Tillotson, *Pope and Human Nature* (Oxford, 1958), pp. 182–8.

('like') and its dullness is emphasized by the force of the word with which it rhymes ('strike'). Would it not be ungenerous to Pope to suppose that he could, without conscious contrivance, arrive at a diction of such bland nullity?

Pope's intentions may be irrecoverable and, as some would hold, irrelevant in considering the actual merits of the passage, but the attempt to take a bearing on his treatment of metrics by reference to his treatment of diction and rhyme, and to relate the metrics, the diction and the rhyme to the explicit and implicit sense of the passage, may serve to make the point that the sense borne by a passage is closely related to the technicalities of the medium and also to make the further point that any attempt to relate the thing done to the manner of doing it rapidly involves the critic in a desperate scamper to keep pace in prose words with the articulateness of the poet's manifold techniques. Poetry's means of imitating the thing it talks of go far beyond what Pope called 'style of sound' (complex though that, in his hands, was) and they include the poetic management of linguistic necessities not peculiar to poems, as rhyme and metre are.

Of all the elements necessary to make an utterance meaningful, the most powerful is syntax, controlling as it does the order in which impressions are received and conveying the mental relations 'behind' sequences of words. And since we naturally tend—except when checked by a difficulty—to take in without effort the relations conveyed by syntax, its operation as a cause of poetical pleasure is often the last cause we recognize, if indeed we recognize it at all. The result is that syntax is important to poet and to critic because it produces strong effects by stealth; these remain 'inexplicable' so long as the power of the syntax goes undetected. For instance: many people have observed the sublime effect of the passage (Genesis, i, 3), 'And God said, Let there be light: and there was light', but it was left to Spitzer[1] to trace the sublime effect to its cause—in the fact that the syntax in which the fulfilment of God's command is described is as

---

[1] Leo Spitzer, 'Language of Poetry', in *Language: An Enquiry into Its Meaning and Function*, ed. Ruth Nanda Anshen, Science of Culture Series, VIII (New York, 1957), p. 210.

close as possible to the syntax of the command itself. (In the original Hebrew, as Spitzer points out, the parallelism of command and fulfilment is even closer: *jĕhī aur vajĕhī aur.*) In this instance the cause of those strong effects which the reader naturally perceives but cannot explain to himself lies in the fact that because of the compelling syntactical relations in each passage, the reader's mind receives not only the information the passage may be said to communicate but also and at the same time the significance of the information. The Genesis passage informs us of the fact that, and of the manner in which, God created light; the exact form in which this information is conveyed compels us to regard it as meaning, further, that what God willed was forthwith brought to pass exactly according to His word as the consequence of that word; these significances proceed from the relations, apprehended in a flash by the reader's mind, between the parts of the command (and their organization) and the parts of the fulfilment (and their organization).

Some such apprehension in a flash is a mental event the reader cannot avoid experiencing, since as a user of language he is conditioned to attach meaning to syntactical relations without conscious effort; the meaning of an utterance as a whole does not reach him at all unless it reaches him already arranged into the set of relations syntax imposes on the words the utterance contains. Consequently syntax, however little it is noted by the reader, is the groundwork of the poet's art. Often it supports a poetic edifice elaborated by many other poetic means and the reader is content to believe that these other means are the cause of his pleasure, but when a passage relies chiefly on its especially compelling and artful syntax to make its effect, the reader and the critic who never expect syntax to be more than 'a harmless, necessary drudge' holding open the door while the pageantry of words sweeps through, will be at a loss to understand why the passage affects them as it does and at a loss to do critical justice to its art.

There is more at stake than the critic's chances of being able to make less inexplicable those passages whose art is primarily syntactical. In many cases there will prove to be a fruitful interplay between syntactical relations and other formal systems—as for instance the rhyme-scheme. This is so in Pope's well-known lines (*Pastorals*, II, 73–6):

> Where-e'er you walk, cool gales shall fan the glade,
> Trees, where you sit, shall crowd into a shade,
> Where-e'er you tread, the blushing flow'rs shall rise,
> And all things flourish where you turn your eyes.

Here the management of the rhymes cannot be fully appreciated unless one relates them to the flow and ebb of expectations set up by skilful management of syntax. The first of these lines balances about the pause after 'walk'; before the pause comes the human action, after it the effect on Nature. The second line repeats this strong pause but introduces a syntactical variation: 'Trees' (which corresponds syntactically to 'cool glades') is put first in the line and is further emphasized by an irregular strong stress; 'where you sit', which follows, makes us expect that this second line will in some way repeat the pattern of the first. So we expect to be told what the trees will do, and because we are made to wait for the verb, this expectation becomes a felt desire for the completion of the pattern—a desire which is then not only satisfied but amply satisfied when the pattern expands ('shall crowd into') and then returns to rest when 'a shade' brings this line into correspondence with 'the glade' in the line before. The opening of the third line reaffirms the formula of the opening of the first, with the words 'Where-e'er you tread', and one interprets this as a recapitulation of theme that must lead to a further variation. When that variation does come ('the blushing flow'rs'), it provides at the same time a dilation of that element of the pattern which had contracted in the previous line (where 'Trees' had replaced 'cool glades'). This third line does not, like the second, return to rest, for it ends with 'shall rise'; here there is no counterpart to 'the glade', 'a shade'. The fourth line is a complex and surprising resolution of this crisis in the pattern. First it sums into a satisfactory climax the sequence 'gales'—'Trees'—'flowers' with the phrase 'And all things'. The following verb, however, still leaves unsatisfied our wish for a counterpart to 'glade' and shade'. Delayed thus, the urge to fulfilment is stronger, and to it is added the pressure of expectation of a counterpart to 'Where[-e'er] you walk/sit/tread'. Suddenly both demands are fulfilled simultaneously: the latter in 'where you turn your eyes', the former in the fact that *this* phrase now provides the transitive verb and the object, so that 'you turn your eyes' is a return to the syntactical pattern of the second half of the first line ('cool gales shall fan the glade': subject—verb—object) and at the same time it brings the quatrain to an end by neatly reversing the initial disposition of the two major parts of the overall pattern:

> Where-e'er you walk,   cool gales shall fan the glade,
>
> .   .   .   .   ✕   .   .   .   .   .
>
> And all things flourish   where you turn your eyes.

It is only with respect to these manipulations of expectancy that one can estimate the art shown in the rhymes. The rhyme 'glade'/'shade' is unsurprising[1] (it rhymes noun with noun, the nouns naming comparable things) and this is suitable for this point in the pattern (for here the second line returns to rest); in contrast, the rhyme 'rise'/'eyes' more surprisingly rhymes a verb with a noun, and the verb occupies a position on the crest of a wave of expectancy whereas the noun occupies such a position in the pattern that it resolves all the remaining expectations of the poem in a simultaneous fulfilment. Moreover it is only with respect to all this activity with patterns of rhyme and syntax that one can estimate the fitness of the diction for its purposes. Such a diction, worn smooth with use, has no anfractuosities to distract us from the witty evolution of the patterns I have discussed; its unruffled surface is almost a necessary condition of our being set at ease to follow the patterns moving beneath it with such agile assurance.

It should be clear from this last example that elements as diverse as syntax, rhyme and diction usually have to be considered together because of their interpenetration of one another. This interpenetration is the prime difficulty encountered in attempts to translate literary language into other terms—whether the terms of critical

[1] For discussion of Pope's interest in telling rhymes (seen in his concern to rhyme different parts of speech, and words from different semantic spheres) see W. K. Wimsatt, Jr., *The Verbal Icon: Studies in the Meaning of Poetry* (Lexington, Kentucky, 1954), pp. 157–64.

language or the terms of a foreign language. As Goodman points out, translation is difficult because every aspect of the language of a poem is, or could be, expressive in itself and in its relation to other aspects:

To be idiomatic in the new tongue, it is always necessary to change the word order, and this must result in new emphases in the sentences and verses; on the other hand, if the word order of the original is retained, the feeling (perhaps of naturalness) is altered. Again, one language is inflected, whereas another uses auxiliary words like "have" and "shall"; then the relation of the thought to the metric feet will be different, for the auxiliaries will, for the most part, be the unstressed syllables. In excellent translations entire systems of relations are altered or neutralized in order to save certain parts that the translator believes to be crucial; the imagery is altered in order to save the rhymes and stanzas, or the rhymes are sacrificed in order to save the imagery. . . . Good translation is grounded in practical formal criticism, for the translator must estimate just what parts are strongly functioning in giving the effect.[1]

In so far as we criticize poetry at all, as distinct from simply reading it, we claim that we have some competence to estimate what parts of the poem are strongly functioning in the production of its effect, and we are not likely to arrive at a just estimate of the parts if we do not make ourselves aware of the ways in which contrivance at the lower levels of poetic language penetrates upwards and affects elements at a level more overtly meaningful.

In many of the instances cited so far, the poetic devices of greatest power are very much on display and a critic is not likely to find difficulty in tracing the poetic effect to its source. But the true source of power in a passage of poetry is, in many cases, very effectively concealed. Effects not avowedly rhetorical (as in the passages I have quoted from Shakespeare) or avowedly elegant (as Pope's pastoral) or avowedly onomatopoeic (as Pope's 'style of sound') may still prove to depend more on manner than on the thought we assume to have been in the poet's mind or the comparison the poet may select in addressing our understandings. As an instance of this I choose one that may serve to illustrate how readily in these days we tend to give to a comparison all the credit for a poetic effect which depends, in fact, on much more than the bare comparison itself. Matthew

[1] Paul Goodman, *The Structure of Literature* (Chicago, 1954), pp. 226–7.

Arnold's poem *Resignation* rises to greatness in the lines comparing a moment of time to a watershed:

> And though fate grudge to thee and me
> The poet's rapt security,
> Yet they, believe me, who await
> No gifts from chance, have conquer'd fate.
> They, winning room to see and hear,
> And to men's business not too near,
> Through clouds of individual strife
> Draw homeward to the general life.
> Like leaves by suns not yet uncurl'd;
> To the wise, foolish; to the world,
> Weak;—yet not weak, I might reply,
> Not foolish, Fausta, in His eye,
> To whom each moment in its race,
> Crowd as we will its neutral space,
> Is but a quiet watershed
> Whence, equally, the seas of life and death are fed.[1]

The analogy used here derives its impressiveness from devices of various kinds—notably rhythm, syntax and consonantal structure. In the line, 'Is but a quiet watershed', the impression of a remote and peaceful agency owes much to the placing of the consonants *t* and *d* (the *t* coming in three times and then deepening into the *d* at the end of the line), which gives the line a steady, distant pulsing like the pulse of the waters. This sound-structure could not of course mean or do by itself what it means and does in conjunction with the sense of the words that contain these sounds, but the sound-structure makes the reader feel, as an immediate experience, what the sense of the words calls up. Its effect is furthered by its placing, for this line is so placed as to strike a contrast with the line immediately before ('Crowd as we will its neutral space'); moreover it is to be followed by a very long line (the longest in the poem) in which there is to be a vast expansion of the contained force of the quiet waters above. The long line 'Whence, equally, the seas of life and death are fed' mirrors in its extraordinary length the vastness of the processes of life and

[1] For the complete poem see *The Poetical Works of Matthew Arnold*, ed. C. B. Tinker and H. F. Lowry (London, 1950), pp. 52–60; the extract cited is on pp. 59–60.

death, but at the same time it contains this vastness within the scope of its source, by the use of 'Whence' at the beginning of the line and 'fed' at the end. 'Whence' explicitly links this line to 'watershed'; 'fed', by its rhyme, returns us to that word. The sense-linkage effected by rhyme is an effect of which Arnold was well aware, as one can see from his comments in his essay *On Translating Homer*, where he criticizes Chapman's translation for setting up connexions, by rhyme, between lines that ought not to be clutched together. He remarks that 'rhyme inevitably tends to pair lines which in the original are independent, and thus the movement of the poem is changed'.[1] He cites a glaring example, and comments:

The moment the word *chance* strikes our ear, we are irresistibly carried back to *advance* and to the whole previous line, which, according to Homer's own feeling, we ought to have left behind us entirely, and to be moving farther and farther away from.[2]

In this comment Arnold makes it clear that a rhyme can take us back not only to the one word with which it rhymes but to the whole line. Just so, 'fed' takes us back to the whole line, 'Is but a quiet water-shed'.

Arnold in this same essay offers some comments on the poetic management of syntax, which make it clear what kind of importance he attached to it. Writing of Newman's translation (whose diction he thought lamentable) he concedes,

Mr. Newman's syntax has, I say it with pleasure, a much more Homeric cast than his vocabulary; his syntax, the mode in which his thought is evolved, . . . seems to me right in its general character, and the best feature of his version.[3]

In those words— 'syntax, the mode in which his thought is evolved'— Arnold expresses a discernment criticism cannot afford to overlook: a discernment of the importance of syntax at the highest creative point, that is, the poet's grasp of the relations inherent in the whole he is about to impart. And one is encouraged, on reading Arnold's

[1] *Essays by Matthew Arnold Including . . . On Translating Homer . . . and Five Other Essays* (London, 1914), pp. 253–4.

[2] ibid., p. 254.

[3] ibid., pp. 270–1.

comment on syntax, to suppose that he did not arrive by accident at the magnificent control of poetic effect by syntax which can be seen in those lines from *Resignation* which I have been discussing. In the last line it is the management of syntax that enables the powerful word 'equally' to do its work. The word may properly be called powerful because it has at least three meanings relevant to the poem and realized within it. The word can mean *with even movement*, and this meaning is realized in the poem by the steady pulse of the line 'Is but a quiet watershed'. The word can also mean *in equal proportions*, and this meaning is realized in the analogy of the dividing watershed dealing its waters equally to the sea of life and the sea of death. The word can also mean *impartially*, and this meaning is also realized in the poem—in this case indirectly, by way of the associations the analogy calls into the poem, associations with the serenity and remoteness of high mountains (the word 'quiet' does much to make us select, out of all possible associations, just these). What organizes the power of all these meanings, by concentrating them into one place in the poem from which they magnificently strike, is the syntax. The line begins, 'Whence, equally', and for the duration of these two words it holds the reader in check, knowing that something must follow to release this suspension, for our normal expectations of language tell us that 'Whence' demands a continuation. Before that comes, there enters 'equally', which keeps the mind in suspense still, but now in expectation that when the suspense is released it will be by something balanced, something characterized above all by some kind of equivalence. It is only when the mind of the reader has been made, in this way, to foreshape the conclusion, that the fulfilment of expectation is allowed to come and the poet releases the line—syntactically and rhythmically—with 'the seas of life and death are fed'. Yet we have still not done justice to this great line until we recognize how much is done by the rhythm. The rhythm of 'the seas of life and death are fed' has nothing facile about it; it is a perfect, internally self-compensating movement, slung across the great pillars of 'seas', 'life', 'death', 'fed', and the rhythm of this phrase is set up by putting a distributed pause near the beginning of the line. (That is to say, no main caesura occurs; instead, we have a pause after 'Whence' and another after 'equally'.) To put a distributed pause in the forepart of a line creates a rhythmical inclination towards distribution of emphasis in what comes after, since a line not organized as a whole (balancing about a main caesura) tends to find its metrical equilibrium by an internal balance achieved within that segment of the line which must counterpoise the distributed emphasis with which the line opens. This of course is no more than a tendency, which the poet can frustrate if he so wishes—for instance, by opening the line with some irregularity so bold or some enforcement of regularity so compulsive that the whole line falls into a submission to the movement its forepart has set up, as in Milton's 'Eyeless in *Gaza* at the Mill with slaves' (*Samson Agonistes*, l. 41), or Pope's 'O'er Hills, o'er Dales, o'er Crags, o'er Rocks, they go'. Any observation one makes, of the tendencies set up in a line by some noticeable feature of it, must always be accompanied by the mental reservation, 'other things being equal', or nearly enough equal to allow the observation to hold good, for the rhythm we 'hear' in a line may be imposed by any one of a number of factors, and the quality we ascribe to it may depend on the relation of this one imposing factor to all other factors upon which it imposes itself.

The rhythm we 'hear' and the quality we ascribe to it are themselves so complex in origin that I might have done better, in seeking to show how one aspect of language affects another, to choose examples affording close comparisons at the rhythmical level, instead of ranging over so many fields (of sound, of rhetoric, of syntax, of sense). But the critical language available for the discussion of rhythm is so unsatisfactory that no such critical point could be made without vast preliminary tedium of theoretical discussion and definition of terms. Not to attempt such a discussion and definition must leave us in the unhappy position of having to refer to 'the rhythm' as though it were a single thing (and as though it were as open to inspection as the syntax, the vocabulary and the specific word-patterns that are 'in' the poem in the sense that one can underline them with a pen or specify them in generally-agreed terms of reference) or of resorting, as I have done, to a merely partial breaking-down of the rhythm in terms no more precise than is necessary to let the reader know what quality I am ascribing to it and what technical reasons I would give (if pressed) in support of my belief that such a quality emanates from the exact form of the line. I must hope for readers who are willing to content themselves with such an operational procedure in a book not primarily concerned with analysing the complexities of rhythm.

But the book is concerned with the complexity of poetic language (of which rhythm is one aspect) and with enquiry after some firm ground on which to stand when challenged in the language of the critic to deliver the kind of response or evaluation that he advocates as proper and just. The reader who stays with me to the end will, I hope, find some reason to agree with me that the firmest ground upon which to stand, when recalcitrant to any particular critical proposal, is simply this: that meaning and value in poems are the product of a whole array of elements of language, all having a potential of eloquence which comes to realization when, and only when, one element is set in discernible relation with another; that, therefore, a disagreement about the meaning or value of a poem is a disagreement about relationships and is likely to be interminable just so long as the relationships operating in a poem are by either or both parties to a dispute inaccurately estimated and described; similarly, general critical discussion of the nature and importance of any one of the elements of poetic language is unlikely to be fruitful unless it focuses on the relationships that characteristically obtain between that element and others. And just because relationships (whether in particular poems or in poetic language in general) have this importance, the reader's ability to make constructive use of the work of critics will depend not only on his ability to appreciate the relationships they note but also on his ability to appreciate and defend as significant those relationships which, in particular climates of critical opinion, it is customary to underrate or ignore. The critic himself (doing his limited best not to underrate or ignore any) can hardly, in talking of individual poems, opt out of the responsibility of making forays into unknown territory; in more general discussion of poetic language as such, his interest is likely to be liveliest exactly where he sees the possibility of critical advance in observation and description

—where, therefore, his methods and his terminology are at their most tentative and experimental. For such reasons as these, the reader may expect that the language of the critic will always fall short of the precision and fullness of the language of poetry and that its main usefulness lies in the fact that its gallant failures cast a light which throws into stronger relief those features of poems most resistant to the best attempts of criticism to reduce them to analytical terms. The good analytical critic is not one who strips the layers off the onion one after another until there is nothing left inside; poetic language has the quality, paradoxical in non-poetic language, that when one layer of it is stripped off, the onion looks bigger and better than it did before—or, to speak more rationally, the process of examining its structure in critical terms sharpens the enquirer's appreciation of the power residing in poetic configurations of words.

We have by now many means at our disposal for studying the complexity of poetic language. The tradition of *explication de texte* offers methods of examining verifiable features of poems. The 'New Critics'[1] of England and America have scored notable successes in handling the multiple implications of diction and symbol; an opposed school of critics[2] has tried to redress what it regards as imbalances in these new methods by studying the proprieties of the particular *genre* to which each work belongs. New developments in linguistics,[3] especially in the working out of methods appropriate to study of meaning, have made it possible to relate enquiries into poetic language to work done on other forms of language, and not the least of criticism's gains from this situation is the fact that modern linguistics discerns complexity of meaning and diversity of modes of conveying

[1] For some of their work see *Critiques and Essays in Criticism, 1920–1948*, ed. Robert Wooster Stallman (New York, 1949); the preface gives some account of the critical trends represented in the collection.

[2] See *Critics and Criticism Ancient and Modern*, ed. and with an Introduction by R. S. Crane (Chicago, 1952). The abridged edition (Chicago, 1957) has a new preface. For further discussion of issues between critics represented in this collection and those in Stallman's, see Wimsatt, *Verbal Icon*, pp. 41–65.

[3] See Stephen Ullmann, *The Principles of Semantics*, Glasgow University Publications LXXXIV (Glasgow, 1957); this, the second edition, has a supplementary chapter, 'Recent Developments in Semantics', and an expanded bibliography.

it in even the commonest forms of utterance.[1] When the linguist, studying the common tongue, can declare that 'each word when used in a new context is a new word'[2] the literary critic may hope to find more general acceptance of the elaborateness of his discourses on the highly organized linguistic structures encountered in the work of poets and he can expect to learn much from the work of linguists concerning the nature of the medium the poet uses.

An instance of increasing *rapprochement* between the interests of linguists and the interests of literary critics is the growing concern of contemporary criticism with the importance of syntax in poetry.[3] The emergence of this interest, in sustained study of the style of a particular writer, can be seen in T. A. Dunn's *Philip Massinger* (Edinburgh, 1957), where management of syntax is made the basis of a comparative estimate of the styles of Massinger and Shakespeare, and very strong claims are made for the importance of syntax in determining the effect of dramatic speech:

However difficult Shakespeare's style may be by reason of the diction, phraseology, and imagery, it is always a speakable style in a strictly elocutionary sense. The thought-elements of it come in an order that is faithful to that of unpremeditated utterance. It observes familiar and colloquial syntax; it runs to principal clauses or their phrasal equivalents, to loose and accumulative rather than to periodic sentences, and to simple constructions; and it resorts little to suspensions, parentheses, and inversions—or, at least, only to such as have a colloquial sanction. (p. 218)
The dramatist who makes his characters speak [in periodic sentences] . . . is defeating his own end more thoroughly than by lapses in *vraisemblance*, plot, or characterisation. Awkwardnesses in plot are not very apparent in a performance, especially if the producer knows his business. And the personality of the actor can carry off unreal characterisation. But there is no escape from the syntax of the dialogue. (p. 223)
I hope by now to have established a first precise and valid ground for a

---

[1] See, for instance, J. R. Firth, 'Modes of Meaning', in *Essays and Studies 1951* (The English Association) [New Series, 4], pp. 118–49; William K. Frankena, 'Some Aspects of Language' and ' "Cognitive" and "Noncognitive" ', in *Language, Thought, & Culture*, ed. Paul Henle (Ann Arbor, 1958), pp. 121–45, 146–72.

[2] Firth, op. cit., p. 118.

[3] See Donald Davie, *Articulate Energy: An Inquiry into the Syntax of English Poetry* (London, 1955); Margaret Schlauch, *Modern English And American Poetry* (London, 1956); Christine Brooke-Rose, *A Grammar of Metaphor* (London, 1958).

comparison of the style of Massinger with that of Shakespeare. It is this fundamental difference in respect of syntax—something which seems simple and not important at the first glance, but which is on the contrary of far-reaching significance. (p. 224)

Though the examination of poetic syntax is at present in an experimental stage, enough has already been done to show that syntax must radically affect other elements of poetic language. Since it controls word order, it controls the order in which impressions are received by the reader. A reviewer of Davie's book on syntax in poetry observes:

We are at a stage in the development of our language when word-order and idiom are becoming increasingly decisive in communication. ... but it may be questioned whether we yet sufficiently recognize how sensitive is the complex of anticipations which is set up at each point in a sequence of words or phrases, and which enables a reader to select the appropriate elements of connotation from the words following.[1]

Upon its successful management depends the placing of a word in a telling position in the line, a telling position in the metrical and rhythmical structure, a telling position in relation to other words in its vicinity. It can produce the kind of effect we more readily associate with the 'tone' or 'atmosphere' of a poet's vocabulary—and do this by stealth, since at the level of syntax we respond (though no less decisively) with less conscious awareness of the immediate cause of our response, to what is implied concerning the *persona* of the poet by the familiarity or impersonality, the simplicity or complexity of his locutions. Indeed, some syntactical forms carry with them a meaning that resides in their usage as special forms expressive of a particular mental attitude in the speaker who adopts them. One such is noted by Holloway: 'There is a special though archaic form ("would that . . .") for expressing wishes that the speaker believes are hopeless and therefore that he does not wish anyone to attempt to promote.'[2] Others are sufficiently characteristic of or reminiscent of a particular kind of context—such as the Psalms, or liturgical prayer—to 'place' the language of a poem as implying such a context—as in Goethe's

---

[1] A. D. S. Fowler, *Essays in Criticism*, VIII (1958), 86–7; cp. p. 20, n. 3.
[2] John Holloway, *Language and Intelligence* (London, 1951), p. 127.

Wanderers Nachtlied, where the first line, 'Der du von dem Himmel bist', recalls the first phrase of the Lord's Prayer, 'Vater unser, der du bist im Himmel'; as Dr Elizabeth M. Wilkinson says, 'in this prayer for peace, the unbearable tension of the soul is neither described, nor yet evoked by image or analogy. It is transmuted directly into the syntactical structure of the verse'.[1] Syntax can, by repetition or carefully controlled variation, function as the prime organizing element in the pattern or movement of a poem—as in Dylan Thomas's *Ceremony after a Fire Raid*.[2] It can put the significance of a situation in a compelling form—as in Macbeth's realization of the irony of his guilt, 'better be with the dead, Whom we, to gain our peace, have sent to peace' (III, ii, 19–20). Though it is often true that a syntactical arrangement, designed to stamp upon the words the poet's evaluation of the situation they describe, will be reinforced by effects at the level of diction and rhetoric (as it is here, by the repetition of 'peace'), it is still true in such a case that the power that enables the poet to concentrate into epigrammatic form the shape of a man's destiny, or the moral status of his acts, is the power syntax has of giving prominence to logical relationships. The *locus classicus* for studying the operation of this power is *Paradise Lost*. At crucial points in the narrative and interpretation of the relations between God and Evil, Milton needs a syntax capable of tying into an immovable knot the powers, acts, metaphysical status, moral responsibility, and past, present and future of all the agents involved, for the whole moral endeavour of the work is towards a vindication of the logic and justice with which God's laws and purpose constrain the freedom of His creatures. For instance, when Abdiel denounces Satan and warns him of impending punishment, the intricate structure of tenses and pronouns is essential; it demonstrates God's justice by defining God's retributive power in a syntactical pattern ('who can uncreate thee') as close as possible to the pattern that defines His creative power ('who created thee'). The

---

[1] Elizabeth M. Wilkinson, 'Goethe's Poetry', *German Life & Letters*, New Series, II (1949), 323. The specific recall of the Lord's Prayer was pointed out to me by Dr B. A. Rowley.

[2] See the commentary in Schlauch, op. cit., pp. 67–70.

pattern is made even more rigorous by its association with the pattern '*Then* who . . .'/'*When* who . . .' and further by the stress on parallel words which results from the corresponding positions they are given in the arrangement of the lines:

> for soon expect to feel
> His Thunder on thy head, devouring fire.
> Then who created thee lamenting learne,
> When who can uncreate thee thou shalt know.
>
> (v, 892–5)

Were it not for this strong syntactical framework, the manipulation of vocabulary (in 'learne'/'know') would be insignificant, as would the alliteration (in 'lamenting learne'), for these derive their force from their relation to the knot of past and future tied and tightened by the syntax. Latinate syntax is important to Milton because it provides him with more ways than a normal English syntax could muster of devising contrasts and correspondences and of marshalling individual words into exactly those places that will set off the meaning each bears in relation to another. Moreover, a syntax based on Latin models gives scope for longer and more intricate periodic sentences than normal English syntax can support, sentences capable of harvesting in one continuous sweep the manifestation of God's will in history and the relation of events and persons to a providential plan extending from the Creation to the Fall and the Atonement, debated in Heaven and Hell and on earth. It should be evident from the example already given that, in order to make his Latinate syntax comprehensible, Milton has to devise markers of the grammatical functions of individual words or phrases. These may be in the form of rhetorical figures (as when the insertion of the alliterative 'lamenting', before the word 'learne', directs our attention to Satan and his future and so prepares us to understand the construction 'Then . . . learne,/When . . . thou shalt know'), or in the form of strong links of sense (as when the sense-link between 'His Thunder' and 'devouring fire' shows us that these phrases are to be taken as in apposition, despite the intervention of the phrase 'on thy head'), or even in the form of contrivance to make a word in one line fall into the same relative position as that word in the next line to which we are meant

to relate it (as in 'Then . . ./When . . .' and in '. . . learne,/ . . . know./').
These and similar devices for supplying the pointers which in Latin
are given by accidence involve some sacrifice of other effects, notably
at the level of diction, for, as the example quoted shows, a diction
instantly comprehensible is in places necessary to prevent confusion
as to the construction of the sentence. 'His Thunder' and 'devouring
fire' instantly claim kindred with one another just because there is no
distracting novelty to delay our recognition of a familiar link in sense.
In addition, this pseudo-syntax cuts Milton off from some of the
rhythmical effects open to poets who play the metre of a line against
the natural rhythms of normal English phrasing. If syntax was indeed of such importance in Milton's handling of his theme that he
was prepared at crucial points to let diction and versification pay
whatever price the dominance of syntax might exact, it would seem
that criticism of his practice at the levels of diction and versification
must, if it is to be just, take strict account of what is achieved and in
turn necessitated by the syntax. Milton's style, however, is only one
instance of a more general consideration which I hope this chapter
may by now have made sufficiently clear: that we must, when reading
as critics, allow due importance to each and all of the levels at which
poetry elaborates its effects, if the reputations of the poets are to be
safe in our hands.

In this chapter's cursory review of some of the sources of poetic
effects, I have tried to give a glimpse of their numerosity and of the
intricacy of their relations to one another; I have made no attempt to
suggest a systematic approach to the problems of describing and
evaluating poetic language. Nor is it the purpose of this book as a
whole to erect a system of analysis or appraisal. Indeed, in what follows, so far from aiming at a mopping-up of successive problems in
one area after another until the whole domain of poetic language is
occupied and systematized under the control of a central critical
language, I shall try to show that in any area one attempts to isolate
and in the problems that most challengingly arise when one concentrates on it, the more closely one looks, the more each problem re-
veals its own stratification into further problems and the more the
areas reveal their overlap. To attack any one problem is to come

nearer, not to a tidy solution of it, but to a clearer sight of the dimensions and intricacy of the problem of talking about poetic language at all. If there is any virtue in findings of this dismaying kind, it will be in their usefulness for the purpose of disembarrassing one's own criticism of some of those unreal dilemmas and paradoxes of critical language, troublesome to one's thinking and writing, which come about when false simplifications collide with one another.

II

Diction

IT was the tenor of the preceding chapter that when a word or phrase enters into the patterns set up in a poem its effectiveness will depend much on the give and take between those patterns and itself. We cannot, however, avoid the question, 'What does the word or phrase bring with it that is constant enough to make it a contributor to as well as a recipient of the poetic power of the structure it enters?' So far, in discussing poetic structures, the discussion has concentrated on formal elements which modify meaning, and has avoided, as far as possible, involvement with what is usually referred to as the 'diction' of the poem—that is (in vague and general terms) the individual words or locutions as bearers of meaning and their fitness for the work they seem to be called upon to do in the poem.

The first question that comes up is a question about the usefulness of the term 'diction'. Is 'diction' a part or an aspect of poetry which can be isolated sufficiently for one to point to it and say, 'That's what I mean by the diction of the poem'? The usage of the term in critical writings reflects the complexity of poetic language as such: as a critical term it has not yet settled down to mean definitely *vocabulary*, or definitely *effectiveness of vocabulary in a particular context*, or definitely *the preferences shown in a particular poem (or in the works, or style, of a particular poet, or of a group of poets, or of poets as such) for just these ways, rather than all the other ways language affords, of letting the reader know what the poet has in mind*. The Oxford English Dictionary under heading 4a ('The manner in which anything is expressed in words; choice or selection of words and phrases; wording; verbal style') gives, as the earliest use of the term in this sense, Dryden's in 1700. Dryden, criticizing Hobbes's remarks on Homer, writes:

Mr. Hobbs, I say, begins the praise of Homer where he should have ended it. He tells us, that the first beauty of an Epic poem consists in diction, that is, in the choice of words and harmony of numbers; now, the words are the colouring of the work, which in the order of nature is last to be considered.[1]

Here it is clear, since 'diction' includes 'harmony of numbers', that Dryden did not use the word to mean simply *vocabulary*. In 1880, we find, the word is used in a passage of Leslie Stephen's in a way which suggests that the sense *effectiveness in a particular context* has dropped out and the sense *choice of words* or *vocabulary*, is now primarily intended:

The style in which a woman is called a nymph—and women generally are "the fair"—in which shepherds are conscious swains, and a poet invokes the muses and strikes a lyre, and breathes on a reed, and a nightingale singing becomes Philomel "pouring her throat," represents a fashion as worn out as hoops and wigs. By the time of Wordsworth it was a mere survival—a dead form remaining after its true function had entirely vanished. The proposal to return to the language of common life was the natural revolt of one who desired poetry to be above all things the genuine expression of real emotion. Yet it is, I think, impossible to maintain that the diction of poetry should be simply that of common life.[2]

In critical writings of the present day the term has the same instability. It is used by critics who concern themselves primarily with the vocabulary of a poet, especially in so far as it contains unusual words or excludes certain classes of ordinary words. It is also used by critics who are concerned primarily with the effective handling of words (whether these are, severally, 'unusual' words, or not). To put the distinction crudely but conveniently: if we were talking not about poems but about rugs we might distinguish the individual lengths of wool used in making the rug from the pattern according to which they were arranged; or if we were talking about machines we might distinguish the parts of the machine from its smooth running; if now we speak of poems, using the term 'lengths of wool' (or 'machine parts') to refer to individual words, and the term 'pattern' (or 'smooth running') to refer to poetic effect, where shall we locate the area of our interest if we interest ourselves in diction—in the 'wools' or in the 'pattern'? in the 'machine parts' or in the 'smooth running'?

[1] *The Poetical Works of John Dryden*, ed. W. D. Christie (London, 1870), p. 496.
[2] Leslie Stephen, *Alexander Pope* (London, 1880), p. 69.

I imagine myself to have readers who would retort that these are unrealistic distinctions—that the finished rug depends on both the wools and the pattern, and the smooth running of the machine depends on the parts and on the way they act together. But this, which is of course true of rugs and machines, is not taken as a matter of course by all critics who write about the words used in poems. In fact, in reading books on diction, we often find that a particular writer will use the term not exclusively to mean a vocabulary or exclusively to mean its poetic effect but to mean now one, now the other. It is exceedingly difficult in practice to discuss diction without hopping about from the wool to the pattern, from the parts to the smooth functioning of the machine, from vocabulary to language. One good reason for this is that some poems deviate ostentatiously from that range of vocabulary likely to be accepted as 'normal' by readers, whilst others do not, and a criticism concerned with the interplay of the words the poet chooses to use must take account of both kinds. Another good reason is that for a man studying a poem it is easier to discriminate the more important from the less important choices than it is to frame a definition of what constitutes an important choice. No one would wish to interdict a project of research simply on the grounds that no satisfactory definition of the field of research could first be framed; we should be the poorer if the critics of diction had all expired in a soundless paroxysm of despair when confronted with the task of explaining why they gave their attention to some words and not to others.

The extreme difficulty of defining diction can be illustrated by reference to recent work. Bernard Groom's valuable study of English poetry opens with a definition which, taken as a whole, gives one to understand that in choosing for critical commentary some but not all of the words used in poems, he looked out for those words which were, of all the words in the poem, those most evidently related to the final difference that obtains between a poetic and a non-poetic representation of reality:

This work deals mainly with the diction of poetry, not with "poetic diction". It is concerned with the outstanding poets of some three centuries whose practice shows them to recognize an "essential difference between the language of prose and metrical composition". The diction of poetry, then, consists of all the words and phrases in true and creative poetic writing which are in any way distinguished by their form or function from those in ordinary use. It includes synonyms which heighten or embellish style; also felicitous phrases which, even if often repeated in later use, still confer honour on their true inventors; and finally, certain imaginative and expressive words which exist only in the world of poetry.[1]

The difficulty with such a definition (though serviceable enough as a form of words indicating generally what the book is about) is that it abounds in terms difficult to pin down: 'true and creative', 'distinguished by', 'form or function', 'ordinary', 'heighten or embellish', 'style', 'felicitous', 'imaginative and expressive', 'world of poetry'. 'Distinguished by their form or function from those in ordinary use', which one might take to be the crux of the definition, contains in itself at least two unresolved difficulties: what is 'ordinary use'? what is meant by 'function'? 'Function' is distinguished from 'form', which would therefore seem principally to mean *variant form* and to cover archaisms, dialectal forms, orthographical variants, idiosyncratic or novel word-formation and freakish occurrences; 'function' would then cover the invention of, for instance, new verbs from old nouns as in Shakespeare's *lip*, *fist*, *knee*, *heel* and *foot* (Groom, p. 43), and similar departures from the norm of syntactical usage or what is taken as the norm in the poet's own linguistic environment. But if we restrict 'form or function' to such senses we shall have to assume that this part of the definition is not meant to cover locutions which, though 'normal' *vis-à-vis* the state of the language at a given historical point, are none the less used in a poem with striking effect; such striking effects as are produced by 'synonyms which heighten or embellish', 'felicitous phrases' and 'imaginative and expressive words'. So perhaps we ought rather to take 'function' in a wider sense, that is in a sense permitting the inclusion of divagations from ordinary use which would not necessarily excite the interest of a lexicographer but which do excite the reader of the poem.

The difficulty of determining what the terms of the definition severally mean is a measure of how difficult it is to break poetic language down into individual components. Even a non-literary con-

[1] Bernard Groom, *The Diction of Poetry from Spenser to Bridges* (Toronto, 1955), p. 3.

text will resist an atomistic approach to its meaning. Literary contexts, for a variety of reasons (some of which this chapter hopes to explore), are even more resistant.

The separate words in a poem are not merely symbols in contextual settings but are themselves equally contexts for each other, modifying each other and combining with each other to provoke a coherent response, so that the significance of the poem is always more than the sum of each separate signification, no matter how carefully these separate significations are determined . . . . the unity inherent in the poem may be so complete that to attempt to break it down into its constituent elements would, like the breaking down of a compound word, only lead us along the path towards literal, i.e. bogus, accuracy.[1]

Some of the difficulties of discussing the functions of words in literary contexts may be illustrated by examining two literary uses of 'etcetera'. One occurs in the opening line of Canto III of Byron's *Don Juan*:

> Hail, Muse! *et cætera.*—We left Juan sleeping . . .

Is this '*et cætera*' distinguished by its function from 'etc.' in ordinary use? The answer would seem to be that in ordinary use—as for instance in a business letter or on a poster announcing the auction of a desirable residence and its contents—'etc.' functions to indicate the existence of a number of further particulars which it is unnecessary to specify, since they can be inferred from what has gone before and from common experience of the issue with which the letter or poster is concerned. And this indeed is what is indicated by '*et cætera*' in Byron's truncated invocation of the Muse: why bother, Byron seems to say, to go to all the trouble of writing it all out, since any reader can make it up for himself? But what '*et cætera*' does to its context in Byron's line is not what 'etc.' does to its context in a business letter or a bill of sale. Byron's '*et cætera*' dismisses the Muse as not worth any further expenditure of paper and ink and time. Because it keeps its ordinary meaning, it functions in this context as derision. A phrase which means, roughly, *and so on and so forth* does something to its context, and the something it does is not the same as

[1] John McFarlane, 'Modes of Translation', *Durham University Journal*, XLV [New Series, XIV] (1952–53), 88.

the meaning *and so on and so forth*. This derisory function cannot simply be ascribed to any inherent unpoetical quality in the word. As evidence that the word cannot guarantee a belittlement of any poetic context it enters, one might cite Wordsworth's lines in *The Prelude* (1850 version, VIII, 437–43):

> Where the harm,
> If, when the woodman languished with disease
> Induced by sleeping nightly on the ground
> Within his sod-built cabin, Indian-wise,
> I called the pangs of disappointed love,
> And all the sad etcetera of the wrong,
> To help him to his grave.

In Wordsworth's lines, 'etcetera' (now doing duty as a noun) is so far from deflating the dignity of the context, which, itself, is a half-rueful account of how the poet's imagination operated to romanticize the lives of those around him, that, on the contrary, it gives the passage more of real human dignity than it has while it speaks of 'the pangs of disappointed love'; the reader who receives an impression of unreality from 'pangs of disappointed love' may well find in 'all the sad etcetera of the wrong' an expression of his own sense of the long pain felt in every humiliating circumstance of suffering. Considering together these two very different poetic contexts, Byron's and Wordsworth's, into which a locution of common life has entered and, without losing its common meaning, has functioned in context to do something novel and striking, one cannot but realize that the function of a word in an artistic context is not the same as, and is not predictable from inspection of, its uses in everyday life. To drive the point truly home one might cite E. E. Cummings's cadenzas on the word:

> my sweet old etcetera
> aunt lucy during the recent
>
> war could and what
> is more did tell you just
> what everybody was fighting
>
> for,
> my sister

isabel created hundreds
(and
hundreds) of socks not to
mention shirts fleaproof earwarmers

etcetera wristers etcetera, my
mother hoped that

i would die etcetera
bravely of course my father used
to become hoarse talking about how it was
a privilege and if only he
could meanwhile my

self etcetera lay quietly
in the deep mud et

cetera
(dreaming,
 et
   cetera, of
Your smile
eyes knees and of your Etcetera)[1]

From this it follows that criticism of a poet's locutions should be inseparable from study of the context in which they occur. The question of the diction of poetry is a question of how words affect and are affected by the artistic contexts they enter. Matthew Arnold, reasserting his objections to the diction of Newman's translation of Homer, writes: 'Of the words which, placed where Mr. Newman places them, I have called bad words, every one may be excellent in some other place'.[2] If we are to discuss a poet's choice and use of locutions we shall have to remember that there are no bad words or good words; there are only words in bad or good places. This is not merely a theoretical assertion. As instances of two extremes of the range of words good poetry can accommodate one might on the one hand cite Kathleen Raine's poem *Water*, which deals with the coming

---

[1] E. E. Cummings, *Selected Poems, 1923–1958* (London, 1960), p. 20. I owe this reference to Dr B. A. Rowley.

[2] *Essays . . . Including . . . On Translating Homer*, p. 387.

into being of individual life-forms and therefore not only permits but demands a specialized biological vocabulary, as in the lines

> Entities, selves, globules, vase-shapes, vortices,
> Amoeboid, ovoid, pulsing or ciliate,
> That check the flow of waters like forms of thought,[1]

and, at the other extreme, the opening lines of the third section of *East Coker* where, to convey the sterility of modern life, many locutions are taken from or closely modelled on the standardized and banal diction used on notable public occasions and in newspaper reports of them:

> O dark dark dark. They all go into the dark,
> The vacant interstellar spaces, the vacant into the vacant,
> The captains, merchant bankers, eminent men of letters,
> The generous patrons of art, the statesmen and the rulers,
> Distinguished civil servants, chairmen of many committees,
> Industrial lords and petty contractors, all go into the dark,
> And dark the Sun and Moon, and the Almanach de Gotha
> And the Stock Exchange Gazette, the Directory of Directors,
> And cold the sense and lost the motive of action.
> And we all go with them, into the silent funeral,
> Nobody's funeral, for there is no one to bury.[2]

Here the banality is the point, and to make the point clearer Eliot makes his diction court comparison with the passionate, sensitive, religious diction of those lines in *Samson Agonistes* (80–105) to which it unmistakably alludes:

> O dark, dark, dark, amid the blaze of noon,
> Irrecoverably dark, total Eclipse
> Without all hope of day!
> O first created Beam, and thou great Word,
> Let there be light, and light was over all;
> Why am I thus bereav'd thy prime decree?
> The Sun to me is dark
> And silent as the Moon,
> When she deserts the night
> Hid in her vacant interlunar cave.
> Since light so necessary is to life,

---

[1] *The Collected Poems of Kathleen Raine* (London, 1956), p. 165.

[2] T. S. Eliot, *Four Quartets* (London, 1944), pp. 18–19.

And almost life it self, if it be true
That light is in the Soul,
She all in every part; why was the sight
To such a tender ball as th'eye confin'd?
So obvious and so easie to be quench't,
And not as feeling through all parts diffus'd,
That she might look at will through every pore?
Then had I not been thus exil'd from light;
As in the land of darkness yet in light,
To live a life half dead, a living death,
And buried; but O yet more miserable!
My self, my Sepulcher, a moving Grave,
Buried, yet not exempt
By priviledge of death and burial
From worst of other evils, pains and wrongs.

And though Eliot's obituary language is set in a context of impassioned thought and imagination, it is as much a part of the poem as the sensitive diction with which it is contrasted.

Yet, though it is easy to point to successful poems containing words characteristic of unpoetic occasions and activities, it is not easy to account for their success. It is unlikely that the simple concept of 'contrast' will satisfy us as an explanation of the interest and pleasure complex poems afford. Eliot's description of the silent funeral of the eminent raises the acute problem of accounting for the fact that a diction which in normal use is stale and suspect of falsity is not stale or false in the poem—and this is not because it is redeemed by the interest of the different diction about it. One is not bored by the lines in which the obituary diction is concentrated. Before we resort to giving, say, the rhythm all the credit for sustaining our interest while diction defaults, it will be wise to ask a few more questions of the diction itself. A closer inspection of it will be rewarded by the realization that this diction does not oppress us with a demand for reverence or acclaim of the dead, for, whilst using obituary or *Who's Who* language, it subtly detaches itself from the social attitudes such language is normally associated with. It detaches itself from these not only by the anticipatory summary, 'the vacant into the vacant', but also by using one kind of eminence to nullify another; as one form of illustriousness is succeeded by another and still another, each diminishes

34

in importance; where there are so many directors of the world's affairs that a Directory of Directors is necessary to keep track of them, importance dwindles into nonentity. This is a manœuvre to allude to contemporary forms of prestige whilst at the same time repudiating the attitudes usually adopted (or simulated) in connection with them, and manœuvres to the same end are found in the detail of the diction. If we examine one by one the phrases that make up the roll-call of the funeral we find many telling deviations from the normal usage of writers of obituary columns and entries in books of reference. 'Chairmen of many committees' is a particularly telling example of the undermining effect of using plural forms of descriptions usually reserved for giving the accolade to a single individual. 'Captains' seems to hover between contemporary language (compare the phrase 'captains of industry') and the semi-biblical (compare, in Kipling's *Recessional*, 'The Captains and the Kings depart')[1] and, similarly, in the phrase 'the statesmen and the rulers', the rulers appear to belong to an older and less secular stratum of language, that of the Bible and of the writings of divines. The 'industrial lords' look one way to 'press lords' and similar usages in which 'lords' means *magnates* and the other way to the lords temporal and lords spiritual who constitute the Upper House of Parliament (with the implication that modern life has introduced a third category—those whose command of industry has helped them to the peerage) and the word 'lords' is even further complicated by its juxtaposition with 'petty contractors'; this latter, though a standard occupational classification, gives to 'lords', by contrast, the sense of lordliness, and takes to itself the sense of pettiness. Eliot's diction here permits simultaneously a recall of contemporary ways of describing status and a criticism of the values associated with such ways of describing. In order to bring about this simultaneous recall and reappraisal, he adheres sufficiently to contemporary usage to establish the reference and deviates enough from it to deflate the pomps to which he refers and to suggest older values of a higher order. Thus the diction, in which the element of reappraisal depends upon significant deviations from the contemporary language he has taken as his ostensible model, is a very delicately

[1] *Rudyard Kipling's Verse, Definitive Edition* (London, 1940), p. 328.

judged mixture of conformity to and deviation from the stereotypes of current usage.

In many respects this manipulation of a contemporary model is comparable at the linguistic level with Eliot's use of literary allusions. These often function in his poetry to give the perspective in which the contemporary scene is to be viewed and often they enter the poem not by overt reference to literary figures but by recall of the diction of a literary work. In order to be manifest, these allusions must consist of phrases sufficiently individual to be recognizable, whilst at the same time the phrases have to be adjusted to the texture of Eliot's own poem to prevent them from sticking out like fossilized remains or ancient monuments. The Milton allusion in this passage is an interesting example of his technique. The passage from *Samson Agonistes* is called into *East Coker* by the opening, 'O dark dark dark'; it is necessary that the allusion be unmistakable, because the development of the passage depends upon it; yet it is equally necessary that it should be integrated into the passage, not allowed to dominate it, and so the unspecified 'They all' are introduced immediately after the Milton quotation, to fix the attention on what is to come, in *this* passage, to explain 'they'. With 'go into the dark' Eliot converts Milton's adjective into a noun and prepares the way for the strong rhetorical pattern which holds together the Miltonic matter and his own and provides the forward movement of the whole passage:

      a   *b*
      ‾‾‾‾‾‾‾‾ ‾‾‾‾‾‾   *a*
O dark dark dark. They all go into the dark,

             a
    ‾‾‾‾‾‾‾‾‾‾‾‾‾‾‾‾‾‾‾‾ *b*   *a*
The vacant interstellar spaces, the vacant into the vacant,

      b
    ‾‾‾‾‾‾‾‾‾‾‾‾‾
The captains [*et al.*] . . .

                   b   *a*
               . . . all go into the dark,

    a
And dark . . .
    a   *a*
And cold . . .   . . . and lost

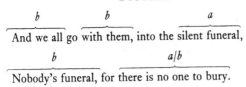

And we all go with them, into the silent funeral,

Nobody's funeral, for there is no one to bury.

Within this rhetorical framework, meanwhile, Eliot executes another manœuvre involving 'interstellar', 'Sun and Moon', 'Almanach' and 'silent', a manœuvre that depends both on allusion and improvisation. 'Vacant interstellar spaces' is based on Milton's 'vacant interlunar cave', but the substitution of 'stellar' and 'spaces' (for 'lunar' and 'cave') both brings the phrase up to date in its astronomy and at the same time adds to Milton's total darkness the horror Pascal expressed in the famous phrase 'Le silence éternel de ces espaces infinis m'effraie',[1] and Pascal's 'silence', now an undertone in the passage, gathers strength from Milton's 'silent as the Moon' and from the passage in Dante's *Inferno* (I, 60) (to which Milton's phrase alludes) where the sun is silent—'dove'l sol tace'—and it is this reiterated and complex undertone that emerges into sudden prominence in the phrase 'into the silent funeral'. This intricate dovetailing of meanings gives an ever-changing and ever-deepening value to the words 'dark', 'vacant', 'cold', 'lost', 'silent', and infuses horror into the contrast between the inanity of the departing and these attributes of the void into which they depart.

What makes this dovetailing possible is the prior existence of literary contexts so strongly individual in content and form that they survive Eliot's alterations without becoming unrecognizable. But literature is not the only source of recognizable configurations or kinds of language. A given social milieu, occasion or activity may provide the poet with a ready-made language easily identifiable from even a few snippets of it—as in Henry Reed's poem *Lessons of the War: I. Naming of Parts*, which begins:

> To-day we have naming of parts. Yesterday,
> We had daily cleaning. And to-morrow morning,
> We shall have what to do after firing. But to-day,

[1] Blaise Pascal, *Pensées sur la réligion et sur quelques autres sujets*, ed. Louis Lafuma, 2nd edn. (Paris, 1952), p. 221.

> To-day we have naming of parts. Japonica
> Glistens like coral in all of the neighbouring gardens,
> And to-day we have naming of parts.[1]

Here a slight verbal alteration effects a decisive change: 'To-day we have naming of parts . . . what to do after firing' comes out of the mouth of the man giving rifle instruction, but it is clear that the repetition in 'But *to-day*, *To-day* we have naming of parts' is not his; these words make a transition from the rifle lesson to the captive audience's private feelings and reflections, and are recognizable as a transition because the reader's experience of different ways of speaking enables him to place a style or a usage without stopping to think, much less to analyse the shift in style.

A number of the problems encountered in trying to think and write critically about diction become easier to approach if we make a habit of reckoning with the swift and unnoticed operation upon the reader's responses of his own experience of the language he is reading—experience which enables him to make differentiations which he does not formulate in analytical terms. In the examples given from Eliot and Reed, differentiations of usage are very prominent and a reader who appreciates the poem at all will be aware that it mixes usages usually kept apart in ordinary life. But in many poems, mixture of usages goes on in a less ostentatious way and the poem may present an apparently smooth surface. If, for instance, we consider two lines from Auden's *Letter to Lord Byron* (II, 19, 6–7):

> And many a bandit, not so gently born
> Kills vermin every winter with the Quorn[2]

we can see at once that this is heightened, interesting language, but it is not easy to identify the manner of its heightening or the source of the interest. Apart from the fact that it is metrical and rhymes, it would seem to owe little to overtly poetic devices. Here is a crucial question about diction as a mode of creating effect: where does the interest come from? what is it that makes a series of words striking, in cases where rhythm and word-pattern are not doing very much (if

---

[1] Henry Reed, *A Map of Verona* (London, 1946), p. 22.
[2] W. H. Auden and Louis MacNeice, *Letters from Iceland* (London, 1937 p. 53.

any) work, and where the individual words considered severally do not derive their interest from their deviation from the vocabulary of common life? To answer such a question one must first do something to bring into the light of critical enquiry the process of placing and interpreting the language carried on by the reader as he reads. If silly questions were asked (such as 'Does the word "vermin" in these lines refer to rats?' or 'Are the lines meant to convey what foxes feel like when they are hunted?'), the reader would recognize the silliness of the questions because he has already interpreted the poem's words in relation to one another and in relation to the linguistic field from which they come.

What we call 'the English language' is not really a single structure; it is made up of a large number of differing structures. Different occupations have differing vocabularies and usages, the various branches of knowledge give rise to differing systems of communication, one social stratum will differ from another in speech habits, and even the pursuits of our leisure may involve the learning of a language peculiar to them. Moreover, the individual human beings who are used to moving about in the various fields of speech they enter at work, at home, with friends, at church, in shops, at the doctor's and so on, can also move without conscious effort through a whole range of differing written conventions (in books, newspapers, crosswords, timetables, letters, cards of invitation, bills) which use the English language in markedly different ways. Even while reading through one newspaper we make these adjustments: we do not read advertisements in the same way as we read the leading article, or that in the same way as the sports page. Further, each of us, whatever the linguistic fields we know best, employs vocabulary which reflects the complex structures in which we think about ourselves and our environment. Being human, we are complex; we make deductions, machines, love; we have property, ideals, faults, troubles; each aspect of experience has a vocabulary appropriate to it, by use of which we can relate our experience to the mental structures useful for thinking and talking about them. Vocabularies and usages may overlap (the overlap too can be exploited by the poet) but the extent to which usage is discriminated gives the poet ample opportunity to select words and phrases that bring into his poem a particular social and cultural context which will interact with other words and phrases in the poem.

This interaction may be so strong and decisive that a phrase as it operates in a poem has a power which seems inexplicable in terms of what the phrase ostensibly refers to. The phrase 'every winter', in the lines just quoted from Auden, serves to illustrate this. 'Every winter', viewed in isolation, would seem to be a familiar enough phrase, referring to the time of year and the frequency with which something or other takes place, though of course if it were really in isolation there would not be anything taking place; if one were to do in real life what one unfortunately tries to do in atomizing a poet's diction— that is, fire phrases off in a vacuum and pretend to hear what kind of bang they make—questions might be asked about one's sanity. But what the phrase really does in its context will appear if we drop the words out of the sentence and put in their place some other words that would fill the metrical gap without producing nonsense (e.g., 'If he's lucky'), for it will now appear that 'kills' and 'vermin' have lost some of their edge and 'Quorn' has lost some of its solidity. The point of 'every winter' lies in its relation to these other words. The nature of the relation may more readily appear if we examine a comparable line from Byron's *Don Juan* (III, xcvii, 4):

An epic from Bob Southey every Spring—

where the force of 'every Spring' is not the information it conveys about the time of year but the information it conveys about the quality of Southey's epics (which is also conveyed by calling Southey 'Bob'). Byron's line suggests that it is a far cry from blind Homer and mighty Vergil to Bob Southey, and it suggests this by playing off 'every Spring' against a context not created by the poem but simply drawn into it—a context in which it is customary to think of great poets attempting as the crown of their life and work the highest literary form of all. 'Every Spring' focuses, out of all we know about the epic, the magnitude of the endeavour to write one, and suggests that epics that come 'every Spring' are not epics at all, except in Southey's use of the term. Similarly with Auden's 'every winter'; the force of the phrase when used along with 'kills' and 'with the Quorn' lies in the suggestion that killing, and talking about it in this way, is done for social reasons.

This same line illustrates another aspect of the question of social context and the idiosyncrasies of poetic language. The phrase 'kills vermin' is not a familiar usage. In unpoetic parlance vermin are kept down, kept under control, cleared out, destroyed, dealt with, got rid of; nobody outside the world of the poem, engaging in this activity, would be likely to reply, to someone who asked what he was doing, 'I'm killing vermin'. He might, if he were asked, 'Why do you kill animals this way?', reply, 'They're vermin'. Auden's diction here telescopes a usage ('kills') which describes the fact and a usage ('vermin') which goes with defence of the fact, and then ridicules the defence by suggesting that the real purpose of hunting is not the extermination of vermin but rather participation in an activity with a high social rating. Such a deviation from the language of common life does not strike us as eccentric or affected when we encounter it in a poem. Similarly, in reading a poem we are not put off by the open expression of attitudes not usually expressed openly in ordinary life. The 'I' of a poem may say, as in Pope's *Epilogue to the Satires* (II, 208–9), 'Yes, I am proud; I must be proud to see Men not afraid of God, afraid of me', whereas such a remark if made in real life would be unlikely to be received with anything other than social embarrassment. But 'poetic licence' to do such things is not an oddity so outstanding as to differentiate language into two opposed worlds, the poetic and the non-poetic. Poetry is one of a number of developed types of utterance, each with its own history and conventions, the nature of the present conventions depending upon the past history of how this type of utterance established itself and upon the continuing pressure exerted on it by contemporary forms of the human activities or needs it grew up to meet. We bring to poetry the expectations it has itself created and the aptitudes for understanding it that we have developed in our previous encounters with it. The common reader, opening a book of poems, expects that the language used in the book will be 'different', because in his experience the language used in poems usually is. But though we must concede to every developed form of language the right to exist without being branded as more odd than any other, we must also concede that poetry has the extreme peculiarity of being able to raid other forms of language at will, taking from them as much or as little as it chooses and doing what it likes with the bits. One reason for this is simple and obvious enough, though the results of such freedom may be endlessly surprising. A poem, in so far as it is a fiction uttered by a poetic 'I', is not tied to any context save the context the poet himself articulates in the poem. A real human being in real life cannot escape from a whole array of contexts: the kind of person he is (or hopes to pass for), which demands of him certain kinds of linguistic behaviour; the kind of people he is addressing (or thinks of himself as addressing); the kind of subject he is treating; often, too, the kind of occasion on which he is discussing it. For instance, it is not open to me, at this present moment of writing, to repudiate my relation to my reader by writing the rest of this book in French, German or Latin, or indeed any part of the book in any of these languages (unless in quotation or in italics to mark a borrowing). But to switch languages in some portions of a poem is allowed to Skelton, Langland, Pound, Eliot. The poet may of course entertain views of poetry which cause him to adopt, say, the *persona* of a frequenter of Mrs Thrale's drawing-room and address himself to an audience hypothetically of the same kind. Or, for the purely temporary occasion of a particular poem, or a poem in a particular *genre*, he may assume a particular *persona*, envisage a particular audience, or carefully fabricate the illusion of a particular real-life setting. Or he may assume a sardonic *persona* who criticizes values, or a volatile *persona* with lightning changes of mood and language. The central fact still is that in so far as a particular kind of *persona* is necessary to the poem, the poet's diction must create it. Moreover the object or situation or experience he means to put on paper has a comparable fluidity until his words fix it—a fluidity that does not obtain in the physical world. In a poem, objects may be related verbally to just those mental spheres the poet happens to be interested in, because objects in the poem are only verbally represented; they have no adhesions to reality except through the words the poet allows into the poem. Roses may 'exist' without thorns, grins without Cheshire cats; a vale may run through Cheapside; there is nothing to prevent the poet from asking, as Blake does in *Jerusalem* (i, xii, 26–33):

is that

Mild Zion's hill's most ancient promontory, near mournful
Ever weeping Paddington? is that Calvary and Golgotha
Becoming a building of pity and compassion? Lo!
The stones are pity, and the bricks, well wrought affections
Enamel'd with love & kindness, & the tiles engraven gold,
Labour of merciful hands: the beams & rafters are forgiveness:
The mortar & cement of the work, tears of honesty . . .[1]

But in order to ensure that objects are considered under those aspects the poet wants considered, the poet must use in his poems the terminology that brings into play those particular mental structures or categories (scientific, historical, moral, religious, psychological, etc.) in which it seems to him interesting to think or feel about an object. The poet is both free of context and bound to create it: free of any binding real context, he is bound to supply verbally the context that gives objects attributes, scale, setting and significance, for if he does not, the very objects he names may be almost incomprehensible, as in a later passage of *Jerusalem* (i, xvi, 1–5) where Blake asserts that

Hampstead, Highgate, Finchley, Hendon, Muswell hill rage loud
Before Bromion's iron Tongs & glowing Poker reddening fierce;
Hertfordshire glows with fierce Vegetation; in the Forests
The Oak frowns terrible, the Beech & Ash & Elm enroot
Among the Spiritual fires.[2]

The clarity and assurance with which the poet can direct us towards his own valuation of an object are often the result of his using a diction which, in the act of specifying the object, pre-selects the point of view from which it is to be seen. This indeed is one of the great functions of metaphor and simile—to determine the reader's point of view by intimately relating the object to some area of experience capable of conferring value upon the object or of attesting the quality of the poet's feelings towards it; indeed it is possible to

[1] *The Complete Writings of William Blake*, ed. Geoffrey Keynes (London, 1957), p. 632.
[2] Keynes, p. 636.

43

write poems which laud, at length, an object about which we are told nothing that would of itself account for the high value set upon it by the poet. As an example of the poet's freedom to impregnate one object with qualities which in real life go with something quite different, one might cite Wallace Stevens's poem *Peter Quince at the Clavier*.[1] The poem is a meditation on the theme of Susanna and the Elders—a theme which might appear to the common man to have nothing to do with music. It begins:

> Just as my fingers on these keys
> Make music, so the selfsame sounds
> On my spirit make a music, too.
>
> Music is feeling, then, not sound;
> And thus it is that what I feel,
> Here in this room, desiring you,
>
> Thinking of your blue-shadowed silk,
> Is music. It is like the strain
> Waked in the elders by Susanna

and it ends:

> Susanna's music touched the bawdy strings
> Of those white elders; but, escaping,
> Left only Death's ironic scraping.
> Now, in its immortality, it plays
> On the clear viol of her memory,
> And makes a constant sacrament of praise.

The poem as a whole depends upon the idea and terminology of music which the poet has ostentatiously chosen to associate with his meditation on Susanna. What is so evidently in this poem an act of free choice on the poet's part—a mental improvisation as experimental as the improvisation of his fingers on the keys of the clavier—goes on to some extent in all poems, though usually less openly. Effective poetry manages its diction so that the words chosen provide the point of view from which the topic of the poem is to be viewed, and does this in such a way as to make the relation between the topic and the point of view an interesting relation. For instance, the poet may

[1] *The Collected Poems of Wallace Stevens* (London, 1955), pp. 89–92.

deliberately treat a certain object in a diction that suggests values other than those ordinarily thought to be proper to the object, as when Pope in *The Dunciad* (IV, 301–2), playing on the conventions of eighteenth-century landscape poetry and painting, and pretending to believe that all that matters about the scene is its purely pictorial value, especially the harmony of its colour tones, effortlessly subdues the complexion of the abbots to the colouring of the landscape:

> To happy Convents, bosom'd deep in vines,
> Where slumber Abbots, purple as their wines

and the quip is enhanced by the fact that it is made in the diction of landscape poetry. In that diction clouds and rivers 'slumber' and 'sleep'; appropriately, in Pope's lines, the purple abbots sleep too—but literally, not figuratively. And however improper this may be from the religious point of view, in the pictorial convention the abbots' part in the whole composition is perfect—or so Pope's diction claims (inviting us to demur).

It is inevitable from the very nature of language that choice of words implies choice of attitude, the choice of a certain kind of mental structure within which the object is seen, or to which it is assimilated, or by reference to which it is explained. The nature of language is such that there can be no such thing as a neutral transcription of an object into words. Even if language is used as in a police description of a wanted man, it is still used from a pre-selected point of view—in this case, from the point of view that it is of prime importance to make identification possible. It is for this reason that we should be chary of describing any diction as 'realistic' or 'accurate'. 'Accurate' for what purpose? 'Realistic' according to what view of reality? Sometimes one is tempted to criticize a diction on the grounds that things are 'not really' what the poet says they are—not really feathered tribes, but really birds. But, whilst one expression may be less usual than another, birds are as *really* feathered tribes as they are birds or about a hundred sparrows or ninety-eight examples of *passer domesticus domesticus*. What matters most about any one way of referring to a thing is the implications of one's referring to it in this way in preference to others; the particular way chosen implies a kind of speaker with a kind of purpose or point of view which relates the sparrows/birds/feathered tribes to some system of looking at such objects. Criticism of diction is most likely to be illuminating if it concentrates on the relation between the object and the point of view and promotes sensitivity to the way in which words are used to induce or define attitudes other than those in which everyday language allows us inertly to rest. It is true that a single word, reverberating against the near-synonyms it has displaced, may imply an attitude— as 'steed' or 'nag' or 'horse' or 'favourite' or 'mount' (whichever is chosen) implies an attitude different from what would be implied by choosing one of the other terms available—and in this respect the single word does matter. But it matters to its context, which means that ultimately criticism of diction resolves itself into consideration of the interplay of certain words in a certain context; single words bring to the poem a potential of power which derives from their usage outside the poem but the power is not set to work until it combines or collides with other potentials brought into the poem by the other words it also uses.

It will be clear both from what has been said and what has so far been left unattempted in this chapter that we have only scratched the surface of the immense question of diction. It is immense because it concerns at one end the whole state of the language from which the poet draws the words that make up his poem, while at the other end —in the poem itself—it may in any given case involve consideration of how the poet uses means available in poetry, but not in prose and non-literary language generally, to modify or reanimate the import of the words he chooses from the whole range of the language. Moreover, a poem is a progressive context: by the time he reaches the last line, the poet's decisions as to what words to use and what not to use will probably involve considerations different from those which swayed his choices in the first line, for, by the time the last line is reached, the poem itself has built up a context of immense individuality and complexity. A passage from *Don Juan* will illustrate the extent to which a context already highly individualized will respond to the simplest-seeming words, as a touch on the controls will change the hum and speed of an efficient machine.

The 'hymn' in the third canto of *Don Juan*, with which Haidée's household poet lauds the Isles of Greece, ends with

> Place me on Sunium's marbled steep,
>   Where nothing, save the waves and I,
> May hear our mutual murmurs sweep;
>   There, swan-like, let me sing and die:
> A land of slaves shall ne'er be mine—
> Dash down yon cup of Samian wine!

and Byron then goes on, in stanza 87,

> Thus sung, or would, or could, or should have sung,
>   The modern Greek, in tolerable verse;
> If not like Orpheus quite, when Greece was young,
>   Yet in these times he might have done much worse.

'Thus sung' is the epic '*dixit*' which marks the termination of a heroic speech and prepares for the move from *oratio recta* to narrative or descriptive verse. To 'Thus sung' Byron adds 'or would, or could, or should have sung' and the purpose of this addition is to deflate, but not too suddenly, the dignity of what has gone before; this sequence, putting ludicrous stress on the auxiliaries of the verb, draws attention to the fact that the sardonic Byron is coming back into the poem, the Byron who casts a cold eye on the Muse and who represents himself as finding it so difficult to write poetry in a modern setting that he is always having involved debates with himself about the propriety or impropriety of what he has just written or what he might write or what other people think he ought to write. This aspect of the Byronic personality re-enters the poem not with a bang but a stutter, a deliberate grinding of the gears of language as the poem changes over again from romantic to satiric writing. The stutter, of course, is not just a metrical filler in a desperate situation; it is only supposed to be that; it is ironically offered as a helpless bit of writing. Its real purpose is to modulate to the satirical tone again and to the already established Byronic manner in which the deliberate exposure of poetic machinery is part of the satiric technique.

Effects derived from striking transitions in diction are not confined to witty poems; the pathetic and the tragic may show them too. When Keats writes, in the seventh stanza of his *Ode to a Nightingale*,

> Perhaps the self-same song that found a path
> Through the sad heart of Ruth, when, sick for home,
> She stood in tears amid the alien corn,

he gives the passage its impact by taking a term used of national and cultural differences and applying it to something in the insentient natural world which knows nothing of these. King Lear in his mental agony ascribes Poor Tom's miseries to the same causes as his own and cries out:

> Is it the fashion, that discarded fathers
> Should have thus little mercy on their flesh?
>
> (III, iv, 74–5)

Lear's bitterness comes out in 'discarded fathers', where a term associated with a practical and utilitarian attitude to things is put with a word implying the deepest human ties and moral obligations. When such phrases strike us we are set busy constructing for ourselves the connecting link between words not usually found in one another's company. We imagine in Ruth a state of such total isolation that even the corn looks alien. We imagine in Lear a state of such bitterness that he sees fathers as being treated like things: used and thrown away. The fact that the reader is made to participate in the poet's insight by working out such a relation for himself is most evident in instances where the yoking together of terms is very violently done, as in the last line of Yeats's *Byzantium*: 'That dolphin-torn, that gong-tormented sea'. What enables the reader to arrive at the right relation is the guidance built into the passage or even into the whole work in which the striking phrase occurs. 'Alien corn' could not do its work without 'sick for home, She stood in tears', nor 'discarded fathers' work without 'Is it the fashion . . .' and, behind that again, the larger context of the whole action; Yeats's epithets for the sea need the whole poem[1] as their preparation.

In saying this, we raise a question beyond the scope of this chapter: the question of how to discuss the structure of a whole work. Before going into this, it is necessary first to repair the most crying omission of this present chapter on diction, by turning now to the study of metaphorical language.

[1] See *The Collected Poems of W. B. Yeats*, 2nd edn. (London, 1950), pp. 280–1.

III

Metaphor

THE word 'metaphor' is commonly used to mean something like *speaking of X as though it were Y*. The poet means his reader to think of a woman but he calls her a rose, speaks of her as though she were a rose. This *speaking of X in terminology proper to Y* was stressed by Aristotle in his definition of metaphor.

μεταφορά in the sense of *transference, the process of transferring a word from one object of reference to another* is defined in *Poetics*, 21,1457 b: 'Metaphor consists in applying to a thing a word that belongs to something else; the transference being either from genus to species or from species to genus or from species to species or on grounds of analogy.'[1]

Aristotle lumped together with what we now call metaphor other transfers to which nowadays other names are given: the transfers now called synecdoche and metonymy. In synecdoche there is a transfer of name from the whole to the part (as when the object *ship* is called by the name 'keel') or from the part to the whole (as when in Shakespeare's *King John* at IV, ii, 108–9 a downpour is called by the name 'weather': 'So foul a sky clears not without a storm: Pour down thy weather'). In metonymy an object is called by the name of something associated or connected with it (as when in *King Lear*, I, i, 41, younger people are called 'younger strengths'; as when in *Much Ado About Nothing*, II, iii, 61, music is called 'sheep's guts'; as when nowadays we talk of reading an author when we mean reading his works). 'Metaphor', which according to Aristotle included these, has come to be restricted to name-transfers based on analogy.[2] But it is

[1] W. Bedell Stanford, *Greek Metaphor: Studies in Theory and Practice* (Oxford, 1936), pp. 9–10.

[2] I. A. Richards, in *The Philosophy of Rhetoric*, uses the term more freely, 'to cover all cases where a word, in Johnson's phrase, "gives two ideas for one", where we compound different uses of the word into one, and speak of something as though it were another. ... further still, to include, as metaphoric, those processes in which we perceive or think of or feel about one thing in terms of another —' (p. 116).

useful to begin with his definition, simply because it does lay emphasis on transference of name and by so doing directs attention to the linguistic aspect of metaphor (as distinct from the mental act of perceiving analogy).

If we call a woman a rose, or speak of anything as though it were something else, we are doing something at the language level; 'calling', 'naming' and 'speaking as though' are expressions referring to linguistic operations. It is important to remember that metaphor is a linguistic phenomenon. So is simile. In the case of a simile the linguistic machinery used to mark similitude consists of special words: 'like', 'as', etc. Verbal machinery is logically distinguishable from the perception of likeness or analogy it conveys, and there is some point in observing the distinction between seeing an analogical relation (an act of thought) and putting it into words: the distinction, that is, between a thought as such and its linguistic manifestation in a figure of speech.[1] That this is a real distinction is clear from the fact that an analogy can be put into words in different ways. If when a poet looks at the sea it puts him in mind of a harp, he can put his reader in mind of a harp by saying, 'The sea is like a harp', or by exclaiming, 'O harplike sea!', or by talking of 'chords played on the wires of the sea' and so on. Many linguistic means are available for expressing a discernment that two things may be compared, as is clear if we think of these: Hopkins's title, *The Blessed Virgin compared to the Air we Breathe*; the first line of Shakespeare's Sonnet 18, 'Shall I compare thee to a summer's day?'; the formula for extended

---

[1] Strictly speaking, the word 'analogy', when used of a relation, indicates relation of the type *A is to B as C is to D*, and when used of a figure of words ought to refer to the expression of such a relation. But in the context of this discussion such strict usage would involve frequent use of cumbrous expressions and I have therefore availed myself of looser usage of the term, using it to refer to various figures of speech involving some form of likening. It seems inadvisable to use 'likeness' or 'likening' as an inclusive term since, as I. A. Richards points out (op. cit., p. 127), the interest of a metaphor usually depends as much on disparity between the two members related by a metaphor as on their likeness: 'the peculiar modification of the tenor which the vehicle brings about is even more the work of their unlikenesses than of their likenesses'; moreover an image may depend 'not upon any plastic resemblance between tenor and vehicle, but on the subjective identity of the emotions each arouses', as Brian A. Rowley points out in 'The Light of Music and the Music of Light: Synaesthetic Imagery in the Works of Ludwig Tieck', Publications of the English Goethe Society, xxvi (1957), 67.

treatment, *Not with more so-and-so does X do something than Y does something else (or the same kind of thing)*; Donne's lines in *The second Anniversarie* (ll. 244–6):

> her pure, and eloquent blood
> Spoke in her cheekes, and so distinctly wrought,
> That one might almost say, her body thought;[1]

in Shelley's line, 'O wild West Wind, thou breath of Autumn's being', the double apostrophizing. Obviously, the likening of one thing to another can take a variety of linguistic forms. It may seem, to some, equally obvious that in calling this roll I have disregarded vital differences; some critics would hold that metaphor embodies deep truths whereas simile merely suggests an aspect under which one might temporarily look at a thing or an idea one might toy with but not care fully to assert. But not infrequently it will be found that in poetry an analogy is expressed first as a simile and then as a metaphor, so there can hardly be much difference between the two, with respect to their truth-claims or imaginative depth. One might reflect on Cleopatra's description of Antony:

> his delights
> Were dolphin-like; they show'd his back above
> The element they lived in[2]

or the vicissitudes of an idea recorded in Stephen Spender's account of the labours that went to the writing of his poem *Seascape*.[3] In such cases it seems reasonable to suppose that there is no superior inner truth in an idea which issues as metaphor, as contrasted with an idea issuing as simile. It seems more profitable to distinguish between metaphor, simile and other forms of comparison, by reference to the linguistic apparatus which conveys the idea and to the relative advantages and drawbacks of each kind of apparatus.

---

[1] *The Poems of John Donne*, ed. H. J. C. Grierson (London, 1929), p. 234.

[2] Shakespeare, *Antony and Cleopatra*, v, ii, 88–90.

[3] Stephen Spender, 'The Making of a Poem', *Partisan Review*, XIII (1946), 294–308; reprinted in Brewster Ghiselin (ed.), *The Creative Process: A Symposium* [published as a Mentor Book by arrangement with the University of California Press] (New York, 1955), pp. 112–25. For the final text of *Seascape* see *Collected Poems, 1928–1935, by Stephen Spender* (London, 1955), p. 172.

Metaphor is not easy to deal with; before considering how best to define it, one must make some preliminary observations. Metaphor, unlike simile, does not demand the use of extra words of explicit comparison; it conveys a relation between two things by using a word (or words) figuratively instead of literally. But the terms 'figurative[ly]' and 'literal[ly]' are themselves in need of clarification. It is a commonplace to students of semantic change that a language extends its range by using words in transferred senses, linking what is new in men's environment, and in their thinking, to words already available in the language, using them in a way at first figurative but in course of time becoming well-established as the usual way of referring to something, so that the usage is then thought of as merely literal. One may give as examples the 'bonnet' of a car, or its 'hood'. Paul Henle, in a discussion of the use of metaphor to extend language, and of the subsequent fading of metaphor into a literal sense, remarks:

Metaphors of this type tend to vanish, not in the sense that they are no longer used, but in the sense that they become literal, so that today no one would think of saying that 'plastron of a turtle' or 'hood of a car' were metaphors.[1]

This process has so deeply affected the development and state of our language that, as Ullmann remarks, 'in the semantic sphere, the fading of metaphors is almost proverbial'.[2] It is, therefore, difficult to fix the meaning of the terms 'figurative' and 'literal' except by reference to general usage in the state of a language at a particular time. Henle (op. cit., p. 174) suggests using the terms in the following way:

By the *literal sense* of a word we may mean the sense which a word has in other contexts and apart from such metaphoric uses. By *figurative sense* we may mean that special sense on which the metaphor hinges. . . . the literal sense most often would be the meaning of a term given by a dictionary or, if there is more than one dictionary meaning, the meaning which is appropriate in context.

However difficult it may be to give a precise definition of the terms, I

---

[1] *Language, Thought, & Culture*, p. 187.
[2] *Principles of Semantics*, p. 91.

think we can hardly, in practice, go far wrong if in any particular case we settle the question of whether a use is or is not 'figurative' by reference to our own impression of it; if it strikes us as 'normal' (another shifty word, but meaningful enough for our purposes) we can call it 'literal'. This attitude to the question of discriminating between figurative and literal uses, however rule-of-thumb it may be, is reasonable enough if we take the view that much of the impact and interest of metaphor in poetry depends on our sense of a gap between the two members of the relationship: the object pointed to (known as the 'tenor' of the metaphor) and the terms in which it is alluded to (known as the 'vehicle' of the metaphor). For, as Ullmann remarks,

> It is an essential feature of a metaphor that there must be a certain distance between tenor and vehicle. Their similarity must be accompanied by a feeling of disparity; they must belong to different spheres of thought. If they are too close to one another, they cannot produce the perspective of 'double vision' peculiar to metaphor.[1]

This curious situation, where there has to be a similarity between two things sufficient to hold them together and a disparity between them sufficient to make their encounter exciting, raises considerable difficulties of terminology. We need a term with which to refer briefly to *the capacity of one object for entering into metaphorical relation with another*, a term to cover *the degree to which one object brought into a metaphor resembles the other object brought in*, and yet a third term for *the degree to which this 'similar' object excitingly differs from that other object*. We might in a rough-and-ready way get out of the latter two difficulties by speaking of the 'plausibility of connecting two objects' and 'the interest of connecting two objects' but the problem of finding a term with which to describe the potential of two objects for entering into this plausible and interesting relationship is much more difficult. Ordinary language does not easily provide us with words in which to describe briefly a relationship of a Yes/No kind, or the quality of a figure of speech whose success depends on a Yes/No relationship between the two objects it connects. But if we do not agree on a term, we shall either find ourselves talking in cumbrously-qualified phrases, or else using a term which stresses the Yes

[1] Stephen Ullmann, *Style in the French Novel* (Cambridge, 1957), p. 214.

at the expense of the No, or No at the expense of Yes. For instance, if—as in what follows in this chapter—it is necessary to talk at length about the resemblances between two things (or the 'plausibility' of connecting them) then the sheer frequency with which the word 'resemblance' (unqualified) appears on the page creates a disposition to think that this is the most important aspect of the relation between the two things brought together in a metaphor. What we need is a terminology which in the act of pointing to the resemblance reminds us that it is only a partial resemblance. For this reason I would suggest that my reader should enter into an agreement with me that we shall speak, when we want to refer to resemblance (i.e. to what makes the connection plausible), of 'the link' between the two members of a metaphorical relationship. And since the last seven words of the sentence I have just written would have to be used over and over again if no shorter means of reference were found, I shall speak, instead, of 'the extremes' of a metaphor. If we use this terminology of 'linking' the 'extremes' we shall all the while be safeguarding ourselves against taking a distorted view of the nature of metaphorical language.

Using these simple words, and using 'literal' and 'figurative' in the way explained above (that is, 'literal' use is, roughly, 'normal' use, and a 'figurative' use is one that makes us aware that a linkage is being effected) I can return to a discussion of the linguistic apparatus involved in metaphor and simile, beginning with examples made up for the purpose of showing how these terms apply.

In simile, words are used literally; essentially what is said is 'This thing is like that thing'. If, looking at a telephone, one is suddenly put in mind of a black pug dog—or, looking at a black pug, one is irresistibly reminded of a telephone—(the mouth- and ear-pieces of the telephone corresponding to the pendulous ears, and the centre of the receiver-rest corresponding to the snarl on the face of the pug), one might put into words the link between these two extremes, pug and telephone, in a simile: 'Telephones are like pugs' faces', or 'Pugs' faces are like telephones'. Turning now to metaphor: if the radiator of a car approaching one suggests bared teeth, this, meta-phorically expressed, might appear as 'The radiator came at me with bared teeth'. Here, however, it is much more difficult to say what is being compared. What are the extremes of the metaphor? 'Radiator' and 'teeth', perhaps. Why not 'radiator' and 'bared teeth'? Or 'radiator coming at me' and 'bared teeth coming at me'? None the less it is clear enough that since dictionaries do not give *bars of car's radiator* as a normal meaning for 'teeth' (let alone for 'bared teeth') we shall have to take 'teeth' as being figurative. The metaphor has a literal extreme and a figurative extreme. And though, as I have indicated, it is only by arbitrary selection from the features of the situation it represents that one can say that the literal extreme is 'radiator' and the figurative extreme is 'teeth', we have no difficulty in distributing the terms 'literal' and 'figurative' to the appropriate extreme, however difficult it may be to describe the exact constitution of the two areas of meaning involved. The greater complexity of metaphor is not confined to the problem of saying exactly where its extremes lie. There is the further problem that one of the extremes ('teeth', in my present metaphor) stands for something not specified: for *something to do with car-radiators coming at me*. It would be very difficult to find a good defence for my easy assumption that 'teeth' stands for the bars of the radiator, particularly if I had to argue the case with an opponent who said that our problem is not to find out what 'teeth' stands for, but what 'bared teeth coming at me' stands for. My opponent might say that the bars of a radiator would have no very plausible resemblance to bared teeth if they were found on a scrap-heap instead of in site in the metal frame on the front of a car which is bearing down on an alarmed pedestrian. In the actual situation described by the metaphor, my opponent might argue, there is something present which is not named in the words of the metaphor but which by its relation to the whole situation suggests to the writer of the metaphor that bared teeth are coming at him; it would be a gross misrepresentation of what was going on in the mind of the writer either in the actual situation or in the act of writing the metaphor to say that 'teeth' means *bars*; obviously the writer does not mean *The radiator came at me with its bars (as is usual) unenclosed.*

What most clearly emerges from all this is the fact that simile does not create difficulties of this kind, and the further fact that if we are to talk about metaphor we shall at some stage need a term with which to refer to this unnamed something which is present in the situation described by the metaphor but is not verbally specified in the metaphor itself. For the present I shall ask my reader to agree with me to call it 'X', should need arise to refer to it before we have decided whether it is important and, if so, what other questions (and terms for discussing them) it has to be related to.

It is one of the main purposes of this chapter to show how the effects gained by the use of metaphor are related to its linguistic form, and this purpose will be furthered if it can be shown that consideration of its linguistic form makes it easier to deal with problems such as those touched on in the last few paragraphs. The linguistic form of metaphor has been carefully characterized by Paul Henle. He writes:

In a metaphor some terms refer literally to one situation and figuratively to the second while other terms refer literally only and refer to the second situation only.[1]

To relate the definition to an instance: in the sentence 'the ship ploughs the waves', some words ('ship', 'waves') have literal reference, but the word 'ploughs' refers literally to ploughing and at the same time figuratively to the movement of a ship.

What is the use of propounding this definition?

Its use is that of any valid definition: to enable us to agree what comes into our discussion and what does not. It is useful too for the analysis of complex passages. Most important of all, this description of the linguistic configuration of metaphor brings out the truth of what some writers on metaphor have been at pains to point out: that is, that with a metaphor one can make a complex statement without complicating the grammatical construction of the sentence that carries the statement. For if we say, 'the ship ploughs the waves', this is tantamount to saying, 'The action of a ship in the waves is like the action of a plough in the soil', or to saying, 'The ship goes through the waves; the plough goes through the soil; the two actions are in

[1] Henle, op. cit., p. 181.

one or more respects the same', or 'The ship is to the waves as the plough is to the soil'. Ezra Pound described the poetic image as

that which presents an intellectual and emotional complex in an instant of time. . . . It is the presentation of such a 'complex' instantaneously which gives that sense of sudden liberation. . . . It is better to present one Image in a lifetime than to produce voluminous works.[1]

No doubt it is a very far cry from an 'Image' of such a quality to the pot-bound metaphors prevalent in 'homely' sermons and in the columns of fireside philosophy in some magazines. We have of course to distinguish between metaphors in which the linking of extremes is ham-fisted, and the result is boring or embarrassing, and metaphors in which the linking of extremes gives a 'sense of sudden liberation'; it depends on what sort of a 'complex' is presented, whether we are impressed or not. But the linguistic form of metaphor as such is what makes it possible for the 'complex' (whether it is a pot-bound bit of dreariness, or Birnam Wood coming to Dunsinane) to enter the mind in an instant of time. In a metaphor, the usual syntactical frame of a sentence is at some point filled up with a figurative word or phrase. The resulting impression must be complex, since two sentences are implied. The sentence 'The ship ploughs the waves' implies *The ship does something to the waves* and *The plough ploughs the soil*. For, if we had to 'explain' the metaphor, we could do so by writing out a wholly literal sentence about what the ship does (substituting for 'ploughs' some literal phrase—such as 'goes through') and then on the model of this literal sentence about the ship we could write out another sentence literally describing the parallel operation of the plough. I have said that these two sentences are 'implied', because of course neither of them is actually written when the metaphor is used. These implicit or unwritten sentences function simultaneously to provide a parallel action or reflected image. If this account of the working of the metaphor sounds far-fetched, it may be because this metaphor is so obvious that it is understood instantly without any consciousness of having had to work at it. In order to show that one does in fact work at a metaphor in some such way as I have suggested, I must take a less obvious metaphor.

[1] *Literary Essays of Ezra Pound*, ed. T. S. Eliot (London, 1954), p. 4.

Let us then consider the line, 'Afternoon burns upon its wires'—a line written and then rejected by Spender in the course of composing *Seascape*, as he tells us in 'The Making of a Poem'.[1] 'Its' refers to 'the sea' in the first sketch of the poem (in the final version, 'the happy ocean' replaces 'the sea'), so we may treat the metaphor as though it ran:

Afternoon burns upon the wires of the sea.

Before we can begin to get at the metaphor in this line we must 'translate' its other figurative devices. 'Afternoon' can stand for [*afternoon*] *sun* because *sun* and *afternoon* are associated with one another. So are *tea* and *afternoon*, and *nap* and *afternoon*, but we interpret 'afternoon' to mean [*afternoon*] *sun* because we make an inference from 'burns'—an easy inference, since we are familiar with the phrase 'burning sun[shine]'. Now we have the burning rays of the sun shining or striking upon 'the wires' of the sea. Since seas do not literally have wires (if we exclude submerged cables), the word 'wires' must have taken the place of something else; 'upon the wires of the sea' must therefore mean *upon the something-or-other of the sea*. We have now completed the first of the unwritten sentences implied by the metaphor.

If we had no further directions for locating this *something-or-other of the sea* we might suppose it to be spray or floating seaweed or even a rainbow, or anything—to do with the sea—in any respect resembling wires upon which a burning sun shines. Fortunately the antecedent context (both in the first sketch and in the final version of the poem) supplies more grounds for inference, since the sea/ocean has already been said to be 'like a harp'/'Like an unfingered harp'. Our second implicit sentence will therefore be to the effect that *the afternoon sun shines on the wires of the harp*. Visualizing this, we have a mental model in which the wires are taut, thin lines, are metallic, occur at regular intervals, etc. From this mental model, we have to supply to the *something-or-other of the sea* a particular reference. I take it we should all agree that the thing having to do with the sea that corresponds most nearly to all the specifications would be the crests,

[1] See Ghiselin, *The Creative Process*, p. 117.

ridges, backs, or swell of the waves; we can therefore, fairly confidently, take it that this must be the sense of 'wires'.

All this pother about a single line may serve to bring home the fact that the interpretation of a metaphor is a complicated process. It involves linguistic inferences—as to a *something-of-the-sea* corresponding to *the wires of a harp*—and, when these have been made, a sorting of our knowledge of sea-structure and our knowledge of harp-structure until we come up with whatever particular aspect of sea best corresponds to harp-wires and best meets all the other specifications given by the utterance we are interpreting—the wires must be wires upon which 'afternoon' can be said to 'burn'. A metaphor is thus a set of linguistic directions for supplying the sense of an un-written literal term. (This is why metaphor can 'say' things not provided for in the existing literal vocabulary of our language.) We should note that metaphor directs us to the *sense*, not to the exact term. The directions lead us, not to the term 'ridges', not to the term 'swell', not to the term 'humps', not to the term 'crests', but to that which in nature is the common target of all these verbal shots. By not using any of these terms, metaphor allows us to supply an uncontaminated image from our own experience of the physical world. What we supply, because it is free of terms and of their special senses, doesn't have to be hard like ridges or white like crests or humpy like humps; all it has to be, is the way the sea looks when afternoon burns upon its wires. Hence the much-vaunted physical immediacy of metaphor. Metaphor indicates how to find or to construct the target but it does not contaminate the mental image of the target by using any one of the literal terms available in ordinary language for referring to such a target. The reader pieces out the metaphor by something supplied or constructed from his own experience, according to the specifications given linguistically by the utterance in which the metaphor occurs. This is why metaphor has physical immediacy. Physical immediacy enters to supply the place of the missing literal word, to supply the thing pointed at by the something of the sea which is at the same time the wires of the harp.

It is worth while to stress the fact that this feature of metaphor is not shared by simile. In a simile there is no 'X'. In metaphor, where there is an 'X', the reader must supply from his own store a concept or image of 'X'. This has certain implications as to the general usefulness of these two linguistically-different ways of linking. It would seem to be implied—and it would be interesting to see how far this would be borne out in practice by the work of any one poet—that metaphor would be particularly useful for dealing with phenomena and experiences not so far named by common language. I need not labour to make the point that most of us have at some time noticed phenomena or had nuances of emotion for which ordinary language does not provide an identifying name. Stephen Spender's *afternoon burning upon the wires of the sea* is a case in point. No word exists that refers exclusively to the phenomenon of bright light striking a particular small area of a reflecting surface and seeming to blaze or burn in the object it strikes. 'Glint' is not a good enough word for this phenomenon because it does not do justice to the appearance of precise location (of the little blaze). 'Blaze' won't do because the word suggests too large a conflagration. As with the physical world, so with the world of private emotion; that world is in particular need of metaphor because the vocabulary of emotion is comparatively little developed—no doubt because emotions cannot be pointed to and identified as one can point to and identify shades of colour. Metaphor is therefore a useful means of dealing with the area of unnamed experiences. It is also useful for supplying a model on whose lines we can construct our own concept of what the poet is talking about, especially in cases where what he is talking about not only has no name in common language but is moreover an insight or configuration of experience peculiar to the poet and thus not already within the experience of the reader. To give a simple example: poets on the whole seem readier than the average man to recognize that conflicting or 'contradictory' feelings can be simultaneously entertained; one does not in all cases either love or hate, for there are some cases where one does both at once, cases where feelings fight a battle with one another. In saying 'fight a battle', I have myself resorted to metaphor in order to describe an emotion that cuts across the rational 'opposites' of common language. The metaphor of a battle of love or hate is not, perhaps, a very good one: a better one is Shakespeare's in

Sonnet 35 where, describing a very complex emotional and moral situation, he uses the metaphor of civil war ('Such civil war is in my love and hate') to describe the emotional aspect of the experience.

So far I have not stressed the fact that metaphor by its very form tends towards the diagrammatic. It must do so because the metaphorical sentence is a compacting of two implicit sentences standing in a close relationship which, set out in abstract form, consists of the analogy *A is to B as C is to D*. To say, in so many words, 'A is to B as C is to D', is explicitly to state the relationship implied in metaphor. Poetry, it is true, can accommodate explicit analogy, as in Shakespeare's Sonnet 75:

> So are you to my thoughts as food to life,
> Or as sweet-season'd showers are to the ground;
> And for the peace of you I hold such strife
> As 'twixt a miser and his wealth is found;

but the drawback of naming both members of the relationship is that there is then a tendency towards stereotyped linkage or towards diffuse explanation. 'So are you to my thoughts as food to life' is stereotyped; it depends for its working on the prior existence of a standard relation between food and life. No food, no life. This does not tell us very much about the poet's feelings, except the very general thing *No youth, no thoughts*. If the poet wants to make the analogy both unstereotyped and explicit, it will probably become diffuse and complex in syntax, as in Shakespeare's Sonnet 52, where the poet wants to say (roughly speaking) that though the youth is absent for a time the very thought that he will come back is a consolation, and absence will make his return the sweeter. In order to make clear the relation between a miser with a key to treasure locked up and the poet whose friend is kept away from him by absence, complex syntax has to be used:

> So am I as the rich, whose blessed key
> Can bring him to his sweet up-locked treasure,
> The which he will not every hour survey,
> For blunting the fine point of seldom pleasure.

Even with this rather strained syntax, the poet so far has dealt with only a part of the whole situation: *you are to me as treasure is; I am to my treasure as a miser is.* As yet he has not explained the 'blessed key' or the 'sweet up-locked treasure'. In order to relate the key and the treasure to the situation the poet has to call in the further assistance of 'time that keeps you as my chest, Or as the wardrobe which the robe doth hide'. The harder the poet tries to specify a precise relationship as a model for interpreting an individual emotional issue, the more diffuse and complex the syntax tends to become. The extreme point in extended syntax which goes on and on specifying particulars is the epic simile. Metaphor need not involve itself in complex syntax, because its form, permitting allusion to the unspecified, enables it to leave much to inference and implication. It is often the case in Shakespeare's sonnets that when he makes analogy explicit, one pair (of the four terms in *A is to B as C is to D*) tends to be standard (as in *miser to treasure*, or as in *food to life*, or *rain to earth*). The reason for this I assume to be that unless one of the pairs is a standard exemplar of a recognizable relationship familiarly occurring in real life, considerable syntactical difficulties will be encountered in referring to it. We may consider what happens in *The Tempest* when Shakespeare does use in a simile something which is not a familiar example of a rational activity in real life. What has to be said is that Prospero's brother acted as the Duke's substitute for so long that he began to believe he really was the Duke, and in so believing (says Prospero, attempting to clarify this irrational phenomenon), he was like a man who tells a lie so often that at last he comes to the point of believing in it himself. The syntactical result of trying to clarify an irrational act by likening it to another irrational act, is this:

> like one
> Who having into truth, by telling of it,
> Made such a sinner of his memory,
> To credit his own lie, he did believe
> He was indeed the duke; out o' the substitution,
> And executing the outward face of royalty,
> With all prerogative: hence his ambition growing—
> Dost thou hear?
>
> (1, ii, 99–106)

This dire syntax[1] is the natural result of Prospero's using, as a model to explain his brother's perfidy, another situation which itself requires explanation. In trying to explain how it is that a man can tell a lie and ultimately believe it himself, he involves himself in consideration of sins of habit and of consequent corruption of memory and the syntax never really recovers from the load of explanation it is called upon to bear. But usually, when Shakespeare uses simile as a model of relationship, the thing cited as a model is already familiar enough to be in no such need of explanation or definition. Shakespeare commonly uses the simile to enable the reader to refer to something with which he is already familiar in actual or linguistic experience. Simile very often acts for Shakespeare as a way of establishing the conceit he intends to develop. When this slips over into reducing a complex experience into a forced correspondence with something already known, and understood as 'rational', the result can be a repetitive and heavily argumentative sonnet, as Sonnet 118 is:

> Like as, to make our appetites more keen,
> With eager compounds we our palate urge,
> As, to prevent our maladies unseen,
> We sicken to shun sickness when we purge,
> Even so, being full of your ne'er-cloying sweetness,
> To bitter sauces did I frame my feeding
> And, sick of welfare, found a kind of meetness
> To be diseased ere that there was true needing.
> Thus policy in love, to anticipate
> The ills that were not, grew to faults assured
> And brought to medicine a healthful state
> Which, rank of goodness, would by ill be cured:
>   But thence I learn, and find the lesson true,
>   Drugs poison him that fell so sick of you.

By contrast, the superiority of the companion sonnet on the same theme, Sonnet 119, stands out clearly:

> What potions have I drunk of Siren tears,
> Distill'd from limbecks foul as hell within,
> Applying fears to hopes and hopes to fears,
> Still losing when I saw myself to win!

---

[1] The *Globe* gives it up as a bad job, but the text is not in fact corrupt.

What wretched errors hath my heart committed,
Whilst it hath thought itself so blessed never!
How have mine eyes out of their spheres been fitted
In the distraction of this madding fever!
O benefit of ill! now I find true
That better is by evil still made better;
And ruin'd love, when it is built anew,
Grows fairer than at first, more strong, far greater.
    So I return rebuked to my content
    And gain by ill thrice more than I have spent.

There is no doubt that the latter is the better sonnet. It uses metaphor to figure the unusual and the irrational, and emphasizes the paradoxical nature of experience; the result is much better poetry than we get in the other sonnet, the one which tries to fit private experience into rational patterns in the public world.

In addition to the aspects of metaphor so far discussed (how it achieves physical immediacy and how it acts as a diagram or model of relationships) we have yet another to consider: the power of the metaphorical term to bring associations and suggestions with it. The figurative words bring with them a diffused aura of their literal use; I say 'aura' deliberately, to emphasize that it is rather indeterminate. What a word brings with it depends for each individual reader on his associations: his word-associations and his associations in the actual experiences of his own life. Obviously some words have more standardized associations than others and some have more vivid suggestions than others. The poet can to some extent control the aura, by being careful what analogy he chooses and by carefully selecting the other words he uses in the passage in which the metaphor occurs. But his power to control the aura is not unlimited. For example, if he wanted to find a model of grace and flexibility and silent movement he might reject some objects which do have these qualities, simply because the objects have powerful repulsive associations for most people, as the snake has. The well-chosen model, however, can contribute its associations to the effect of the passage. When Shakespeare writes, of Antony, 'For his bounty, There was no winter in't; an autumn 'twas That grew the more by reaping'[1] he draws on our

---

[1] *Antony and Cleopatra*, v, ii, 86–8.

approval feelings about autumn, and makes sure that these come into play, by using words which call up the idea of mellow fruitfulness. We feel about Antony roughly as we feel about the season of abundance, autumn. In this case, the constructive use of associations does not preclude strong emphasis on the diagrammatic aspect of the metaphor, for, at the same time, Shakespeare emphasizes Antony's quality of doing everything so superlatively that he is more bountiful than whatever is most bounteous in the natural world; the metaphor is so handled as to make it clear that Antony is unlike autumn in one important respect: his bounty has no limit or decline. This particular metaphor is a special case; it would be easier to match it with other metaphors in *Antony and Cleopatra* itself than to find parallels in other works. It is the nature of the subject—Shakespeare's conception of Antony—that causes him to invent metaphors which are simultaneously strongly associative and strongly diagrammatic. His task is to make Antony at once amply physical and superior to the merely physical, so we get metaphors which draw on two different possibilities of metaphor: the force of association and the force of the relation *better than that, not merely like that*. There is a comparable metaphor in the same speech: 'his delights Were dolphin-like; they show'd his back above The element they lived in'. Here again the aura of associations is constructively used: dolphins sport, are lusty, live in the open sea, they suggest freedom, vigour and enjoyment, to see them is an event which is remarkable and excites a sense of wonder. Yet in addition to all this a clear logical relation is conveyed. Dolphins are to the waters of the sea as Antony's spirit of enjoyment is to his pleasures: in them, but not subdued to them, as the dolphins show joy in their element precisely at the moment when they leap up out of it. This diagrammatic aspect of the metaphor is even more telling than its aura of associations. However, as I have remarked, *Antony and Cleopatra* is a special case and we must expect to find that metaphor cannot often be used in such a way as to realize its different potentialities simultaneously, with equal force to each. Metaphor can be used to pull into the poem a real-life experience which is a complex of different qualities, but in many cases this will tend to diminish precision, vividness, or physical particularity. Even

Shakespeare, brilliant as he is at swooping on perfect natural analogies, cannot in the autumn metaphor or the dolphin metaphor make us see a physical phenomenon so visually sharp as, say, the sun striking burning metallic fires out of the swell of the waves. We can't have everything at once.

Suggestion, then, is one potentiality of metaphor. It may, however, well be true that suggestion is usually better done by simile. Simile (when simple) does not indicate the respect in which one thing is like another thing. It says the things are alike; it is up to us to see why; the things may be alike in a large number of ways. Thus simile in turn has its own advantages. It may be a considerable advantage to the poet to claim that likeness exists without indicating where it lies. And if the poet goes beyond simple simile (beyond *this is like that*) he has open to him a great variety of effects. The simile in the first stanza of Blake's *Infant Sorrow* contrives to be both specific and mysterious:

> My mother groan'd! my father wept.
> Into the dangerous world I leapt:
> Helpless, naked, piping loud:
> Like a fiend hid in a cloud.

Before Blake presents the simile, he specifies the qualities he has in mind: the child is 'Helpless, naked, piping loud'; this is very definite. Then comes the mysterious simile, 'Like a fiend hid in a cloud'. The words 'naked' and 'piping loud' induce us to visualize the fiend of the simile as the face of the wind represented in the corners of old maps: a fierce child-face.[1] The result of linking the adjectives of the third line with the mysterious fiend simile in the fourth is that though there is nothing helpless about the fiend-face and, so far, nothing fiendish about the newborn child, we are induced to link 'Helpless' with 'piping', and 'fiend' with an image of a child, and so we become obscurely convinced that there can be such a thing as a helpless fiend—that a helpless fiend is what the newborn child really is. (Having made the point by these tortuous means, Blake can

---

[1] Joseph H. Wicksteed in his *Blake's Innocence and Experience* (London, 1928), compares this with the sixth *Job* illustration and suggests that 'the association of the fiend and the cloud. . . . probably originates in the image of a thunder-clap' (p. 174).

then say, 'Bound and weary I thought best To sulk upon my mother's breast'.) We accept the mysterious connection, *a child like a fiend*, because we have already accepted the specified likenesses (*naked, piping loud*) between a baby and the babyfaced wind. Free effects of this and presumably of many other kinds are open to the user of simile. Just because simile is not so peculiar in form as metaphor is, it leaves open a much wider range of ways of comparing one thing to another. It is hardly to be imagined that one could make a survey of the various things simile can do.

It has been my purpose, in such detail as I have gone into, to put forward the argument that what can be done in poetry by the use of the various devices discussed in this chapter depends very closely upon the linguistic configuration of the device itself: linguistic forms themselves can do much to control the process by which the reader interprets and responds. The differences in the effects poets achieve are no less a linguistic affair than they are an affair of hitting on a good mental analogy. In conclusion, it seems proper to remark that the vast power of metaphor in poetry (and the fashionable belief that metaphor is *the* language of poetry) should be set in relation with simple linguistic facts. One reason why metaphor is common in poetry is that metaphor vastly extends the language at the poet's disposal. Since metaphor uses terms in a transferred sense, this means that, subject to some not very serious limitations, a poet who wants to write about object X but finds its terminology defective or resistant to manipulation, can simply move over into the terminology of Y. By using Y-terminology to describe X, he opens to himself the linguistic resources available in connection with Y. The merit of a particular metaphor from the poet's point of view may be not simply that there are 'links' between love and a journey in a boat, but also that there is a much larger range of specialized terminology connected with boats and the sea than there is with love; once he chooses this as his analogy, he makes available to himself the whole terminology of seafaring—and, if he likes, of fishing and swimming and marine ecology too—as in Dylan Thomas's *Ballad of the Long-legged Bait*. The importance of this bare linguistic fact is inexhaustible. To look at metaphor as a linguistic phenomenon is to begin to suspect that the basic explanation of the prevalence of metaphor in poetry lies in the fact that metaphor, by extending the range of terminology at the poet's disposal, offers him a magnificent array of solutions to major problems of diction.

It is well to remember, when talking about metaphor, that in order to work an analogy into a poem the poet has to reckon with the configuration of ordinary language. Not all analogies can be made to work, linguistically. Earlier in this chapter, for instance, I was alleging likeness between a telephone and a pug, and though this went easily into simile I found it necessary to take evasive action when confronted with the linguistic difficulty of devising a metaphor to convey it. The difficulty is that there are no terms, except 'pug', which inevitably bring pugs into the picture. If there were any puggy verbs I could easily have made my analogy into a metaphor. But as there is not enough terminology exclusively connected with pugs it is impossible to express that particular analogy except by citation of the things and explicit comparison machinery. It would seem that very often the real reason why a poet chooses a simile instead of a metaphor is simply that common language does not provide him with terminology recognizably connected with what he wants to use as the figurative extreme of the metaphor. Probably one reason why, in our poetry, there are so many cases where the poet begins with a simile and goes on to a metaphor, is that he must first introduce his comparison explicitly, otherwise nobody would recognize it. In the case of Stephen Spender's comparison of the sea to a harp, the comparison has first to be made explicitly because though there is a verb 'harping' it happens to have usage which does not suggest harps. There is a noun 'harpist' which could be figuratively used, but here the associations are wrong, and moreover, had the poem tried to establish its analogy by a phrase such as 'the harpist, the sea' we should be saddled with a personified sea. The poet has to take the system of common usage as it stands. In order to get out of literal description he has to find for figurative use another field of discourse whose established terminology meets his needs. One of those needs, if he intends to be metaphorical, is that the object used as a model must be such that some sufficiently recognizable terminology is already associated with it. And not only this; it is also necessary that his model should not defeat his purposes by bringing in the wrong sort of context. Sometimes poets are criticized for sticking to traditional metaphors—as though the world were all before them where to choose, and as though they could draw their analogies from contemporary innovations as soon as ever those innovations come into the world. The truth is however that those innovations must also come into being in the linguistic system, with a sufficient range of terminology associated with them, before they can provide metaphorical language. Television sets can provide metaphors any time now, because their related terminology ('viewers', 'channels', 'screens') is now established in common usage. Of course a new invention can become a simile as soon as its name is recognizable by whatever audience the poet thinks of himself as addressing, but simile does not give the poet the advantages metaphor does, and a poet may prefer traditional metaphors over contemporary simile on the grounds that he can do more linguistically with a metaphor than he can with a simile. It may go against our grain as readers to think of the poet casting a calculating eye on the linguistic resources associated with an object before he decides which object to compare something to. But the poet has to be realistic about the linguistic resources associated with an object, for if he is not he will simply find himself with a number of unfinished poems on his hands. He might for instance find himself, while working along one metaphorical line, wholly at a loss for a rhyme, and have to abandon his poem or rearrange its whole development to avoid the difficulty. The poet is not, therefore, wholly free to go to any area of experience when he is in search of a metaphor; he can choose only from areas which provide language resources capable of meeting all the technical necessities of his poem.

However, even with these restrictions on his scope in using metaphor, the poet will find it the best means for using language to cover the unusual situation and the unnamed phenomenon, for the simple reason that metaphor frees him from the necessity of referring via conventions of reference; i.e. via the names already established in common language. Metaphor permits him to use, if not any, then almost any area of the whole system of our language.

A further advantage of metaphor to the poet (simile shares this) is its power to play in with the faded metaphors of ordinary language and to draw special effects from the interplay. A simple instance is found in Shakespeare's Sonnet 30:

> When to the sessions of sweet silent thought
> I summon up remembrance of things past,

where the metaphor of 'the sessions of . . . thought' plays in with the faded metaphor in 'summon up', which itself would not be felt to be figurative if it did not appear in contiguity to the metaphor of the sessions of thought. 'Summon up' thus regains the force of metaphor: one realizes anew that to summon up one's mental powers refers to an act of choice and command. What however is more important is that the familiarity of the phrase 'summon up' acts as a guarantee of the propriety of the metaphor of the sessions of thought; the old metaphor ratifies the new metaphor, supports it, gives one the conviction that some real activity is really going on. In this case the relating of new and old metaphor means that the poet is able to give his poem vivid particularity and novelty by the metaphor of the sessions whilst at the same time—since the metaphor is supported by ordinary usage—retaining an appearance of speaking easily and familiarly and in a convincing way. The reanimation of 'dead' metaphor may become a means of contriving effects of great subtlety and power, as I hope to show in Chapter VIII. For reasons which will sufficiently appear in the concluding pages of the next chapter, I have not tried in this one to clarify the question of whether it is possible to distinguish between metaphor in poetry and metaphor in the general stream of language. For those same reasons I have not attempted to cover or to classify the range and diversity of meanings and effects that ray out from that whirling and flaming sun. As the word 'sun' serves us for referring to a phenomenon out in space, known to us only through its inexhaustible effects, so the word 'metaphor' serves us only as a label. By using it we can delimit, to some extent at least, one area or form of language.[1] But, as the next

[1] There is an extensive literature on the subject of metaphor. Stanford [op. cit.; see p. 49, n. 1] is especially informative on the views of classical philosophers and rhetoricians. Studies in metaphor and related topics are surveyed in Chap. XV ['Image, Metaphor,

chapter maintains, what can be done in that area, or what the form 'really is', always depends on what else is in the area and what *that* 'really is'. In this chapter I have tried to keep at least one foot on the earth (and my sunglasses on) in order to fix attention on the fact that metaphor and other forms of comparison can be studied at the linguistic level and in relation to certain general problems of diction, and to fix attention too on the related fact that however far the soul of the poet may soar into the empyrean when he thinks in metaphors, it is only because that thinking is embodied in a linguistic structure of meaning (related no less to the state of the language as a whole, than to the thoughts of men) that the reader is in his turn empowered to fire his jets and blast off with him. If in this chapter metaphor seems to have had much less than justice done to it, the next chapter may make it clearer why the judgment seat is a perilous place to ascend at all.

Symbol, Myth'] of René Wellek and Austin Warren, *Theory of Literature* (London, 1949); see also pp. 373–5 of their bibliography. Ullmann's *Style in the French Novel* [see p. 53 n.1] has a valuable survey of problems (pp. 210–17) and useful references; his *Principles of Semantics* [see p. 19, n.3], primarily linguistic, contains invaluable reference matter and gives (p. 306, n.1) a list of recent studies of metaphor; for passages of especial relevance to literary problems see, in the Index, 'ambiguity', 'analogy', 'association', 'metaphor', and, in Chap. V, the section on synaesthetic imagery, pp. 266–89. For a useful survey of differences between various theories, and their implications, see Monroe C. Beardsley, *Aesthetics: Problems in the Philosophy of Criticism* (New York, 1958), pp. 134–144; see also the excellent critical bibliography, pp. 159–63.

IV

Metaphor and Poetic Structure

THERE is a sense in which it might be said that this and the next two chapters are at the centre of the web of topics treated in this book. In speaking of a 'web of topics' rather than of an argument, I use a figure which will perhaps serve to disclaim any intention of tidying up the intricacies of meaning discussed in the book; until more is known of the nature of linguistic meaning generally, it seems better to feel one's way along the filaments of the web than to cut bits out of it, label them separately and arrange them into a show of orderliness. If, however, there is one centre to which many of the filaments seem to lead, it is more likely to be glimpsed in these central chapters than anywhere else in the book. For in this present chapter, while continuing the topic of what metaphor can do, I shall be trying to say what kind of thing it is I mean when I speak of 'poetic structure', and in the next two chapters I shall have occasion to show how various kinds of structuring may be used to overcome the limitations or redress the tendencies of the language the poet shares with the rest of us. These chapters together, then, may put some substance into those terms which, if I were pushed to give a succinct statement of my point of view, I should have to use—for I should have to say that in my own opinion the chief difference between language in poems and language outside poems is that the one is more highly structured than the other, and the more complex organization set up in poems makes it possible for the poet both to redress and to exploit various characteristics of language at large. What is meant by the term 'poetic structure' is discussed at length in this present chapter; what is referred to in the phrase 'various characteristics of language at large' will be made clearer in Chapters V and VI.

When we try to move on from observation of the several workings of the components of poetic language to consider the whole continuum of a poem, we meet many difficulties. In the first place it is doubtful whether critical language can deal fully with the complexities of the various poetic modes of meaning at that level where, as Shakespeare says in Sonnet 8, 'one string, sweet husband to another, Strikes each in each by mutual ordering'; secondly, even if this difficulty might somehow be met, it would still be advisable to calculate, beforehand, what one might hope to achieve by pushing theoretical criticism to this level, since the poem (incalculably more complex than any one sentence in it, and each sentence probably more complex than comparable sentences in ordinary discourse) would seem, by definition, to preclude the making of useful generalizations about the ordering of the whole. The structure even of ordinary language is, above the level of the sentence, 'free', so far as linguistic analysis is concerned. As John L. M. Trim remarks,

When subjected to proper methods of analysis, the language of every community investigated has proved to possess a fully developed, regular structure. The types of structure encountered vary widely, but all share certain fundamental characteristics. All operate with a small repertory of basic sound units (phonemes), which are combined together in set ways to form morphemes, the basic meaningful units of language, roots and affixes. These in turn are combined to form an ascending hierarchy of units (such as 'word', 'phrase', 'clause', 'sentence') each having its own set pattern of subordinate units, each in turn longer, more complex, and with a larger inventory. Above the word level, the inventory is too extensive to list. Instead, statements of combinability are generalized in grammar. Above the sentence, permitted sequence is so free that no attempt is made to state the possibilities. Any substantial sequence of sentences will probably constitute a unique utterance.[1]

Above the level of the sentence the structure of the language itself does not constrain a speaker's choice of the best way to arrange his discourse; the arrangement will depend on his situation and purposes, the nature of his material, and his whole past experience of how to utter himself so as to make sense to other people—and here I am deliberately vague in order to avoid defining or enumerating possible ways in which sentences when put together may make sense. Logical relations may play an overt part but often it is the context of

[1] John L. M. Trim, 'Who Taught Me Language?' *The Listener*, 25 February 1960, p. 340.

an utterance that makes sense of it, and when we reflect on the diversity of considerations involved in getting the hang of what is uttered (one may for instance have to make a rapid estimate of a speaker's attitude and motives in order to grasp the relevance of one sentence to another) we are discouraged from supposing that any systematic account could be given of the various ways in which discourse may cohere. How much less then is the likelihood that any systematic account could be given of the various ways in which poetic discourse may cohere? What, rather, must be sought if we are to talk usefully about the structure of poems, or even of any one poem, is some procedure for locating and illuminating what it is, in the organization of poetic discourse, that is characteristically poetic, and this itself will come within the scope of our present purposes only if it is likely to help us, in reading poems, to see the point, or, in criticizing them, to talk more intelligibly about poetic language. Each 'if' is a large one. Indeed I hardly know which is the more appalling to attempt, for in the first case one would seem to be looking for a way of talking that may bring to earth what it is that peculiarly enables poetry to do things as improbable as 'to see a World in a Grain of Sand',[1] and in the second case one attempts hardly less than to demonstrate the power of poetic structure to confer upon its own components meanings more individual than anything those components ordinarily have. There is a puzzle here, in that we seem to be concerned with two very different things at once: in thinking of the poem as a whole we are thinking about vastness of meaning, whereas in thinking of its parts—of the impact of a word, a phrase, a line and so on—we are thinking of vividness of meaning, and it is not easy to explain how vivid meaning may exist without precision and definiteness. So in pursuing the idea of 'the structure' of a poem we seem to be pursuing something with the extraordinary capacity of being able to confer, on its parts, meanings that are somehow palpable, individual, concrete—or anything the reverse of generalized—whilst at the same time this something-or-other which we call 'structure' brings about a spread of the meaningfulness or felt importance of the poem as a whole. To such an extent does it do this that one is made to feel

---

[1] Blake, *Auguries of Innocence*, l. 1.

that no exhaustive definition can be given of the meaning of the whole poem, that its significance as a whole cannot be summed up or adequately restated. And there is something unsatisfying about our criticism if this paradox of vastness-in-the-whole and particularization-of-the-parts cannot be resolved. If it is not resolved, we shall find ourselves, in talking about the parts, going into endless particularization of the niceties of contextual meaning, without being able to show how those niceties got there, or even that we have not invented them ourselves, and in talking about the whole our criticism may collapse into rhapsodic general tributes to the complexity and simultaneity of the mental processes activated by the continuum of the poem—again, without our being able to say how they are activated. Worse still, we shall have retired from the struggle to understand the workings of poetic language exactly at the point where these workings are at their most characteristic: that is, at the point where we realize that the inner circle of vivid meanings has to be related to the outer circle of vast significance. If poetic language can indeed close its own circuit so as to individualize the meanings of individual phrases, and yet at the same time so successfully expand the significance of what is said that the stars in outer space seem to return an echo to its beam, it would appear that there cannot be anything more important for us to do than to find out how this can be.

It may of course be true of this paradox, as of others, that what ties us in a knot is our own language, and that like other paradoxes it can be resolved by restatement. I suspect that we might do something to resolve this one firstly by enquiring whether, when we speak of 'the meaning in the parts' and 'the meaning of the whole', we are perhaps using the word 'meaning' in two different senses; secondly, by enquiring whether the vividness or particularization of the parts really has got anything to do with precision, with verbal limiting and defining. But the trouble about trying to resolve the paradox by restatement on such lines as these is that we have too many tricky concepts to juggle with at once. An example is always useful to bring theory to earth, and before we tackle the problem of this paradox in a theoretical way, it may be useful to try to slice the knot open and inspect the raw ends, by taking one example and asking what peculiarities we find in it. I propose, then, to prod the problem of structure at points where it notably involves the use of metaphor, in the hope that the resultant upheaval will throw into prominence some concealed oddities of poetic ways of discoursing. One may hope for a large and not random upheaval, on the grounds that 'the paramount importance of the image in poetry is beyond dispute', as Ullmann says in concluding an enumeration of critics and poets who have testified memorably to this effect.[1]

Shakespeare's Sonnet 73 is a promising case, since its first twelve lines are devoted to the elaboration of three related metaphors; moreover, it has received particular acclaim, and a recent critic observes that 'Shakespeare's method in these sonnets may best be observed in No. 73'.[2]

> That time of year thou mayst in me behold
> When yellow leaves, or none, or few, do hang
> Upon those boughs which shake against the cold,
> Bare ruin'd choirs, where late the sweet birds sang.
> In me thou see'st the twilight of such day
> As after sunset fadeth in the west,
> Which by and by black night doth take away,
> Death's second self, that seals up all in rest.
> In me thou see'st the glowing of such fire
> That on the ashes of his youth doth lie,
> As the death-bed whereon it must expire
> Consum'd with that which it was nourish'd by.
>> This thou perceiv'st, which makes thy love more strong,
>> To love that well which thou must leave ere long.

I hope it will not throw my reader into irremediable confusion if I begin by quoting Hallett Smith's comment on Sonnet 73: 'The richness of the sonnet derives more from its metaphorical involutions than it does from the clarity of its structure'.[3] 'Structure' in this quotation seems to mean the same as 'general design', for this paragraph, whose concluding sentence I have just quoted, begins:

Sonnet 73 is clear in its general design. The three quatrains have a

---

[1] *Style in the French Novel*, p. 211.

[2] Hallett Smith, *Elizabethan Poetry : A Study in Conventions, Meaning, and Expression* (Cambridge, Mass., 1952), p. 182.

[3] op. cit., p. 185.

relationship to each other and a natural development. They proceed from the declining of the year to the declining of the day to a declining of the fire, bringing the metaphorical point closer to the subject as the poem progresses.

I have begun with these quotations for two reasons. The first reason is that the clarity seen in the 'general design'—let us call it the 'ground-plan'—is the clarity of abstractions: the relationship between a declining and a declining and a declining. Inspection of the particulars specified in each quatrain makes it abundantly clear that though this is on the one hand the abstraction that best fits all the metaphors, it is for any one of them a slightly uneasy fit—though it is equally clear that the ground-plan of the sonnet provokes us to believe that all three sets of particulars are in fact intended to illustrate a common abstraction. The second point of interest in these quotations is that though one can see in this sonnet a ground-plan which is clear, yet at the same time it can be asserted that the 'richness' of the sonnet derives not so much from this, as from the 'involutions' of something else. Here then we have the interesting situation that the sonnet provokes us to see a clear ground-plan consisting of a clear relation between clear abstractions but this ground-plan leaves richness out. I cannot think of a better way of putting the difference between a poetic and a non-poetic structure than to say that poetic structuring consists of more than a clear relation between clear abstractions, giving a general continuity to an utterance. Though this kind of clarity and continuity, obviously, is a marked and carefully contrived feature of this sonnet, it is equally obvious that to describe this clear and continuous ground-plan does not throw any light on the causes of the excitement we feel on reading the sonnet; there is nothing exciting in merely being told that the onset of winter and the coming of night and the dwindling of a fire are all examples of decline and that they metaphorically describe what the poet feels. If that is all, who cares? We care because of the way in which these examples are particularized. The ground-plan, continuous and clear, permits the particularizing but it does not of itself effect it. What it does effect is some of the relating of the particulars to one another. The ground-plan relates the particulars to one another by provoking us to abstract from them a common formula and so it makes us relate all three metaphors to one another as examples of the same thing. But while the ground-plan says that the metaphors exemplify 'the same thing', the particulars of the metaphors themselves hang together in such a way that they say something else, as I shall try to show. And if I succeed in showing it, I shall then argue that it is very important to the poet to be able to drive his poem along by more than one set of reins at the same time, and that a characteristic way in which poets equip themselves with extra reins is by using the difference between, on the one hand, the concretion of verbal particulars and, on the other, the abstractions those particulars can be guided to suggest.

We are guided in Sonnet 73 to impose a common factor on the three particular metaphors by the clear repeating formula 'thou mayst in me behold'/'In me thou see'st'/'In me thou see'st'/'This thou perceiv'st', and this strong suggestion of sameness is extended firmly into the subsidiary formula 'That time of year . . . When'—'twilight of such day As'—'glowing of such fire That'. The particulars which inhabit these schemes, though extraordinarily difficult to summate, permit themselves to be assimilated to a common ideogram of decline (of the year, of the day, of a fire). But that common ideogram, however compulsively given by the poem, leaves out other movements going on within the particulars of the metaphors, moving as they do from a cold, bare, ruined season to a glowing fire, from a time of year to a crucial moment, from what has gone to what is imminent, from the separate perceptions and simple reference in the first quatrain ('yellow leaves' . . . 'boughs which shake against the cold') to the one complex image, highly figurative in expression and irradiated with intellection, in the last quatrain. These movements are no less controlled than is the emergence of a 'common' abstraction under the impetus of the 'in me . . .' formula. For if we inspect the second quatrain closely we shall see that in the case of each of the movements (from cold to fire, past to future, diffuse to concentrated, etc.) the second quatrain occupies a stage intermediary between the first quatrain and the third. The glide from 'cold' through 'fadeth in the west' to 'glowing of . . . fire', easiest to point to, is not more important than the other glides the quatrain executes, though these take longer to translate into critical language and are perhaps not so readily accepted as being important—because they are not visualized, and because they embody relations rather than references. But the tenses glide too (from 'sang' through the ambiguous 'by and by . . . doth take away, . . . seals up all'—these hovering between present and future—to 'must expire'); without this glide we could not be disposed to grasp in the last quatrain the simultaneous annulling of tense (for the fire is made to symbolize continuous process) and the irradiation of the one remaining moment of unextinguished vitality with passionate importance and concern. More important still, the second quatrain increases the degree of figuration superimposed upon the basic metaphor. In the first quatrain extra figuration was applied only to one distinct element of the time of year, that is to the boughs, which were metaphorized as 'Bare ruin'd choirs'. In the second quatrain it is 'black night', swamping all the afterglow in the west, that is given extra figuration—not only as 'Death's second self' but also as that which 'seals up all'; this extra load of figuration prepares the way for the almost unanalysable intricacy of

> such fire
> That on the ashes of his youth doth lie,
> As the death-bed whereon it must expire
> Consum'd with that which it was nourish'd by.

It is worth remarking too that in this last image the extra figuration is inseparable from the definition of what kind of fire this is. Again it is the second quatrain which, by being an intermediary stage in the degree and treatment of extra figuration, enables us to glide easily from the descriptive definition of the first quatrain to a definition, in the third quatrain, so highly figured as to attain the status of the metaphysical. This heavy load of figuration, intellection and metaphysics in the language of the last quatrain is received without any jolting sense of sudden thinness in its relation to ordinary reality; perhaps the highest compliment we can pay the poem is to say that the succession of its various kinds of language is so controlled that we take in the language of the last quatrain, so distanced from the language of common life, without recoil.

Something more particular than this still remains to be said, if we are to appreciate the precise handling of this extra figuration. The last quatrain achieves a confrontation of the idea of imminent death by the idea of glowing fire and so brings the concern of the poem to its climax; in this respect too, one can see a steady progress from the first quatrain to the last. The 'time of year' in the first quatrain is only *in posse* a metaphor for a state where death is imminent; if this quatrain stood alone, its metaphor would then more probably be taken to relate to regret for diminished powers or joys, to a feeling that the glory is departed, rather than to a feeling that soon one must die. It is the second quatrain that speeds the evolution of the tenor of the metaphor from lost joys to imminent death by introducing, firmly, the word 'Death'. The introduction of this word does not seem arbitrary, or to have designs upon us, since it occurs in the secondary, familiar figuration of night as 'Death's second self', but once the word is in the poem it influences our interpretation of the metaphor in each of the other quatrains. A modification of the first abstraction—collected from the particulars of the first quatrain—is called into play in the second quatrain (as, again, in the third), by the necessity of relating new particulars to the abstraction one made at first. This retrospective redefinition can be of massive importance to the total effect of a poem. Is it not the case that the image of glowing fire, in the third quatrain of this sonnet, retrospectively redefines for the poet, for his friend, and for us, what we are to make of a state first described as bare, cold and ruined? For he has carefully induced us by the arrangement of his ground-plan to believe that what is described in the three quatrains is the same. The sameness is a deliberately-provoked abstraction, which endures even though the successive particulars of the poem throw up, in series, abstractions only precariously alike. The 'sameness' insisted on by the ground-plan is the indispensable premise of what is successfully argued in the particularized language of the poem.

It seems fairly clear when one studies this sonnet that though its metaphoric sequence has the particular virtue of giving rise to malleable abstractions, the continuity and the moulding of these depends both on something outside the metaphors (that is, on a ground-plan of repeating elements) and on something inside the verbal particulars of the metaphors themselves. In so far as one can isolate and report on the controls built into the continuous procession of meanings, one finds that these controls have to be discussed in terms of their interaction with one another; the purpose of the controls is to bring about at the end of the sonnet a confrontation of those strains of feeling which at the beginning were only diffusely suggested. When these diffusely-suggested and mixed strains of feeling have been more clearly brought out, and brought to the point where they challenge one another to a verbal duel, the poet devises a peculiar kind of language wherein each strain of feeling, each duellist, as it were fires with the other's pistol. This may be paradoxical, but so is the language of the third quatrain. And it is worth noting that the strains of feeling get to duelling-point because of what has been done with the *natural* particulars ('cold' becomes 'fire'), and they swap pistols—talk paradoxically—because the *artificial* particulars (that is, the extra load of verbal figuration imposed on the natural scene) have been brought to a condition where meaningful paradox is possible. On the one hand, the natural particulars prove to be analogical not only of the same thing (decline) but also of very different things (of lost warmth, of still-enduring vitality). On the other hand, the artificial particulars prove to have been a stealthily-advancing army of occupation which in the last quatrain successfully overruns the quatrain's whole area so that the language there, by becoming a network of figures, is able to reconcile, in figurative terms, feelings whose co-existence and interpenetration of one another could not in literal language be expressed.

If we consider the means by which, in this sonnet, metaphors provide the poet with a continuously-changing language, we realize that much of the importance of metaphor as a form lies in its variableness. The metaphor of 'That time of year . . .' is something like an objective correlative: it calls up a diffused sense of what one might naturally feel in and about such a scene and time. The metaphor of the sunset, whilst having something of this same quality, is made, by the addition of the passage about black night, into something nearer to an emblem—an image plus a moral or interpretation.

The metaphor of the glowing of fire is itself a tissue of figures of comparison and paradox, one being used to interpret another, and the effect of this is extraordinarily difficult to analyse. One at least of the functions of the structural elements in this sonnet is that they provide the strategy by which the poet manœuvres himself into a position where this kind of language is possible. The question of how we are to discuss the effect of language such as this, I shall reserve for consideration in another chapter. In this chapter we have already enough to do, if we confine ourselves to asking, simply, what useful generalizations can be made from the findings of our close inspection of the structure of the sonnet as a whole.

It will be best first to note that though this structure is very complex it should not be thought of as untypical of linguistic processes in poems in general, or even as being discontinuous with linguistic processes in ordinary life. It has, in common with other poems discussed in this book, the feature that it individualizes the meanings of the words it uses and the concepts it calls into play; it does this by giving to word-meanings and to concepts a new, immediate, particular, complex fundament in the concreted particulars of the poem.[1] And, so far from vaulting into a sphere above that of ordinary linguistic processes, it goes out of its way to call them decisively into play. It is natural for a user of language to abstract from the particulars of any utterance an idea of how it hangs together; this sonnet, as I have shown, provokes, and fixes in a ground-plan, the abstraction of a common factor from all three metaphors. But its peculiarity is that this provocation and fixing of an abstraction is done in order to set up a tension between the abstraction itself and the other processes elaborated within the successive particulars of the successive metaphors. It is at this point that we see a striking difference between non-literary and literary organization. In ordinary discourse we expect that the discourse will hang together in one main way; that

[1] Ullmann, discussing 'the process of *abstraction* by which our "concepts" are evolved' and 'the gap between the virtual sense in the language-system and the actualised sense of speech-contexts' (*Principles of Semantics*, p. 93), quotes, from H. Delacroix's *Le Langage et la pensée* (Paris, 1924), p. 205, the observation: 'Un concept est toujours ouvert; il "attend" de nouvelles déterminations de sens: il est le produit d'une dissociation, d'une analyse qui l'isole d'expériences globales'.

what it means as a whole will come to us if we see its ground-plan. But in this poem the ground-plan is only one element in a larger organization, a larger organization by virtue of which we derive from the poem as a whole a verbal experience more exciting than, and not reducible to, a reiteration of a common idea of declining. To say that a poem has a higher degree of organization than we find in ordinary discourse, is, then, not a rhapsodic tribute to the excitement we have on reading poems but a sober statement of fact. What in ordinary discourse is the highest level of organization—the 'hang' of the utterance—is in this poem only one level; the poem hangs together this way but also in other ways as well. Within the very particulars which clothe the ideogram of decline with individual body and detail, there is a continuous process of change, of multiple relationships undergoing multiple transformation; the sense of vastidity of meaning in the sonnet derives from these many transformations of old into new.

It seems fairly obvious that multiple organization is possible only in a medium whose matter or substance (if I may speak in this way) is itself possessed of diverse properties. In many of the poems discussed in earlier chapters we have seen the poet using diverse properties of words and word-meanings. But in this poem we see more clearly that he uses properties of meaning whose diversity we find it even shocking to have to admit. We do not, in ordinary talking, recognize that an abstraction is an entity of a different order from that of the particulars from which we abstract it. Yet in this poem, it is clear, the difference is so great that an abstracted pattern can compete with other patterns inhering in the very particulars from which it is abstracted. For the purpose of ordinary discourse this discrepancy between what we abstract (and think of as 'the meaning') and what we abstract it from (the particulars and relations which mean) is scandalous, and better not thought of at all—or we might all retreat into silence. For the purposes of literary art the stratification of meaning, its fissure within itself, is of crucial importance. In this poem the common abstraction which unifies and the particulars which diversify are forced apart, to such effect that

> a thing inseparate
> Divides more wider than the sky and earth,
> And yet the spacious breadth of this division
> Admits no orifex for a point as subtle
> As Ariachne's broken woof to enter.[1]

Each element of that 'thing inseparate', the meaning, is not only separated out but given individual organization. By doing this the poet enables himself enormously to multiply the number and complicate the interaction of the patterned relationships spanning the whole sonnet. It is at this point, perhaps, that we can do something to restate the paradox of illimitable meaningfulness seeming to emanate from clearly-articulated detail. Perhaps the sense of vast meaningfulness derives from the numerosity and the tensions of organized relationships, whilst the sense of vivid individual meanings derives from the power of those particulars which are used—as 'ashes' for instance is used—like an optical glass, to focus our seeing at those successive points in the poem where knots of relationships are most tightly tied and most expertly untied, or where feelings most notably collide, argue, negotiate, and shake hands. But it is important to bear in mind that the verbal experience afforded by the poem, however firmly it is organized, is not fixed like an algebraic equation. Both in the means of organization and in the particulars organized there is much that is unverbalized, not tied down in a sign. Intellectual relationships are not verbal statements; they shape, and are apprehended as shapely, but they do not enter into the fixity and the limitation of verbal statement. The particulars, however definite in themselves and however definite in the analogy they build up, bring into play an aura of their suggestions, the 'feeling-tone' of their adhesions in the world of non-linguistic reality; this feeling-tone, though it may be as individual as a taste or a scent, is also, like those, too idiosyncratic and rich to pin down in verbalization. It may be even more important to observe that these crucial words—the 'optical glass' words—may serve as escape-hatches from conceptual terms, because of their power to refer us out of language to an object (such as ashes, or a death-bed) which in real life is a visible crisis-

[1] Shakespeare, *Troilus and Cressida*, v, ii,148–52.

point or declaration-point in a complicated history of process, a natural symbol with all the advantages over language of being in itself a simultaneity of opposites. We should not, of course, forget that it is up to the poem to suggest *what* opposites are involved. Indeed, many of the problems of discussing structures of meaning originate in the very fact that words provoke unverbalized processes, such as the apprehension of relationships, and they refer us to objects in real life which as it were express in shorthand the long stream of our consciousness of process.

I do not know how far, if we went to non-metaphorical poetry, we should still find it true that the cleavage between abstraction and concretion plays a vital part in complicating the structure of relationships that plays across the verbal surface of the poem. But whether or not we found this to be displayed equally clearly in non-metaphorical poetry, it seems fair enough to draw from our study of this sonnet the conclusion that the study of meaning in poetic structures will cast light on the nature of meaning in ordinary language, just as much as the study of ordinary language casts light on the nature of poetry. If poetry is language at full stretch, the stretching must help us to see more clearly the nature of the fabric stretched.

If this is so it may be profitable, before we break off from considering poetic structures in which metaphor is prominent, to examine another kind of complexity which metaphor is characteristically able to promote—namely a traffic between the real and the contrived, between what comes into the poem as a member of the 'real' situation under discussion in a poem, and what comes into the poem as extra verbal figuration imposed at the will of the poet. The sonnet we have just discussed will make the distinction clear enough: the words,

> such day
> As after sunset fadeth in the west,
> Which by and by black night doth take away

refer us out to 'reality as it is', but 'Death's second self' adds figuration to that reality. 'Death's second self' at once interprets the analogy of the light fading in the west and controls the tendency of the extended metaphor to swing too far away from contact with what it metaphorizes; we take one step away from the invisible reality of the poet's inner state, to the analogy of the sunset (which itself refers us to the kind of reality we know) and another step back towards the reality with which the poet is concerned—to 'Death'. But it is the peculiarity of these steps away from and back to reality that we cannot pinpoint, at the second step, exactly where we are. Is this to be taken as a death in the ordinary sense of physical obliteration, or in a metaphorical sense, referring to the death of something unspecified —poetic powers, or vitality, or joys, rather than to the literal death of the body? Metaphor shakes our bearings on the question of how we stand in relation to 'objective reality', and a metaphor inside a metaphor unfixes those bearings altogether; it makes us lose our direction-fix on the position of what is 'out there' in 'reality' and the position of our own consciousness of that. I have said elsewhere in this book that the relation we assume to exist between our own consciousness and what is 'out there', is only illusorily clear; the conventions of language foster the illusion that objects 'out there' can be reliably identified and referred to by proper use of their accurate names; the illusion is convenient for practical purposes. But for the purpose of finding one's way through the intricacies of personal consciousness the convention has not even the virtue of convenience. Metaphor metaphorized—the double jump outside the convention—breaks the hold of the convention and enables us to become aware of the subjectivity of objects and the objectivity of subjective processes. At this level poetic language can speak convincingly despite the 'irrationality' of what it says; its 'irrationality' is the obverse of the falsity of ordinary language. The paradoxical or irrational features of poetic language are a means of short-circuiting the détour of consciousness through the polarized concepts of normal language—or perhaps we should rather say that they are a means of revealing the alternations of that current which runs from subject to object and from object to subject. Here too, as in the case of the fissure between abstraction and particulars, metaphor in poetry casts light on the nature of language in general.

In Shakespeare's Sonnet 73 the double jump out of the convention is done within the doubly figurative language of each quatrain. But it is possible to execute the double jump at another level—for instance, by framing the statements of the poem with one ostentatiously-contrived comparison. Marvell's poem *The Gallery* begins:

> *Clora*, come view my Soul, and tell
> Whether I have contriv'd it well.

The great speech of Shakespeare's Richard II (v, v, 1 ff.), where he soliloquizes in prison, begins:

> I have been studying how I may compare
> This prison where I live unto the world.

In both cases, the first contrivance is complicated by a second. The successive pictures set up in Marvell's gallery are themselves emblematic or allegorical pictures; the allegory is a second frame. In Richard's comparison, the world becomes a stage on which Richard 'play[s] . . . in one person many people'. In both, the upshot of the doubling of the move away from literal description is the presentation of the ambiguity of the relation between consciousness (the contriver of the metaphor) and what it encounters or contrives. In order to get to grips with this problem of loaded language inside a frame— a problem expressible visually as:

$$\boxed{\text{`Frame-up'}}$$

—we must, in the present state of criticism, make a strong effort to rid ourselves of the current attitude to metaphor—an attitude visually expressible as

$$\boxed{\begin{array}{c}\text{BEYOND}\\\text{LIES}\\\text{REALITY}\end{array}}$$

Current criticism often takes metaphor *au grand sérieux*, as a peephole on the nature of transcendental reality, a prime means by which the imagination can see into the life of things; this attitude makes it difficult to see the working of those metaphors which deliberately emphasize the frame, offering themselves to us as deliberate fabrications, as a prime means of seeing into the life not of things but of the creative human consciousness, framer of its own world. What goes on inside an ostentatiously-displayed frame, may then be worth closer attention. Shakespeare's Richard II, alone with himself in prison, is discovered soliloquizing:

> I have been studying how I may compare
> This prison where I live unto the world:
> And for because the world is populous ·
> And here is not a creature but myself,
> I cannot do it; yet I'll hammer it out.
> My brain I'll prove the female to my soul,
> My soul the father; and these two beget
> A generation of still-breeding thoughts,
> And these same thoughts people this little world,
> In humours like the people of this world,
> For no thought is contented . . .
>
> (V, V, 1–11)

and he goes on to describe how every train of thought he takes up encounters difficulties and gives place to thoughts of a contrary kind, which in turn break down too; thoughts of religion, thoughts of escape, thoughts of resignation all peter out in dissatisfaction:

> Thus play I in one person many people,
> And none contented: sometimes am I king;
> Then treasons make me wish myself a beggar,
> And so I am: then crushing penury
> Persuades me I was better when a king;
> Then am I king'd again: and by and by
> Think that I am unking'd by Bolingbroke,
> And straight am nothing: but whate'er I be,
> Nor I nor any man that but man is
> With nothing shall be pleased, till he be eased
> With being nothing.
>
> (V, V, 31–41)

It is strikingly clear in this passage that the resemblance between the prison and the world is admitted to be a deliberate fabrication ('I'll hammer it out . . . I'll prove . . .'). And even if we concede that the prison had to be mentioned, in order to explain to the audience where Richard is supposed to be, we may still reflect that presumably Shakespeare could, had he so wished, have begun with a different comparison, or even so treated this particular one as to conceal rather than so sharply to stress the difficulty of establishing it. Though the comparison of the prison to the world, and his thoughts to people, serves to lead on to an enumeration of the many changing rôles Richard mentally plays, it is conceivable that some other comparison, much less 'difficult' to make out, could have been used to lead into the same enumeration. The manner of making the comparison, if it has any function in the whole, has one that we cannot confidently explain as merely that of introducing the main substance of the speech. What then is gained by making Richard begin by stressing the consciousness of the process by which he arrives at a resemblance between the prison and the world? One might of course say that because Richard admits that he is making it all up, the audience is less likely to be irritated by this obvious fact; his admission serves to forestall a reaction, by voicing it for those who might otherwise feel like voicing it themselves. But it is still true that all this could have been avoided. Richard might, to take one of a myriad possibilities, have been displayed denouncing Bolingbroke's turpitude. So we are forced back to the position that Shakespeare tells us Richard is making it all up because this is something he wants us to know from the beginning. The whole speech in fact is about Richard's experience of veering from one unstable rôle to another, with the pace of the changes speeding up all the way, and his discovering in the process the sickening truth that all these rôles are unstable fabrications of his own mind, so that whether in or out of any particular rôle he is essentially nothing other than a consciousness which is simultaneously theatre and author. This realization is articulated most clearly at the climax of the passage where the pace and violence of his changes from one rôle to another are at their height ('. . . wish myself a beggar, And so I am') and so too is the sense of the irruption into his play-world of intractable segments of reality ('treasons make me wish myself . . ./. . . penury Persuades me . . .') and the memory of his actual unkinging by Bolingbroke becomes, in this climax, indistinguishable from the fantasy that wilfully re-enacts it, for 'Think that' means equally *remember that* and *see myself as*. Thus the passage, beginning slowly, 'I cannot do it; yet I'll hammer it out', gradually accelerates until the rôle-making reaches maximal speed, whilst at the same time the brute facts which make each rôle untenable and frustrated are brought into closer and closer relation with the element of conscious willing in his idea of himself, so that finally the self dissolves into nothing under the double burden of its own Protean selfmaking and the recalcitrance of fact. When in the light of the climax of the whole passage we re-consider its opening, that opening is seen to be not an embarrassed and forced lead-in to a technically necessary comparison but rather a first and major step in the development of the whole.

At the climax of the speech it is impossible to separate Richard's one meaning—that as soon as he has an impulse to pretend, the pre-tence takes possession of him—from his other meaning, that his tragic predicament makes every rôle short-lived; nor can we separate, from these, his meaning that there are enough mutually contradic-tory facts in his situation to make every rôle equally possible and impossible. This many-meaninged language articulates his experience of the relation between his personality and the facts of his situation. His rôles and the facts are prevented from separating into silly sheep and hard-headed goats because the whole flock is enclosed by a doubly-ambiguous pen. In the hammering-out of the comparison of the prison to a world, the parish of invention and the parish of reality march together, with Richard figuring as one who beats the bounds; then the world becomes a stage, and Richard figures as the reviewer of the play as well as the actor in it. Beginning with a conscious con-trivance to palliate reality, he is nothing if not critical of his own con-trivance, and, contriving a further comparison to evaluate that, he finds that his double contraption has collapsed the walls between reality and invention and that he is now neatly inside a fourth-dimensional trap. The language spoken by the man in the trap would not have its volleying echoes if we, the audience, had not accom-panied him through every involution of his course. Shakespeare, the contriver of all, has carefully manœuvred the speech into a state in which it is, finally, possible to make the words of the climax echo and re-echo against the structure in which they are set. Indeed one useful way of considering the structure of a passage is to regard it as a means of making it possible for forms of language used in it to have more meaning than they would otherwise have; the structure is a solution of the problems involved in getting a particular thing said. To offer this as a useful attitude to structure may not, perhaps, suggest any definite method of identifying the principles on which any particular passage is constructed, but it has the merit of bringing into the open the fact that the causes of a sudden efflorescence of poetic vitality, apparently at some precise point in the course of a passage, often have to be sought as much in what has preceded that efflorescence as in the form and substance of the lines in which it is apparently located.

Many difficulties confront us when we attempt to apply such a concept of structure to the understanding of particular poetic effects. In a very extended structure, such as that of a play by Shakespeare, the force behind a particular group of lines may have been accumulating throughout vast stretches of the play. In the instance we have just considered, the whole contrast between Richard and Bolingbroke does something to direct our understanding of this particular speech, and one aspect of that contrast—Bolingbroke's attitude to hard facts—has been suggested as far back as Act I, scene iii. There, when Gaunt advises him to lighten his exile by pretending it is something else—'Call it a travel that thou tak'st for pleasure' (l. 262)—he refuses to 'miscall it so', and when Gaunt tries to comfort him with something like the fancy-spinning of Richard:

> Look what thy soul holds dear, imagine it
> To lie that way thou go'st, not whence thou comest:
> Suppose the singing birds musicians,
> The grass whereon thou tread'st the presence strew'd,
> The flowers fair ladies, and thy steps no more
> Than a delightful measure or a dance;
> For gnarling sorrow hath less power to bite
> The man that mocks at it and sets it light
>
> (286-93)

Bolingbroke explicitly rejects the idea that imagination can make any difference to the facts or be of any use to the man who has to deal with them, and retorts,

> O, who can hold a fire in his hand
> By thinking on the frosty Caucasus?
> Or cloy the hungry edge of appetite
> By bare imagination of a feast?
> Or wallow naked in December snow
> By thinking on fantastic summer's heat?
> O, no! the apprehension of the good
> Gives but the greater feeling to the worse.
>
> (294–301)

In the speeches of Gaunt and Bolingbroke, the wall between reality and imagination still stands intact. No doubt in these speeches Shakespeare put as much art into shoring it up as in Richard's speech he put into making it collapse. For in both their speeches, our sleep as prisoners in the convention of language is troubled by a nudge from one of our giant captors—Thinking, Wording, and Being—who, even if we should wake up, keep the keys of the prison out of our grasp by passing them rapidly from one giant hand to another. In Gaunt's speech, Wording gives us a nudge ('*Call* it . . .'); in Bolingbroke's, Thinking gives us a dig in the ribs. But to bring us wide awake something more than this is necessary—something like the structure, and within that the ambiguous wording, of Richard's speech.

A comparable case is Marvell's poem, *The Gallery*:

I

> *Clora* come view my Soul, and tell
> Whether I have contriv'd it well.
> Now all its several lodgings lye
> Compos'd into one Gallery;
> And the great *Arras*-hangings, made
> Of various Faces, by are laid;
> That, for all furniture, you'l find
> Only your Picture in my Mind.

II

> Here Thou art painted in the Dress
> Of an Inhumane Murtheress;
> Examining upon our Hearts
> Thy fertile Shop of cruel Arts:
> Engines more keen than ever yet

Adorned Tyrants Cabinet;
Of which the most tormenting are
Black Eyes, red Lips, and curled Hair.

III

But, on the other side, th'art drawn
Like to *Aurora* in the Dawn;
When in the East she slumb'ring lyes,
And stretches out her milky Thighs;
While all the morning Quire does sing,
And *Manna* falls, and Roses spring;
And, at thy Feet, the wooing Doves
Sit perfecting their harmless Loves.

IV

Like an Enchantress here thou show'st,
Vexing thy restless Lover's Ghost;
And, by a Light obscure, dost rave
Over his Entrails, in the Cave;
Divining thence, with horrid Care,
How long thou shalt continue fair;
And (when inform'd) them throw'st away,
To be the greedy Vultur's prey.

V

But, against that, thou sit'st a float
Like *Venus* in her pearly Boat.
The *Halcyons*, calming all that's nigh,
Betwixt the Air and Water fly.
Or, if some rowling Wave appears,
A Mass of Ambergris it bears.
Nor blows more Wind than what may well
Convoy the Perfume to the Smell.

VI

These Pictures and a thousand more,
Of Thee, my Gallery do store;
In all the Forms thou can'st invent
Either to please me, or torment:
For thou alone to people me,
Art grown a num'rous Colony;
And a Collection choicer far
Then or *White-hall's*, or *Mantua's* were.

VII

> But, of these Pictures and the rest,
> That at the Entrance likes me best:
> Where the same Posture, and the Look
> Remains, with which I first was took.
> A tender Shepherdess, whose Hair
> Hangs loosely playing in the Air,
> Transplanting Flow'rs from the green Hill,
> To crown her Head, and Bosome fill.

The strategy in this poem is to raise a question about his relation to Clora, real or posed, firstly by accentuating all that is *voulu* in Clora and in his own attitude to her. A tone of non-commitment is established at the very beginning by the evident wilfulness of the conceit of making the soul into a gallery of portraits of Clora. One does not view the soul, nor contrive it at will, nor invite people to inspect it and say whether they are pleased. All that follows this opening must be felt as subtly non-obligatory, a polite fiction. If the poet chooses to contrive his soul in this way, that is his business. Various pictures of Clora follow; we are never allowed to forget that they are merely pictures, and all different. Marvell is at pains to make it clear that Clora is not really what any one picture shows her to be: 'Here Thou art painted in the Dress Of an Inhumane Murtheress' (stz. 2); 'But, on the other side, th'art drawn Like to *Aurora* in the Dawn' (stz. 3); 'Like an Enchantress here thou show'st' (stz. 4); 'But, against that, thou sit'st a float Like *Venus* in her pearly Boat' (stz. 5). The sixth stanza brings into explicitness the reiterated suggestion that these pictures are only pictures and that they are mutually-contradictory inventions:

> These Pictures and a thousand more,
> Of Thee, my Gallery do store;
> In all the Forms thou can'st invent
> Either to please me, or torment:

and these lines are followed by a conceit so outrageous that it is a contradiction in terms:

> For thou alone to people me,
> Art grown a num'rous Colony;

94

then follows a description of the lady as a gallery far more interesting to a connoisseur than either Whitehall or Mantua; the citing of real places deliberately underlines the unreality of the gallery he has made—or allowed Clora to make for his benefit. There is not one stanza of the poem in which Marvell does not labour to suggest that the picture gallery is a figment and every picture in it is only a picture: he wills the gallery and Clora wills the contents. Indeed it is uncertain who is responsible for the attitudes struck in the pictures—Clora, or the poet who appreciates them. It is all a highly-civilized game, which will last only as long as both of them want to play.

Having built up all this, both by the diction and by the displayed unreality of the conceit, Marvell now beautifully places the *volte-face* of the poem. It is still a gallery, still a game; one could pull it down, one could refuse to play; and yet—as the last stanza suddenly reminds us—there are degrees of unreality:

> But, of these Pictures and the rest,
> That at the Entrance likes me best:

the picture he chooses as the best is the one at the entrance, at the beginning of love. Here, what is familiar in the diction and what is simple in the picture suggest that there is something artless about this picture. Its effect on the poet is that he is no longer the wholly detached connoisseur of unreal attitudes: he has made a choice, he is affected. What affects him is what is completely unaffected, a purely visual object. But yet, a visual object *in a gallery*. Is it quite un-affected? Was she not, even at the beginning, affecting to be the picture of simple beauty, adorning herself with innocent flowers? No doubt it doesn't finally matter whether or not that was affectation too; he liked her when she pretended to be simple and was just there to be looked at. And despite all the subsequent pictures, the first one is still there, and somehow more real than the others—despite the fact that the first lured him into an experience which turned out to be very different from what it promised. The tone of all this—the detachment at once ironic, tender, and willingly deceived—depends for its achievement firstly on the displayed artificiality of the conceit and of the pictures described within it. But it depends too on a structural element which stands, in a sense, outside the display of contrivance and the stressed artificiality in the diction. This structural element is a relational element. The tour round the gallery returns to the picture at the entrance; the last picture in the poem is the first in the gallery—which is to say that the last stanza of the poem alters all that has gone before by introducing a *da capo*, the relation *to go back to the beginning*. To remove the last stanza would be to take away the base on which the whole poem proves to have been standing. The effect of this element on the whole poem is difficult to pin down, for the good reason that the relation *to go back to the beginning* is, like all relations, clear in one way and infinitely ambiguous in another. The relation itself can be stated. *Da capo* states it. But what it means (means to anybody) depends on the members it relates. Here it relates members who have no definition except *vis-à-vis* one another. The first five pictures are more artificial than the sixth; yet the sixth is also inside a gallery, and an invented gallery at that. So the meaning of the relation *da capo*—when it relates members as ambiguous as these—is one that may well 'tease us out of thought', as Keats said of the Grecian urn.

In this poem, then, metaphor's power to collapse the wall between fact and fiction and between subject and object is brought into full play firstly by displaying the element of contriving, or of invention, which says of the contents of the poem, 'These contents are "framed" '. In this, it has the same strategy as Richard's speech in prison. But something else in such cases has to say, 'These contents are real'. Richard says this by reviewing his own performance—by being outside the frame (or trap) as well as inside it. In Marvell's poem, however, the poet stays inside the gallery—but at the same time outside the frame of each picture, by being free to walk about in the gallery, and choose. And whereas the crucial ambiguity—the 'pay-off'—in Richard's speech is concentrated at the level of a play on words capable of more than one interpretation (as in 'Think that I am unking'd by Bolingbroke'), Marvell's poem has its 'pay-off' in the ambiguity of the *da capo* with which the poem comes to a conclusion in which nothing is concluded.

Looking back over the examples discussed in this chapter, we can see that 'vastidity' of meaning in poems depends on the setting-up of tensions between the various meanings—the various patternings of experience—infused into its language by the power of the poem's structure. To say that there is a tension between meanings in a poem is only another way of saying that its structure impels us to see that the constituents of the poem can be related to one another in more than one kind of way, and impels us too to see something exciting and significant in the fact that these ways are simultaneously opened to us. The concept of 'tension' will be discussed further in ensuing chapters, where it will be seen that there are, at every level of poetic organization, features of language which can be structured in more than one way at a time, so as to set up tension between the various structurings; metaphor is not the only source of multiple relationships. Ensuing chapters should also make it clear that it is no empty figure of speech to assert that the language of poems can make us see an interplay of relationships or that relationships seen by the mind are not immovable, like the bricks of an edifice. Relationships are not so much like bricks, as like a Maenad's hair floating in the wind, and in a poem many winds blow at once. It has been the concern of this chapter to open this vast and difficult area of our concern by treating metaphor as an example of the fact that any one feature, device, or configuration of language is not, itself, a single thing; metaphor easily allows of the illustration of this, because its range of remarkable effects is so great; metaphor is not so much a single Maenad, as the three witches of *Macbeth* rolled into one:

> [*First Witch.*] . . .
> I'll do, I'll do, and I'll do.
>   *Sec. Witch.* I'll give thee a wind.
>   *First Witch.* Thou'rt kind.
>   *Third Witch.* And I another.
>   *First Witch.* I myself have all the other,
> And the very ports they blow,
> All the quarters that they know
> I' the shipman's card.
>
>   . . . .
> Though his bark cannot be lost,
> Yet it shall be tempest-tost.

(I, iii, 10–25)

97

For in metaphor Abstraction can give one kind of wind, Concretion another, and if one metaphor is complicated by another they can together untie the bag of all the other winds that toss us between reality and imagination. The difficulty of discussing poetic structure in a theoretical way, and the fascination of considering particular instances, both depend on that fact which above all I hope this chapter has brought to the fore: that is, that in poetic structures a constituent itself intricate brings out, when married to another, the potential of both; these constituents, common enough in ordinary language, but present there in a relatively inert form, produce—when they are used to develop and offset one another—that 'mutual' ordering to which I referred at the opening of this chapter. As the chapter's main conclusion I would proffer the suggestion that the best approach to the understanding of language in poetic structures is by way of an awareness of this mutual ordering of constituents or devices each in its own right vast in its range of potentialities. Whilst there is no prospect (so far as I can see) of categorizing the offspring of these marriages between one form of meaningfulness and another, there is much still to be done by learning more about the nature and range of each constituent. And if, as I have suggested, the real peculiarity of poetic structure is that in it one constituent is used to develop the potential of another, it would seem to follow that our more general understanding of how meaning works in any kind of language could be extended by study of how it works in poems—where one constituent acts upon another almost like an X-ray.

V

Language in 'Artificial' Forms

THE preceding chapter should have done something to show the meaning of the contention that when items from the common vocabulary enter into a complex structure they partake of the power of the structure and function in an arresting way. If my attempt to discuss the concept of 'structure' without recourse to a discussion of the structure of verse or of patterned word-play has indeed succeeded in making it clear that structuring may be imposed without the importation of systems not found in ordinary prose, the way is now clear to go on and consider some of the more conspicuous ways in which poetic organization of language may differ from the non-poetic. This chapter discusses some relations between the artificiality of language and the artifice of verse form, and the next will discuss some aspects of conspicuous word-play—or, to use a more convenient term—of 'verbal schemes'. There are points of close contact in the kind of material treated, and the considerations set out, in these two chapters. Their common concern is with the uses a poet may make (by way of verse form or by way of verbal schemes) of the regimentation of language into patterns which in various ways offset the limitations of our common stereotypes of meaning and reduce their resistance to poetic purposes. The chief problem considered in both chapters is that of the relation between these forms of regimentation and 'the meaning' in the poem. Though these chapters are entwined with one another in many ways, there is one large difference in the nature of their topics which warrants their being separated. The large difference between regimentation into verse form and regimentation into verbal schemes is that the latter are apparently more open to the objection that they impose formalization on the substance of what is said; verse form, however much it may in fact constrain the poet's freedom to put any words he likes anywhere he likes in the poem, easily allows him to preserve the illusion that he has not wantonly sacrificed the meaning to the successful execution of a move in a word-game. Objections which might be shown to be as relevant to verse form as to the schemes are in fact more strongly felt and more frequently voiced in connection with the latter. In other words, verse form allows us still to assume or pretend to ourselves that the meaning has been poured intact into an available and 'suitable' receptacle—as one might pour tea into a cup without spilling a drop or altering the constitution of the tea—whereas verbal schemes have their very identity in repetitions and variations involving the central apparatus of meaning: syntactical patterns and individual words (or word-stems). On the other hand, verse form, if it is regarded as not interfering with the meaning, may be suspected of being merely extraneous to the 'content' of the poem.

It will be seen from this preamble that these two chapters will involve considering the notion of artificiality in poetry and of the sacrifice of matter to manner and so they can hardly avoid at least some skirmishes with theoretical questions about the relation of content to form. In chapters such as these the pressure of theoretical problems is strong:

> The glacier knocks in the cupboard,
> The desert sighs in the bed,
> And the crack in the tea-cup opens
> A lane to the land of the dead.[1]

At the outset of two chapters where we shall be lucky if we get through before visibility is reduced to nil, it may be a good idea to clear the air by firing a general broadside at the artificiality of language as such.

The efficiency of language, as a system serviceable to the needs of all its users and capable of stability and flexibility sufficient for their purposes, necessarily results in its having on the one hand a fixity, which makes it in many respects incommensurate with the phenomena with which it has to deal (in proportion to its success in reducing them to standard terms), and on the other hand a shiftiness, which makes it indeterminate and slippery to handle (in proportion

---

[1] *Collected Shorter Poems, 1930–1944, by W. H. Auden* (London, 1950), p. 228.

to its success in preserving its ability to meet new situations without continual revision and supplementation of its apparatus). The slipperiness of language will figure more largely in later chapters. Here we may consider some of the ways in which its very stability and familiarity involve its users in complex manœuvres to maintain a satisfactory relation between the system and the non-linguistic reality which has to be manipulated through it.

Because we all have an acquired familiarity with the intricacies of language, we are not habitually conscious of its artificiality. We all play complicated language games without having to stop to think. But if we try to analyse the scoring of points we have to teach ourselves how to pierce through our familiarity with this very artificial thing, language, and to realize that even in its apparently simple forms it is at a great remove from non-verbal reality, and that, on the other hand, some of its more evidently artificial forms may be created not so much out of a wilful fancy for elaborateness as out of a necessity to make a uniquely resonant assertion of the quality of one's own experience. One may be driven to a new extreme in hyperbolic compliment in the endeavour to assert that what one feels is not the same as what lots of other people have already said on a similar subject. One of the poet's great problems is how to lay claim in words to intensity of feeling. ('If it be love indeed, tell me how much', was Cleopatra's command to Antony.) To lay claim to intensity is very difficult because the words of intensity have already been so much used; in this, poetry is subject to the law of diminishing returns. The poet who wishes to advertise the fact that his feelings go beyond the ordinary has a very difficult linguistic problem to solve, for, however much he claims to approach infinity or an ultimate in feeling, the formula for infinity is still $n+1$. One way out of this kind of difficulty is to use abnormal vocabulary. In the satiric vocabulary of Marston, bent on conveying an ultimate in hate and scorn, the violence and unacceptability of the words serves as an index of the intensity behind them; in this, the vocabulary operates much on the principle of swearing—there has to be a tabu, so that one can express one's sense of outrage by breaking it. A satiric vocabulary of this kind is expressive in measure as it is a conspicuous departure from the norm of acceptable language. A different way out, but again one involving a rejection of the standard vocabulary of feeling as being inadequate just because it is standard, is to play a formal language game. Such a game is played in the first speeches of the lovers in Shakespeare's *Antony and Cleopatra*:

> *Cleo.* If it be love indeed, tell me how much.
> *Ant.* There's beggary in the love that can be reckon'd.
> *Cleo.* I'll set a bourn how far to be beloved.
> *Ant.* Then must thou needs find out new heaven, new earth.

(I, i, 14–17)

Here are four moves towards a successful assertion that feeling has reached the ultimate. These moves, as contrasted with the use of abnormal vocabulary, have the advantage that the effect will not become pale by comparison with the floridity of subsequent efforts in the *genre*. A clever language move to express infinity is made in Satan's assertion in *Paradise Lost* (IV, 76–7) that

> in the lowest deep a lower deep
> Still threatning to devour me opens wide,

where the device is to run language back on its tracks by making 'lower' worse than 'lowest'; infinity is given a linguistic index by unfixing the given fixities of grammar. Many complimentary poems, especially those written in a very highly developed tradition, can hardly be appreciated at all unless we treat them as refinements of a stylization; so far from pretending to be direct, untouched reports on reality, they go out of their way to point to the brilliance of their own moves or the tentativeness of their efforts to find the best move for trapping reality in the apparatus currently available. 'Shall I compare thee to a summer's day?' Shakespeare asks at the beginning of Sonnet 18, where he represents himself as casting about vainly for an adequate comparison. Or, in so developed a convention as this, where the sonneteers,

> Full of protest, of oath and big compare,
> Want similes, truth tired with iteration,[1]

the best way to assert the rarity of one's own feelings may be to re-

[1] Shakespeare, *Troilus and Cressida*, III, ii, 182–3.

mark on the falsity of the language used by others who have laid claim to feel as much. Shakespeare does this in Sonnet 130 ('My mistress' eyes are nothing like the sun'), where he devotes the first twelve lines to faulting the lady all the way through a list of the standard comparisons[1] and then in the couplet makes his own assertion about her and his love for her by implying that he has more right than others to the language the others have used:

> And yet, by heaven, I think my love as rare
> As any she belied with false compare.

This is a strategy which uses a convention by alleging that one repudiates it. The brilliance of the strategy is evident by reference to our experience of other uses of the convention, for experience of it equips us with an idea of what is 'normal' inside it and gives us an appreciation of the expressiveness of the moves made on the board— however far the 'norm' of the convention may be from other 'norms'. Gombrich makes this point in discussing the art criticism of Jonathan Richardson who, he remarks,

took it for granted that every medium and every convention has its own level of normality that determines the expectations of the connoisseur who would register any subtle emphasis in one direction or another. The identical tone, therefore, that would strike him as expressive of gloom in a water color might have impressed him as calm and serene in an ink drawing.[2]

What we tend to forget, when we are passing judgment on lapsed conventions, is that the norm by which we judge them is the norm of another convention—whether we judge by some norm we have established for ourselves as a result of our own experience of other kinds of poetry or whether, even more unthinkingly, we judge by the norm of language as we speak and write it ourselves. This latter norm itself undergoes constant change, and among the many reasons

[1] See *Shakespeare Survey*, 6 (1953), p. 83, where J. W. Lever points out the resemblance between Shakespeare's enumeration of over-worked comparisons and the satirical enumeration in John Eliot's *Ortho-epia Gallica* [1593] of the jaded hyperboles of the language of love.

[2] E. H. Gombrich, *Art and Illusion: A Study in the Psychology of Pictorial Representation*, A. W. Mellon Lectures in the Fine Arts, v (1956) (London, 1960), p. 373.

why this is so, the one important to our present discussion is the need the individual speaker or writer may feel for an individual and idiosyncratic use of standard equipment. We encounter and realize the artificiality of this equipment when the thing we want to say comes out as banal or somehow 'wrong' when we put it into familiar words; too many people have said the same before us, and all we can find to say is, somehow, not what we mean. In such a situation we are approaching the situation of the poet.

The inadequacy and artificiality of language, its alienation from the vividly experienced qualities of being alive, has been very acutely realized by some great poets. For some, the impurity of the medium has become almost obsessional. Mallarmé in his sonnet on the swan ('Le vierge, le vivace et le bel aujourd'hui')[1] sees the poet under the symbol of the swan trapped in the freezing lake; the lake is his element, yet at the same time it is the lake itself that traps and freezes him and pins him down, so that, haunted by the thought of '[les] vols qui n'ont pas fui', he sees himself as 'Magnifique mais . . . sans espoir', cut off by language itself from pure reality and frozen in a cold dream of scorn for the language he cannot escape. However earnestly the poet tries to purify himself from all desire to make a show with the trappings of language, he finds after all that the very medium he has to use is the product of the human mind and the human heart. The dream of a wholly naked encounter with reality, without the interposition of language, is always frustrated by entanglement in a 'fictive covering', as Wallace Stevens says in his fable of the encounter of Nanzia Nunzio and Ozymandias:

> On her trip around the world, Nanzia Nunzio
> Confronted Ozymandias. She went
> Alone and like a vestal long-prepared.
>
> I am the spouse. She took her necklace off
> And laid it in the sand. As I am, I am
> The spouse. She opened her stone-studded belt.

[1] Stéphane Mallarmé, *Œuvres complètes*, ed. Henri Mondor et G. Jean-Aubry (Paris, 1951), pp. 67–8.

I am the spouse, divested of bright gold,
The spouse beyond emerald or amethyst,
Beyond the burning body that I bear.

I am the woman stripped more nakedly
Than nakedness, standing before an inflexible
Order, saying I am the contemplated spouse.

Speak to me that, which spoken, will array me
In its own only precious ornament.
Set on me the spirit's diamond coronal.

Clothe me entire in the final filament,
So that I tremble with such love so known
And myself am precious for your perfecting.

Then Ozymandias said the spouse, the bride
Is never naked. A fictive covering
Weaves always glistening from the heart and mind.[1]

The ultimate despair of language, one may suppose, is reserved for those who have in each age done most to make it bend to their will, and poetry, which may finally take the love-hate relationship with language to such extremes as this, has none the less made many successful misalliances on the way and concealed the difficulties of the relationship so well that it is possible for some readers of poetry to believe that poets in their dealings with language are most effective when they merely do what comes naturally. But 'natural' or 'simple' language in successful poems usually proves, on reflection, to conceal unique arrangements for achieving that very illusion. It can usually be assumed to be the case, that a poet who appears to speak 'the language of the heart', or 'the language of common life', has gone to considerable trouble to invent it; the difficulty for the critic, especially where there is no conspicuous innovation at the level of vocabulary, is to arrive at an understanding of those processes in the poem which enable familiar words to convey unique quality. It is obvious enough that in order to make them do this the poet has done something specific to overcome both the generalizing quality and the

---

[1] *Collected Poems*, pp. 395–6.

great range of indeterminacy of words in very frequent and varied use. Of these characteristics of items of vocabulary, Hospers remarks,

words refer only to *types* or *classes* of things—universals—and the poet's task is much more specialized and difficult than merely to indicate class-inclusions; the poet must make the vision much more precise, and this he can do only by the appropriate juxtapositions of words with an eye to just the right evocation. The situation might be improved if there were, for example, a million synonyms for "joy," and we all knew just what shade of feeling was denoted by each of them . . . but since our language is not so richly stocked, we can only use the portmanteau-words we have and put them together in evocative ways, thus serving a purpose which was far from their intention when the words were coined.[1]

But it is arguable whether a million synonyms for joy, or any number of millions, would come near to solving the problems presented to the poet by the nature of language. Even if we were to assume that the poet's purpose is to package his private experience so that it does not get damaged in transit from him to us—or, if that is a wilfully misleading metaphor, that his purpose is to use language to give us a maximally accurate map-reading to enable us to place what he is talking about—we still have to face the fact that a vocabulary however extensive can do nothing of itself to communicate the particularity and concretion of living experience. I use the word 'concretion' to refer to the phenomenon my reader may observe merely by lifting his eyes from the page and looking about him. What he sees will present a simultaneity of attributes, and complexity of relationships, with which referential language hardly attempts to deal. To describe a view from a window, or even a flower in a jug inside the room (a wallflower, dark red, darker at the centre, wilting at the edges, lit by the morning sun, spraying out of its jug, reflected in a mirror), one might go on for ever and still fail not only to put into language all that the flower is in its own particular qualities and in its relationships to other things, but more notably fail—fail in entirety—to register the simultaneous interpenetration of each attribute or quality by every other, the mutual modifications operating over the whole network of relationships inhabited by a thing. And if the

[1] John Hospers, *Meaning and Truth in the Arts*, 2nd printing (Chapel Hill, 1948), p. 183.

particularity, concretion, 'thinginess' even of what we call 'concrete objects' is so inaccessible to the probe of our common language, how much less accessible is that of a moment in the mind, or a mood, a vision, or an attitude?[1] It could be argued that all good poems in some way evoke a sense of sharpness and richness of quality, at once definite, in the sense that it is strongly felt to be 'there' as one reads the poem, yet indefinite in the sense that attempts to verbalize what is felt to be there are, themselves, felt to be imperfect, to fall short of all that the poem evokes—to falsify it, even, in the act of specifying it. The difficulty of accounting for the fact that such responses are evoked is most acute when the words on the page, taken individually, are common and plain. Where the individual words are as common and plain as words in a poem can ever be and yet there emanates from the poem an individual complex of vivid qualities, one has the illusion that the common tongue presents no problem to the poet, and, like Sidney's Astrophel at a loss for language ('others' feete', he complained, 'still seem'd but strangers in my way'), all he has to do is to recognize that the way out of his troubles is as simple as Astrophel concluded it to be:

> Biting my trewand pen, beating my selfe for spite,
> 'Foole,' said my Muse to me, 'looke in thy heart and write.'[2]

It is difficult to discuss the nature of the illusion Astrophel contrives when he pretends that he writes in the simple language of the heart. How far such a language may be from ingenuousness I shall try to show by recapitulating in my own words something at least of the

[1] Cf. Elizabeth M. Wilkinson, ' "Form" and "Content" in the Aesthetics of German Classicism', in *Stil- und Formprobleme in der Literatur*, ed. Paul Böckmann, Vorträge des VII. Kongresses der Internationalen Vereinigung für moderne Sprachen und Literaturen in Heidelberg, 1957 (Heidelberg, 1959), p. 21: 'Art, for Goethe and Schiller, is expressive of the life that goes on within us all the time but which we are never able to communicate as it is lived. . . . This inner life, in the form we experience it, is not accessible to language. When we reduce it to concepts and propositions, it has already changed its character. In vain do we struggle . . . to convey the rhythms and contours, the *feel* of this inner life, not only the feel of our emotions, of our joy or our grief, but the feel of our thinking too, its involutions and convolutions, its ramifications and tensions, its sudden compressions when a long and complicated train of thought seems to condense into a single moment. It eludes all language save the language of art'.

[2] *The Poems of Sir Philip Sidney*, ed. William A. Ringler, Jr. (Oxford, 1962), p. 165.

concretion of qualities present in the words of a short poem and by enquiring whether the means the poet has used to convey this concretion are inaccessible to the critical act. The poem is the simply-worded and very successful elegy on the Countess of Pembroke, usually attributed to William Browne of Tavistock:

> Underneath this sable Herse
> Lyes the subject of all verse:
> Sydney's sister, Pembroke's Mother:
> Death, ere thou hast slaine another,
> Faire, and Learn'd, and good as she,
> Time shall throw a dart at thee.[1]

The effect of this poem as a whole is highly individual. To take a few shots at describing it, I might say, 'The poem gives an impression of superb arrogance', or 'an impression of the most powerful restraint of powerful grief' or 'an impression of the finality of death' (but it both gives that impression and refutes it), or 'an impression of magnificent compliment, so assured of the worth of its subject that it does not condescend to particularize or to use any but the most general terms of praise ("Faire", "Learn'd", "good"); more important than all this, an impression of a gesture made in the face of death, a gesture at once passionate and cool'. Even to call it a gesture wrongs the simplicity of the language; it is not so much a gesture as a long haughty look, a kind of 'I am Duchess of Malfi still'. All these pot-shots are inadequate; but all these impressions, or something like them, come from thirty-four words in a fixed order. Why?

Chiefly, because the poem veers round in the middle, where there is a dramatic turn as violent, in its own way, as the moment when Hamlet leaps into Ophelia's grave. The poem starts in the marmoreal manner, in the tone of public statement, with a *Hic requiescat*: 'Underneath this sable Herse Lyes . . .'. But we are not told the name of the dead at once. This is a death of maximum concern to poets: the death of the 'subject of all verse'. The words 'Sydney's sister,

[1] *The Oxford Book of Seventeenth Century Verse*, ed. H. J. C. Grierson and G. Bullough (Oxford, 1934), p. 339. [A second stanza, usually treated as being an addition by another hand, appears in Lansdowne MS. 777; for this addition see *Poems of William Browne of Tavistock*, ed. Gordon Goodwin (London, 1894), II, 294.]

Pembroke's Mother' call into the poem the ambience of the Countess's name in life: patroness of poets, inspiration of Sidney's *Arcadia*, a woman whose rank and family, personal gifts, and patronage of letters, all made her stand as a grand exemplar of one to whom Poetry was indebted for inspiration and encouragement; now she is dead, there is no more for the poet to do, save with simple finality to record her death. It is at this very point of simple, final recording that the poet himself—as it were—leaps from the tomb, and addresses Death with superb contempt. The poem and its fictional speaker come to passionate life precisely at the very word of address, 'Death'—Death which has done its worst until the end of time when Time will at last turn upon Death and destroy it. It is implied that the end of the world (when Time and Death end too) is the only conceivable parallel to the death of the subject of all verse. This, itself a stupendous compliment, is at the same time the implicit *consolatio* of the elegy: eternal life is implied. But the power of the poem does not lie in its implied religious consolation or in the stupendous compliment paid to the Countess. The power comes from the sudden reversal of attitude that occurs at the word 'Death', the violent explosion of life, passion, compliment and affirmation. The violence of this explosion depends for its effect upon the poet's having first carefully constructed the marmoreal weight it explodes. In order to construct this, the poet has used many hidden devices. Rhythm and metrics are important. The beat in

Underneath this sable Herse

falls as unarguably as it does, because the metrical accent coincides perfectly with speech accent in a solemn, falling rhythm. (What determines the metrical structure is the phrasing imposed by sense and normal stress.) In the first three lines, where the basic rhythm is trochaic [DOM de/DOM de/DOM de/DOM], every stressed word is a blow. The march of the lines is ponderously retarded, because a pause has to be made between the stressed syllable at the end of one line and the stressed syllable at the beginning of the next ['. . . Herse/ Lyes . . .'; 'verse:/Sydney's . . .']. This solemn pause between the end of one line and the beginning of the next does not occur at the turn of the poem: there is no pause before '/Death' because the preceding line ends with a light stress, in 'Mo'ther'. This is the turning-point of the metrics. The whole metrical structure is delicately poised between trochaic and iambic, and what is crucial in the poem's effect is that whereas in the first three lines the metre is predominantly trochaic, in the following three lines it is predominantly iambic. The first three lines insist on being read

DOM de/DOM·de/ DOM de/ DOM,
DOM de/DOM de/ de de/ DOM
DOM de/DOM de·DOM de/ DOM de

but the following lines insist on being read DOM/de DOM/de DOM/de DOM, for obviously it would be ridiculous to read them:

Death, ere/thou hast/slaine a-/nother,
Faire, and/Learn'd, and/good as/she,
Time shall/throw a/dart at/thee.

The diction in the first three lines plays in with the crushing weight of the trochaic scheme; it is a diction concerned with solemn, ponderous facts; the only word that forsakes the factual is the word 'all'. Contrast with this the diction of the ensuing lines, which contain invocation, personification, indirect hyperbole, value-words, metaphor and the future tense; this is essentially convictional language. And whereas in the first three lines everything is so arranged as to make the tomb press down to the extinction of personal identity (she is not even named except as 'Sydney's sister, Pembroke's Mother'), in the other three lines her personal qualities are asserted, and at the height of compliment. Most subtle of all is the way in which the turn of the poem is so placed as to derive, from its relation to the rhyme-structure, the maximum effect of surprise: it is placed exactly in the middle of the central one of the three couplets. One usually expects of couplets that the sense of the passage will fall into two-line chunks, with the second line acting as the clincher of the first. In this poem the central couplet splits apart in the middle; its first half concludes the record of the facts of death, its second half opens the defiance of death. Thus at every point where one examines this brilliantly subtle poem written in such simple vocabulary, one sees that the reversal of death's triumph (which is its action) is achieved by pressing into service that which in each mode—rhythm, diction, verse-form—is capable of giving force to the vocabulary. The progression of attitude in the poem, from the recording of death to a cool contempt for it, is the recipient of contributions from everything else in the poem. The action of the poem is not something agglomerated out of the successive sense-contents of each line. The action becomes effective because of, indeed is effectuated by, the formal relations in the poem: a violent change of attitude owes its violence to its position in the metrics and in the couplet, it owes its force to the great weight of grief it must throw off (a weight created by rhythm and diction), it owes its triumph to the overthrow of the metrical structure dominant in the first three lines, it owes its arrogance of compliment to the rhyming of 'she' and 'thee', and it owes its coolness to the last line's relation to what has gone before—for in the space of one line, Time with a little flick of a dart undoes the mighty Death who in the preceding five lines had managed to do so much. The result of all this is a poem in simple vocabulary—but not a simple poem.

I have treated this short poem in considerable detail because it seems to me to exemplify some facts that the student of poetic language cannot afford to overlook. One is that language is deeply deceptive. It has so many modes of affecting us that under the plainest of surfaces there may prove to be highly intricate formal relations whose effects are the more powerful for being difficult to trace back to any single cause. Secondly, the tracing of an effect back to its causes is often difficult just because the effect is the product of the whole structure: that is, of many relations working together to produce a progression with a very definite shape; the poem is not a collection of phrases, but a dramatic action, the actors being such things as metrics, alteration of tone and so on. Once this is realized, the concept of 'simple language' begins to look like a critical delusion. Simple vocabulary is often the mask of sophisticated art. We may ask ourselves how far our critical vocabulary takes account of the poet's power to do this. What word is there in critical terminology to refer to what the poet does when he constructs a drama which gives us the feel of his subject ? 'Imitation' seems a possible term, but this is misleading, for the word 'imitation' tends to suggest a copying of reality, as if the poet were attempting to use words as simple mirrors of 'components' of reality—the word 'red' to mirror the fact of redness, the words 'great' and 'solemn' to mirror greatness and solemnity. The poet however is not content to use language in this way. His 'imitation' in language is much more devious. He often prefers to enact his meaning: to make a pattern which, when it plays itself through in the reader's mind, enacts the quality of the experience or movement of consciousness he is writing about. The enactment in the elegy on the Countess of Pembroke depends much on values established in the systems of metre, rhythm and stanzaic form, but I should not like to suggest that these are the only elements capable of serving such a purpose. Any mode in which structuring is strongly marked may contribute, to what is said in the mode of statement, an accompanying enactment of individuality. There may be innumerable ways of engineering, by the use of words in systematized relations, forms of individuation outside the range of any vocabulary. It would be foolish to talk as though one could construct a typology of what goes on in the human mind as it responds to language in which overt meaning is accompanied by the enactment of individuated processes which, though assimilable to the meaning, do not themselves state a meaning but rather give coloration, shape, form, tone, or quality. These words are used for want of better ones; it is hard to find a term that will not seem to reduce 'enactment' to the level of a make-up man adding trivia to meaning's face. The difficulty is that the longer I go on using words to describe the outline of unverbalized experience, the further I shall fall through the soundless abyss between linguistic and non-linguistic reality. Perhaps it will be best to make an end, here, of the verbal pursuit of the non-verbal, and recall myself and my reader to a sense of the simple difference (without any inequality) between the two, by saying that the term 'enactment' is used as a reminder of the difference between an action and a verbal statement: enactment escapes the reductive specification of verbal statement. Similarly, to try to write any further gloss on what 'enactment' means, would only serve to clutter up, as words will, the idea of fluid gesture, of an eloquence beyond vocabulary, which I am trying to attach to the term. To avoid this, I must resort to a parallel, and quote the words in which a writer on drama describes the climax of Yeats's play, *A Full Moon in March*: 'The feeling at this point is so intense that speech is too crude, too circumscribed, to express it. Instead, the Queen's commitment is enacted by means of silent, symbolic gesture'.[1]

Of course, in order to bring enactment about—that is, to endow what is said at statement-level with the fullness of an unverbalized particularity—one need not write of a drama of changing attitudes (though the poem I chose as an example is of this kind) and there is no reason to suppose that particularization must always depend on the interaction of the many components at work in verse structure. Nor is it to be supposed that the only work that verse structure will be called upon to do, is the work of lodging the poem's 'statement' in that verse structure which attaches a unique quality to it. In considering enactment as effect, and verse structure as cause, we have, as always with questions of cause and effect in literary forms of language, to remember that 'stylistic elements . . . are "polyvalent"; the same device may produce several effects, and conversely, the same effect may be obtained from several devices'.[2]

It may be asked how one can speak almost in the same breath of unique quality and of 'the same device', the 'same effect'. The first and obvious answer is that one may for the purposes of classification and theorizing use an inclusive term—such as 'metaphor'—for a certain kind of linguistic relation, whose effects will vary according to what kind of words and meanings it relates. A second answer is that when one speaks of 'the same effect', one may, again, be speaking in broad classifying terms or, conversely, one may be speaking with one's eye on the immediate operation of a device on the meaning of the words involved in it, without reference to the larger effect, in context, of the meaning so affected. For instance, one may use the device of giving one word a line to itself and though whenever this is done the effect will be 'the same' in that the word acquires promi-

[1] Denis Donoghue, *The Third Voice: Modern British and American Verse Drama* (Princeton, N.J., 1959), pp. 56-7.
[2] Ullmann, *Style in the French Novel*, p. 20.

nence, the effect of this prominence in any particular passage will depend on the nature of the passage. Obviously the effect of a device does not terminate in its immediate effect on the few words most closely involved in it; in a poem, we are concerned with a network of meanings. But apart from the question of the levelling and limiting effects of critical language we have the further question of the shifting substance in which 'the same' features of verse form are embodied. For, though to some extent words have what Yvor Winters calls 'mechanical properties'—i.e., 'trick' will always sound more like 'track' or 'brick' than like 'pudding' or 'jam'—they have fluid properties too, and even the 'same' word will vary in pitch, duration, stress and force according to the sense of the phrase in which it is found, and, in verse, it will also vary in these respects according to what metrical structure we conceive ourselves to be 'fitting it into'. For such reasons, no two rhythms can be identical, though they may be very broadly comparable. Dealing with some of the fluid properties involved in rhythm, Yvor Winters makes the point that no two lines can correspond exactly in rhythm:

no two syllables ever have the same degree of accent—that is, so far as versification is concerned there is no such thing as an inherently accented or unaccented syllable, but syllables which count technically as accented can be recognized as such only with reference to the other syllable or syllables within the same foot; secondly, although quantity or syllable-length has no part in the measure, it is, like accent, infinitely variable and it affects the rhythm. . . . rhythm results from the proper control and manipulation of these sources of variation.[1]

He goes on to say that 'the rhythm of the poem permeates the entire poem as pervasively as blood permeates the human body: remove it and you have a corpse' (p. 83). One might develop the simile into a conceit, making stanzaic form the skeleton, lineation the muscular development, rhyme the co-ordination of the muscles, and so on. The point that the 'body' of the poem becomes a corpse if its unity is dismembered, will remain.

If the 'body' is unique (as I have tried to show that it must be,

---

[1] Yvor Winters, *The Function of Criticism: Problems and Exercises* (Denver, 1957), pp. 82-3.

despite the fact that we can classify the organs) it may still be asked
how this uniqueness can be meaningful. How can the 'blood', for
instance, add to the meaning of the poem? I hope that my example
has shown that it does add to the meaning; I am concerned now to
find some tolerable terms in which to explain how it can do this. I
have claimed in my commentary on Browne's poem that its verse
form (in alliance with other systems, notably variation in the diction)
does something much more specific than merely to provide interest,
excitement and individuality; it provides surprise, reversal, triumph,
coolness and so on. I think it is at this point that we encounter the
hardest problem of 'form'. It does not need arguing that we habitually
see for ourselves attributes such as grace, or fury, or tenderness, in
the outline of a vase, in the race of breakers bursting over the rocks,
in what Wordsworth called

> that deep farewell light by which
> The setting sun proclaims the love he bears
> To mountain regions.
> (*Prelude*, 1805–6 version, VIII, 117–19.)

Exactly how and why we read these qualities into the world about us
is not a question to be attempted here. I suppose that our reading a
quality into rhythm and into other formal relations is of the same
order but with the differences that in a poem there are incentives, of
a more specific kind, supplied by the sense of the words and our
sense of the situation they refer to, which predispose us to interpret
the rhythm, the formal reversals and the like, into 'attributes' con-
gruent with the situation. Besides this, what takes place in the verse
system of the poem can be interpreted in a much more highly-
differentiated way than what takes place when a breaker crashes on a
rock. The verse system itself contains highly-differentiated 'events',
such as the bold inversion of a foot, the delicate balance of a line,
because it is in itself a system of many components giving rise to
many expectations, many emphases, many crises and resolutions of
pattern; we may perhaps call these 'values', which we appreciate
within the framework of the verse system. The fineness with which
we appreciate these values and relate them to one another is, like
most other advanced operations of the human mind, beyond our

powers of recapitulation in verbal terms, since our vocabulary and syntax are not themselves discriminated with the same fineness; language is man's tool, man's invention, and the invention cannot be as fine as the powers of its maker. A formal structure capable of articulating, in its own terms, fine differences beyond the discrimination-level that is possible in blunt verbal terms, charges those merely verbal terms with precise values of another order of existence. It should perhaps be added that in relating these 'values' to the sense of the words, we probably tend to pick out from among the myriad events occurring in a stream of verse those which most successfully 'enact' the sense; we disregard the irrelevant aspects of the total particularity of what is occurring. One might add, too, the consideration that it is, naturally, a most moving experience when the 'values' of a formal system succeed in proving the sense of the words upon our pulses (to adapt Keats's phrase), for this is an experience of making a kind of contact with the particularity of the (unverbal) world, which the very nature of language ordinarily denies to us. When, for instance, Keats writes, in the Ode to Autumn, 'Thy hair soft-lifted by the winnowing wind', he brings the image of autumn suddenly and intimately close, as the line's own contour traces the first soft touch, then the lifting stir, then the lessening tremor of the 'winnowing' as the breeze moves away, all with such delicacy that it is as if real to us. But this sudden and moving intimacy, so different from the distanced opening of the stanza, is vital not only because it is intimate but because it suddenly brings the distanced image near, and that by no manifest effort or overt lessening of the distance, but by the silent touch of enactment, brought quietly to bear at the exactly necessary turn.

We need not, then, try to imagine a state of affairs in which constantly and without intermission the verse structure must particularize the sense of all that is said in it; there may be much to be gained by calling upon it to do this only at important points. Indeed it may be true that what we feel as the inner movement of a poem may be discernible to us chiefly because the poet controls that movement, by concentrating the force of the verse structure, and the several powers it holds, at decisive nodal points where the flow of meanings turns another way, or where there is one of those 'sudden compressions when a long and complicated train of thought seems to condense into a single moment'.[1] In this way the 'values' in the verse structure can be constitutive of the total form of the poem, in a sense not the same as saying that the verse structure *is*, itself, the form of the poem.

The concept of 'the form of the poem' is an elusive one and perhaps many words here will do nothing but darken counsel. We might say that a poem is not merely a series of statements, however effective the statements are severally and collectively; in a successful poem there is a sense of going somewhere and of knowing when one has arrived. This may amount to the same as saying that in a successful poem the interests it excites are all satisfied within the boundaries of the poem. Whether or not this is only a successful illusion I shall not pretend to know, but it is not impossible to see something of the way in which the satisfaction of all interests excited, or the illusion of satisfaction, may be brought about. If the values of the verse structure may be brought to bear more sharply at some points than at others, it should be possible to make use of this to give prominence to certain interests, both in their raising and in their satisfying, by linking them to some formal feature of the verse—and of course, other systems too, such as verbal repetitions, if necessary. A simple example is to be found in one of Dryden's songs in *The Spanish Fryar*:

> Farwell ungratefull Traytor,
>   Farwell my perjur'd Swain,
> Let never injur'd Creature
>   Believe a Man again.
> The Pleasure of Possessing
> Surpasses all Expressing,
> But 'tis too short a Blessing,
>   And Love too long a Pain.[2]

In the fifth and sixth lines the combination of the feminine rhyme with the concentration on similar vowel and consonant groups gives

[1] See p. 107, n. 1.
[2] *The Poems of John Dryden*, ed. James Kinsley (Oxford, 1958), I, 208.

an effect of delightedly dwelling on the same experience over and over. But after a transition line in which only a trace of these sound-groups survives, and an *l* prepares for the 'Love . . . long' alliteration in the last line, we are suddenly deprived, at the word 'Pain', of this dancing rhyme, and at the same time 'Pain' takes over the *p*-alliteration found in the fifth and sixth lines, dropped in the seventh, and nowhere echoed in this line except on the word 'Pain', which therefore makes a sharp antithesis to 'Pleasure'. Even the contrast between the monosyllabic 'Pain' and the weaving polysyllables 'Possessing', 'Surpasses', 'Expressing', contributes to the sense of sharp loss. (And, just as 'Pain' takes over the *p*'s, so 'short . . . Blessing' takes over the *s*'s.) It can be seen, then, that the 'mechanical properties' of the words are first pressed into a rhythm, a rhyme-scheme and an alliterative system whose values are linked with 'Pleasure', then after a transition these properties are changed, with the effect of a shearing-away of what went before and its recurrence only as 'Pain'. The variations in the formal systems of verse and rhetoric work out in an unexpected but mournfully satisfying way and they give the lines the force of an epigram, since these formal values and their variations are linked with the implicit antithesis of 'Possessing' and 'Love' as well as with the open antithesis of 'short'/ 'long' and of 'Pleasure'/'Pain'.

In speaking of verse structure and its potentialities I have used the term 'formal relations'. One might well hesitate to use it at all, since it has the double drawback of being wide in application and perhaps portentous in tone. Wideness of reference is hardly to be avoided if one maintains, as it is maintained in this book, that any prominent relationship between the parts of a poem will so modify and in turn be modified by other prominent relationships that the final unique-ness of the poem is the result of their total interaction, and where mutual modification of this kind takes place the total meaning of the poem is inseparable from this structure of relationships. The useful-ness of the term is that it enables one to imply, without wearisome repetition of a point of view, that any marked relationship in the poem may modify any other: that, for instance, an intellectual relationship, as between *black* and *white*, may be modified by any of he relationships in which the words 'black' and 'white' stand in the poem, even though these other relationships obtain in systems (such as rhyme) apparently at a remove from the kind of meaningfulness possessed by items of vocabulary. However, since no one is likely to deny that relations at the level of vocabulary and syntax are meaningful, there is a natural tendency for those who use 'formal relations' as a shorthand way of saying, 'All kinds of relationships have meaning and modify other meanings' to be most particularly concerned to defend the meaningfulness of relations occurring in systems that the man-in-the-street might call 'formal' in the bad sense of *extraneous to meaning, merely ornamental*, etc.

Some suspicion of portentousness may still attach to the term and it may therefore be as well to consider a poem where, though a formal relation worked out in the lineation sharply modifies the meaning of the words in the lines, the result is not impressive poetry; this should at least make it clear that I am not advocating the view that good poetry automatically comes into being if formal relations are used to modify word-meanings. I am concerned at present only to show that—for good or ill—modification does in fact take place; it is one of the facts about regimented language. The poem I have chosen to illustrate one effect of sustained contrivance at the level of lineation is *The Red Wheelbarrow*:

> so much depends
> upon
>
> a red wheel
> barrow
>
> glazed with rain
> water
>
> beside the white
> chickens.[1]

This poem tries to present the power of art to make us see things in a non-utilitarian way, making us dwell on properties of ordinary

[1] *The Collected Earlier Poems of William Carlos Williams* (Norfolk, Conn., 1951), p. 277.

objects usually passed over in our ordinary dealings with such things. Nowhere in the poem does the poet explicitly say that art emphasizes the intrinsic qualities of an object; instead of saying this he tries to do it—to make words achieve the condition of pictorial art so that we see visual properties in their individual particularity. The method he adopts is the eccentric placing of line-endings, so that they cut compound words into their separate elements ('rain/water', 'wheel/barrow'), elements as it were separately perceived. Stanza divisions are used to separate the qualifying phrase from what it qualifies ('barrow'//'glazed with rain'). The poem attempts to make words do what a painting can do: to make us see not a vaguely-generalized barrow in vaguely-generalized rain but redness and wheel and glaze and rain and water. Spatial relations too are emphasized: 'upon' gets a line to itself and is followed by a break between stanzas. Similarly colour-relation has a line to itself ('beside the white'). It appears too that we are meant to treat the poem as though it were a picture, by moving about inside it and seeing different groupings in turn, since the link in sense and the separation by line and stanza endings pull us in different ways. If the line and stanza endings were nullified by reading out the poem, to someone who had never seen it on the page, as though it were continuous prose, the poem would lose its point. To say this, is to point out the paucity of formal relations in the poem, not to condemn the particular use made of such relations as there are. The paucity was perhaps unavoidable; the conflict between the lineation and our tendency to read continuously, automatically practising grammatical subordination, and abstraction, as we go, has to be decided by a very strong stress on the peculiarity of the lineation—a stress achieved by keeping out of the poem other relations which might interfere with it. A particularly unfortunate result of this technique is that the word 'red' and the word 'white' are not given qualitative immediacy; they remain almost as inert and general as in ordinary contexts, since there is nothing in the poem to fill in the mere conceptual outline they afford.

Because this poem confines its exploitation of verse form to one main kind of formal relation—the relation between certain words and the incidence of the lineation—it simplifies some of the problems of discussing the bearing of formal relations upon meaning. For instance, reference to this example makes it clear that though the relations between particular words and the incidence of the lineation can be stated (e.g., line splits compound word, preposition stands alone, etc.), it is a long way from such a statement to the inferences I made in my comments on the pictorial character of the poem. To describe a relationship is not the same as saying what it does to the meaning—that is, what construction it causes us to put upon the words it involves. We do not in fact put a construction at all similar upon a comparable relation in the following lines from a poem by Marianne Moore, where one word (though not a compound word) is split by a line-ending:

> All
> external
>> marks of abuse are present on this
>> defiant edifice—
>>> all the physical features of
>
> ac-
> cident—lack
>> of cornice, dynamite grooves, burns, and
>> hatchet strokes, these things stand
>>> out on it; the chasm-side is
>
> dead.[1]

And though in these lines the word 'of' is separated by a stanza-division from the following word, its separation has nothing like the effect of the separation of 'upon' in the poem quoted before. Formal relations do not have meanings as words have meanings; it would be more like the truth to say that they are formative of meaning. As elements leading to the formation of meaning, they are much less determinate than the meanings of words, and are much more dependent, for the nature of their effect, on the strength and character of other formative elements in their vicinity, and dependent too on the extent to which they are asserted by some kind of device to draw

---

[1] For the complete poem see Marianne Moore, *Collected Poems* (London, 1951), pp. 37–8.

attention to them. (Repetition serves this purpose; *The Red Wheel-barrow* repeatedly uses line-endings to interfere with the normal phrasing we would otherwise give to the sentence.) This cannot but mean that a formal relationship of any considerable importance to a poem must involve, in a higher degree than ordinary language usually does, regularity, recurrence, or mirroring in comparable and collaborating relationships. If there is not, in any respect at all, a recognizably higher degree of patterning than ordinary language affords, there will not recognizably be a poem.

VI

Schematization and Abstraction

It is hardly likely to have gone unnoticed that the preceding chapters have been concerned to show that poetry is language at full stretch, bringing into maximal interplay the various potentialities afforded by linguistic forms in artistic structures. In the chapters that have gone before, the general picture is one of the poet doing better what the ordinary man does with his language: using it for the articulation of meaning. Even though the poet has been seen combining common elements and devices of meaning into uncommonly striking utterances, making much of potentialities not often fully realized by the everyday user of the language and exploiting too the potentialities of systems (such as metrics and verse-lining) not used in ordinary communication, he has not yet figured as one who soars into a sphere where diction takes forms so conspicuously unprosaic, so conspicuously deliberate and schematized, that the ordinary man is puzzled to know what relation these forms have to the conveyance of meaning. It is my purpose now to begin to enquire at what point levitation into such a sphere may be said to have taken place and what goes on up there.

Some readers may feel that levitation is to be assumed whenever a critic is driven to talk of poetic language in terms of its 'formal relationships' or of its 'ambiguity'. 'Ambiguity' will be the subject of the following chapter. 'Formal relationships' have already appeared in Chapter V, but there in connection with verse structure, not with schematization at the level of diction. It should be clear from Chapter V that formal relationships of the kind discussed there can be very powerfully operative in poems without any sacrifice of the illusion that the poet's diction is 'simple' and 'sincere'; the surface of the language remains sufficiently continuous with 'language such as men do use' to allow the poet to get by without being challenged to explain why he chooses it. But there are poems in which the setting of

123

words into schemes or systems clearly affects the poet's choice of words and invades the area in which meaning is ordinarily articulated: the area of vocabulary and syntax. It is the purpose of this chapter to discuss some aspects of this 'invasion'. It may be as well to remark at the outset that I shall not be concerned in this chapter with verbal patterns used for the purpose of emphasizing a meaning plainly given by the sense-content of a passage—these are an underlining of, rather than a tampering with, the main trend of what the poet has to say. I shall be concerned, rather, with verbal patterns for which no such easy explanation can be given, whether these take a form suggesting that the poet practises repetition for repetition's sake, or whether—a more complicated and interesting problem— the patterns into which the words are arranged seem to interfere with or cut across or compete with ordinary procedures of conveying meaning.

It is likely enough that anyone addicted to talking of the 'formal relationships' in a poem would find, if relentlessly pressed by an enquirer, that a definition of what he meant by this term would involve him in exposing not only his own theory of what a poem is, but also his own theory of what linguistic meaning is. Yet however wide the domain straddled somehow by the use of such a term, the fact is that some people who expound poems find the term useful and some people who have poems expounded to them remain obstinately convinced that though they can concede the occurrence in poems of those things pointed out to them as instances of 'formal relationships', they do not see the usefulness of recognizing their presence and they do not see what connection they have with 'what the poem actually says'. (We had better ignore the accidental irony in that 'actually'; I was trying not to darken the issue with phrases such as 'the content of the poem', or 'the information conveyed by the poem'.) This kind of difficulty is best approached by limiting attention in the first place to one broad type of formal relationships, that is, to patterned word-play in the 'schemes' familiar to us in the rhetoric of some Elizabethan poets; these have the advantage that the patterns are clearly registered in the diction of the poem; they are unarguably 'there' and their relation to 'what the poem actually says' can be manageably discussed in such a way as to lead on to wider issues.

A simple view of the rhetorical schemes of words which readily suggests itself is that these schemes 'give pleasure', pleasure being conceived of as an extra, superadded to the meaning of the words. It would be foolish to deny that this view may occasionally be in some sense correct, as it would be correct to say that rhythm as such may give pleasure. One can amuse a child with the te-tumming of a wordless rhythm, and minds sophisticated far beyond the child's can derive pleasure from the protracted sonal and rhythmical subtleties in, say, the verse paragraphs of Milton. It is also true that systems other than those of sound can function in an additive way, giving a kind of pleasure which is closely associated with the successful working out of an apparently self-propelling system. The pirouetting syntax of Pope's 'Where-e'er you walk, cool gales shall fan the glade' (discussed in Chapter I)[1] may serve as one example of this. Another example is the double sestina of Strephon and Klaius, performed as part of the shepherds' sports in Sidney's *Arcadia*; in this contest of verbal dexterity the assignment is that each speaker shall in turn outdo the other's manipulation of a six-line stanza in which the changes must be rung on six words which, it is agreed, are the only six from which the performer is allowed to choose the last word of a line and he must arrange the six end-words in a prescribed permutation of the order last used by the other performer. The performers keep this up for twelve full stanzas but two will serve here to show how it works and how pleasant it is:

Strephon. For she, whose parts maintainde a perfect musique,
    Whose beawties shin'de more then the blushing morning,
    Who much did passe in state the stately mountaines,
    In straightnes past the Cedars of the forrests,
    Hath cast me, wretch, into eternall evening,
    By taking her two Sunnes from these darke vallies.

Klaius. For she, with whom compar'd, the Alpes are vallies,
    She, whose lest word brings from the spheares their musique,
    At whose approach the Sunne rase in the evening,

[1] pp. 11–12.

> Who, where she went, bare in her forhead morning,
> Is gone, is gone from these our spoyled forrests,
> Turning to desarts our best pastur'de mountaines.[1]

Yet even in poems such as these, which seem not to claim more for themselves than grace, or the graceful exercise of ingenuity, it would be as rash to assert that we can place them at the low level of mere play as it would be rash to assert that the rhythmical bravuras of Milton afford only a trivial poetic experience. We are far yet from being able to characterize poetic experience and the nature and means of its peculiar satisfactions. All that we may justly say is that poems such as these afford no manageable material for devising a reply to a reader who would object, if asked to consider the formal relationships in a poem, firstly that to do so would merely be to anatomize the causes of a pleasure which if successfully contrived comes to him without study (and might indeed fail to come to him if he inspected the works), secondly that the meaning of a poem does not reside in the poem's formal relationships, and thirdly that if it could be shown that the meaning is not accessible except through diagrammatic contrivances of words, he would promptly enter the objection that the poet had subjected non-linguistic reality to an implausible orderliness, losing in 'truth to nature' what it gained in neatness of verbal presentation.

The third objection, elaborate when critically formulated, is often simply and strongly felt. Shakespeare's Sonnet 28 affords in its closing couplet at once an instance of the kind of scheme under discussion and of the kind of objection to which such schemes easily give rise.

> But day doth daily draw my sorrows longer
> And night doth nightly make grief's strength seem stronger.

'Strength', in the last line, is an emendation; the Quarto text has 'length'. Editors who emend to 'strength' (and most do) do so on the grounds that the successful completion of the scheme (it is an instance of *polyptoton*, the repetition of words derived from the same

---

[1] For the complete poem see *Poems*, ed. Ringler, p. 113.

root)[1] necessitates the word 'strength'; if the poet opts for this scheme, it dictates its own completion. And it may be felt (though I think it could not be successfully argued) that here the poet forces his own experience to fit into a prefabricated verbal mould, or, if we do not go so far as to disbelieve what he says because of the formality with which he says it, that the residuum of sense in this line would equally well be conveyed by saying, 'I feel worse about it at night' and that this alternative, however crude, would at least give the impression that the poet was sincere.

It will be clear, from the immediate rush of questions such a line can bring on, that in approaching the topic of verbal schemes we raise problems not to be sidestepped by taking refuge in the formula 'meaning at statement-level, plus pleasure provided by the formal relations between the words'. The moment the formal relations visibly affect the articulation of the sense—that is, the moment it is perceived that formal relationships take precedence in determining the diction—we have a situation where for some readers the sense is discredited and revulsion rather than pleasure occurs; such a reader feels himself to be confronted with a form of language whose elaboration interferes with transmission from the poet to himself.

One way of dealing with the charge that rhetorical schematization interferes with transmission and repels by its insincerity is to point out that responses to forms of language which conspicuously declare their adherence to conventions of a specific kind ('rhetorical', 'heroic', 'low', whatever it may be) are conditioned responses; they derive, in so far as they remain unanalytical, from current fashions and ways of responding, and when fashions have changed we may easily go astray when we make inferences about the poet's own attitude to matter and words; for him and for his contemporaries the work he was doing within the convention was seen in a different light. A writer on Elizabethan rhetoric has pointed out that though it may now seem to us extraordinary that Shakespeare even at his

---

[1] See Sister Miriam Joseph, C.S.C., *Shakespeare's Use of the Arts of Language*, Columbia University Studies in English and Comparative Literature, No. 165 (New York, 1947), p. 83, where this instance of the figure *polyptoton* is cited as one in which '[the] figure is used . . . for the sake of the sound, which is pleasing in itself, even while it enhances the meaning'.

most rhetorical and 'artificial' impressed his contemporaries with the directness and naturalness of his style, this apparent contradiction may be resolved by accepting, as the Elizabethans did, the convention within which he worked, seeing this particular kind of language as a medium expressive of, rather than resistant to, poetic impulses in no way alienated from the impulses behind the poetry of today:

The qualities which we, as it were, *translate* as spontaneity, even wildness, are conveyed in Shakespeare and in other writers by the zest with which their exacting games were played, by the range of tones and consequent variety, and by the spendthrift energy.[1]

Insincerity, however, is not the whole gravamen of the charge against formalized language. When Elizabethan rhetoric is inspected analytically it does in some of its forms show itself to be interruptive of transmission from the Elizabethan writer to ourselves. But it need not be assumed that what it interrupts is the spontaneous flow of the poet's experience into words. What it interrupts is more likely to be the modern reader's grasp of the sense of the words. In that phrase, 'And night doth nightly', the repetition of the root 'night' obscures the fact that the meaning of the word 'night' in this context is far from being the same as the meaning of the word 'nightly' in this context. Not all rhetorical schemes are of this kind. Those of another kind afford, even for the modern reader, devices quite the reverse of dragging, for they operate as organizers of thought by articulating strongly some intellectual relation, such as sameness, or contradiction, or opposition, or—as in Othello's

> I'll see before I doubt; when I doubt, prove;
> And on the proof, there is no more but this
> (III, iii, 190–1)

—a logical progression; or even, as in the words of Lennox in *Macbeth*, a relation as precise as that of distributing (as Peacham says) 'to everie subject his most proper & naturall adjunct':[2]

> That, by the help of these—with Him above
> To ratify the work—we may again

[1] Gladys D. Willcock, 'Shakespeare and Elizabethan English', *Shakespeare Survey*, 7 (1954), p. 17.

[2] Quoted by Sr Miriam Joseph, op. cit., p. 319.

Give to our tables meat, sleep to our nights,
Free from our feasts and banquets bloody knives,
Do faithful homage and receive free honours:
All which we pine for now.

(III, vi, 32–7)

In cases such as these, schematization (even if it does involve repetition of words) is not complicated by concealed shift of meaning; the point of the scheme in such cases is that it should express the intellectual relation in which the balanced elements of a sentence stand towards one another. If we compare Othello's 'doubt; ... doubt', 'prove; ... proof', with the 'night ... nightly' of Sonnet 28, we realize that 'play on words' is a portmanteau term; the effects covered by it are of very different kinds. The relation between the scheme and the sense of the words in it is not a constant relation obtaining unchanged from one scheme to another, and in the case of any one scheme the relation may call for very delicate statement if we are to achieve any precise understanding of how it works.

In order to have a clearer view of the variety of relations which may obtain between scheme and sense it is as well to consider, first, the extent to which repetition of verbal elements may be forced upon a writer, however unrhetorical. Since language is a highly-systematized convention of registering meanings, it tends to produce verbal repetitions which are unavoidable accidents. The necessity for syntactical relationships, and particularly the occurrence of all-purpose markers (such as 'of', 'to'), will introduce into even the least self-conscious language an element of repetition. This is the inevitable result of our transmitting meanings through a system whose usefulness depends on the power of its meaningful parts to do so much work that by combining them one can discuss anything in the universe. If for any reason we want to pack such a large number of considerations into a few words that it becomes necessary to sign-post the reader on his way through our concentrated discourse, we can provide sign-posts by accentuating the syntactical 'model' inherent in a form of words; by so doing we almost take the reader by the hand and explain to him how he is to set up the meaning of the whole sentence. For instance, in Shakespeare's Sonnet 19 a number of bold and surprising conceptions are put before us, each of which requires some thought before it can be grasped, yet the construction of the whole sentence in which these almost visionary processes are described is never in doubt, because the poet gives prominence to the fact that each conception is introduced by an imperative and that all the imperatives are addressed to 'Devouring Time':

> Devouring Time, blunt thou the lion's paws,
> And make the earth devour her own sweet brood;
> Pluck the keen teeth from the fierce tiger's jaws,
> And burn the long-lived phœnix in her blood.

Our response to syntactical signals ('blunt thou . . ./And make . . . Pluck the . . ./And burn . . .') is so strong that we make the proper response without thinking about it. And our grasp of the principle of repetition of a syntactical form is strong enough to enable us to sort out a passage as complicated in its relationships and as uncolloquial in its expression as the opening lines of Sonnet 68 in Sidney's *Astrophel and Stella*:

> *Stella*, the onely Planet of my light,
> Light of my life, and life of my desire,

for however obscure the content of the individual phrases may be, the syntactical status of each word within them is indisputably given by the repetition of the formula *A of my B* and this common model is clearly recognizable in these various phrases despite the fact that the sense of the words 'light' and 'life' changes in such a way as to permit 'light' to occupy first the *B* position (in 'Planet of my light') and then the *A* position (in 'Light of my life'); similarly with 'life', which is first in the *A* position and then in the *B*. Even if it is argued that Sidney gets nothing out of this word-play beyond a verbal back-stitch which enables him to sew the sonnet's argument together in a fashion predictable by the reader, it remains true, and of importance in the study of poetic language, that the poet can expect the reader of patterned language to notice not only the sense of a phrase but also its pattern, the pattern being grasped quite as clearly as the particulars which fill it out in any one of its repeats. It seems probable enough that patterns based on a syntactical unit will for most readers stand out even more prominently than the actual sense, whereas patterns which are not based on syntactical units, e.g. alliteration, will not be present to the reader's consciousness unless they are very strongly emphasized or intensified, by position, perhaps, or sheer frequency. The poet who needs a complex syntax to carry involved or concentrated subject-matter will find in these syntactically-articulated units of pattern a convenient means of keeping the reader *au fait* with the hang of the sentence as a whole, despite the difficulty of its content, and with the main line of an argument whose parts or steps are not self-evidently simple and logical. Sister Miriam Joseph observes:

The figures of repetition in addition to pleasing the ear have the functional value of emphasizing ideas and the movement of thought, as, for instance, by accentuating parallel or antithetical structure. In an age when books like the *Arcadia* were read aloud in groups, the figures of repetition were especially valued.[1]

In order to understand more fully the potentialities of such figures it is necessary to consider more closely the process of abstraction from linguistic particulars. Though one treads the border of the ridiculous whenever one comes near to dogmatizing about the make-up of an abstraction, and language almost retires, defeated, when it tries to report on the abstraction-processes involved in using language at all, it is clear enough that in the process of taking in the series 'Planet of my light, Light of my life, and life of my desire', we abstract something more complex than the mere relation A *of my* B, B *of my* C, *and* C *of my* D. Though we do abstract this relation sufficiently to enable us to prefigure the syntactical status of whatever occupies positions C and D, and also to prefigure C^2 after C^1, our expectations would not be satisfied if the poet concluded his series with, shall we say, 'life of my attire'. If however we were Eliza-bethan readers, prepared to accept 'aspire' as a noun meaning *aspira-tion*, I take it we would pass 'life of my aspire' as conforming to the specifications laid down by what has gone before; for what is speci-fied is (at least) that the pattern should draw only on words descrip-

[1] op. cit., p. 307.

tive of inner states having something to do with a rather lofty kind of love. To say this is to say that in addition to our abstracting a pattern from the words under their syntactical aspect and under their aspect as repeating units of vocabulary, we also abstract at the level of the sense of the words, so that the resulting expectation is a complex of pattern-abstraction and sense-abstraction.

When however the poet continues:

> Chiefe good, whereto my hope doth only aspire,
> World of my wealth, and heav'n of my delight

he now makes clear, retrospectively, what 'Planet', 'light', and 'life' have in common: they are, each one, some kind of 'Chiefe good', sources or prime movers or true ends of the poet's states of being. To see this is also to see one reason why the circling, contemplating movement of the figure is appropriate to its subject-matter. This retrospective redefinition of a common factor in a repeating pattern is a matter not lightly to be passed over. To think about what makes it possible will bring us closer to a realization of the great complexity of linguistic meaning.

Retrospective redefinition of a unit in a pattern is possible because the pattern we see is an abstraction from all the particulars of the two units between which we see similarity, and it is not the only possible abstraction; when a new member enters the series, it may pick out, by its similarity to disregarded aspects of earlier members of the series, an abstraction it had not previously occurred to us to make. Each new member adds to the abstraction-potential of the others; in introducing a new member the poet can either continue to emphasize the pattern already laid down or pick a new pattern out of the series by using the newest member to emphasize unused aspects of what went before. Lest my reader should think that the weaving of such a nine men's morris of abstractions is an archaic diversion having nothing to do with poetry as it is written in our times, I propose to abandon the example from Sidney at this point and discuss the issue *à propos* of a passage from T. S. Eliot.

In the opening passage of *East Coker* the poet sets himself the task of devising a piece of verse which shall appear to move in a straight line whilst it actually moves in a circle, so that what happens 'in *succession*' to houses will turn out to be a *cycle* of living and dying:

> In my beginning is my end. In succession
> Houses rise and fall, crumble, are extended,
> Are removed, destroyed, restored, or in their place
> Is an open field, or a factory, or a by-pass.
> Old stone to new building, old timber to new fires,
> Old fires to ashes, and ashes to the earth
> Which is already flesh, fur and faeces,
> Bone of man and beast, cornstalk and leaf.
> Houses live and die: there is a time for building
> And a time for living and for generation
> And a time for the wind to break the loosened pane
> And to shake the wainscot where the field-mouse trots
> And to shake the tattered arras woven with a silent motto.[1]

In the fifth and sixth of these lines an Elizabethan rhetorician would have recognized *anaphora* (i.e. the repetition of a word ['Old'] at the beginning of each of a series of clauses), *anadiplosis* (i.e. the repetition of the word ending one clause ['fires'; and again, 'ashes'] in a prominent position in the next, and *epanodos* (i.e. iteration). The function of these devices in this passage is to stitch together in an apparently continuous fabric of verbal repetitions a series of changes which conduct us from 'Old stone' to 'the earth Which is already flesh . . . and leaf'. The steps by which we are conducted are concealed, first by omitting the verb which is 'understood' in each clause; if we actually supply it instead of merely 'understanding' it, we shall find ourselves supplying a series of different verbs (timber *feeds*, fires *sink*, ashes *return to* or *mingle with*); secondly by using a device of repetition ('Old stone to', 'old timber to', 'Old fires to') which suggests sameness of process. But 'Old fires to ashes', under cover of its 'sameness', introduces a change in the formula *Old A to new B*; the change is that 'new' is dropped. To compensate for this, the illusion of continuity is shored up by the continuity of 'new fires, Old fires', a continuity both verbal (in the schematic repetition of 'fires') and extra-linguistic (in that new fires do in fact dwindle into old fires, in real life). In rhetorical terms, 'Old fires to ashes' is

[1] *Four Quartets* (London, 1944), p. 15.

simultaneously *anaphora* (along with the phrase before it) and *anadiplosis* (along with the phrase after it); the same set of linguistic particulars has two different pattern-values, depending on what it goes with. In analysing this verbal conjuring trick I have so far spared the reader some of its complications, e.g. the conversion of 'Old . . . new' into 'new [fires], Old [fires]'. This particular development does not rivet the reader's attention; perhaps it is the quick surreptitious change from hand to hand which the conjurer hopes we won't spot if we are kept busy listening to the patter of the *anaphora* and the *anadiplosis*. One must suppose that Eliot saw very clearly that one phrase can have two simultaneous pattern-values and this permits the poet to move in a new direction under cover of the 'sameness' of the phrase with what has gone before. It can be observed in a later passage where the dance round the fire signifies 'coupling', 'rising and falling' and the round of the seasons and of life and death to boot, that the alleged sameness of these very different movements is foisted on the reader by comparable methods of legerdemain.[1] What, however, is mere legerdemain at the technical level, an illusion which can be dispelled if for the purposes of analysis one artificially arrests its progress, has a different value when it is related to the structure of the whole poem. I chose artificially to arrest the illusion wrought by *East Coker* as a whole because I wanted to show that, startling as it may seem, there is much in common between some of the ancient schemes of repetition and the now more fashionable metaphor, for in both one may observe a linguistic form capable of fastening together an ideogram and a set of verbal particulars in such a way that though the reader himself abstracts the ideogram from the particulars, indeed regards it as given by the particulars, none the less the particulars are capable of unobtrusive transformation into a different ideogram and the ideogram itself is capable of embodiment

---

[1] See below, pp. 167–70. Cf. also J. R. Broadbent's observation that 'rhetoric *is* the verse-form of *Samson Agonistes* and equally of, say, *East Coker*. Consider in the first paragraph of that poem the *prosonomasia* of "removed, destroyed, restored"; the *climax* already noted; the alliterative *synathroesmus* of "flesh, fur and faeces", opposed to stone, timber and ashes. These figures take the place of regular metre, external rhyme and stanzaic form' ('Sixteenth-Century Poetry and the Common Reader', *Essays in Criticism*, IV (1954), 425).

in a different set of particulars.[1] It is precisely because an ideogram is not the same as the verbal particulars which give rise to it that the poet can drive a coach and four through the gap between them and carry the reader off in any direction he likes. The poet, well-versed in the iniquity of verbal particulars (as contrasted with the innocence of extra-linguistic reality) can form and re-form verbal particulars into ideograms, with the freedom of Shelley's cloud:

> I pass through the pores of the ocean and shores;
>> I change, but I cannot die.
>
> . . . .
>
> I silently laugh at my own cenotaph,
>> And out of the caverns of rain,
> Like a child from the womb, like a ghost from the tomb,
>> I arise and unbuild it again.

Meanwhile the reader, busily and unwittingly abstracting (as is his wont) treads the course of ideas successfully mapped out for him by the poem.

We shall not understand the function of abstractions in poetic structures if we forget the fact that our own habits as users of language predispose us to reach out for the commanding abstraction, the likeness, the pattern or the 'point' that makes the particulars of an utterance hang together. For even if we know what the words mean, we still want to know something further: what the writer is getting at. The importance of the commanding abstraction may be illustrated by considering again that same passage which I cited to illustrate Eliot's use of verbal schemes. It would be hard to say what exactly is described in it. As a rough shot, we might say that the passage describes change. In the first four lines especially—

> In succession
> Houses rise and fall, crumble, are extended,
> Are removed, destroyed, restored, or in their place
> Is an open field, or a factory, or a by-pass

—Eliot uses a string of words all having to do with changes which happen to houses. Are we to suppose this to be a seven-fold tautology

[1] Cf. p. 78–9 above.

—that Eliot says some seven times for the sake of emphasis that houses undergo change? At least he has not done anything so simple as to cite seven causes of change; he did not tell us that houses are neglected, flooded, burned, bombed, knocked down by demolition men, collapsed by subsidence of the soil and eaten away by death watch beetles. The inferiority of such an alternative makes at least one thing clear: not all the words referring to change are words to do with falling down; some have to do with building up. The string of words can be distributed into something like a pattern:

$$
\begin{array}{cc}
\text{RISE} & \text{FALL} \\
\text{are extended} & \text{crumble} \\
\longleftarrow \text{Are removed} \longrightarrow \\
\\
\text{restored} & \text{destroyed} \\
\longleftarrow \text{in their place Is} \longrightarrow
\end{array}
$$

where what we get is not seven collapses but, instead, a pattern which runs *Rise/Fall/Fall/Rise/Both(?)/Fall/Rise/Both*. Eliot's lines are, of course, much more interesting than the abstract pattern to which I have just now reduced them. Mine is a clearer pattern than Eliot's lines allow the reader immediately to see—and that is one good reason why Eliot's words are more interesting. His words put some difficulty in the way of making out a perfectly clear pattern; at the same time, they hover so markedly on the verge of assembly into a pattern that the reader is made to feel that there is a pattern there, if only he could get at it. This effect—of a half-hidden pattern, very elusive, hard to define, and yet certainly there—is an effect necessary to the whole poem. By the time we reach the end (or nearly the end) of the poem we are told in so many words that pattern-discerning is a difficult business:

> As we grow older
> The world becomes stranger, the pattern more complicated
> Of dead and living.[1]

At the very beginning of the poem, Eliot gives us the experience of encountering a complicated pattern. If his list, in the second and

[1] op. cit., p. 22.

third lines of the poem, is reduced to the abstractions *Rise* and *Fall*, a clear pattern emerges, but over that clear pattern Eliot has laid an obscuring mesh of other particular considerations through which the reader has to grope. To see how this obscuring mesh is constructed we must look now at the mental categories from which the several words come. 'Houses rise and fall': this is a phrase we might use if we were speaking of the rise and fall of a dynasty, an empire, or a family; it is a term that belongs in histories and memoirs. But the next word, 'crumble', has quite different connections. Here we see the real physical fabric of a small portion of one house mouldering away, crumbling off; we have moved from the historical to the physical. The next word is 'extended', and with this we move into a world of blueprints, of architects throwing out a new wing. Then comes 'removed', which might mean anything. 'Destroyed', which follows, is forceful and implies sudden calamity. Immediately after that comes 'restored', which takes us into the world where noble houses have architectural art-value and people carefully restore them, trying to preserve their style. These are seven different ways of looking at a house: as it has a history; as it is physically there, made of materials; as it has a builder's plan; as a thing which can simply be removed; as exposed to calamity; and as an art-object. These worlds of thinking and acting follow one another in bewildering succession; yet, all the time, the words simultaneously weave the firm underlying pattern of *Rise/Fall/Fall/Rise/Both*(?)*/Fall/Rise/Both*. So the effect of just these words in just this order is an effect, for the reader, of groping among a vast number of particulars to find an inherent pattern.

This seems as good a place as any to pause and take a long, appalled look at the sheer magnitude of the problem of discussing language at all. First of all, our vocabulary is a reflection of the fact that 'reality' itself, as coped with in language, is a vast system of interlocking structures. A house, for example, can be an art-object, or a lump of physical matter, a historical phenomenon, or a home, or a lot of other things—according to how one happens to be thinking (according to what context one puts it in). What we must all use, then, is a structured vocabulary. In addition to this, since we possess mental powers of abstraction and pattern-making, we can, without trying at all, often see an abstract pattern (such as *Rise* and *Fall*) cutting through a large number of particulars of different kinds; the mind is always eager to get diverse particulars organized into simple patterns. Take then our structured vocabulary, with all its possibilities for giving rise to secondary abstract patterns, and use it in a line of poetry. On entering the line it involves itself in new structures: metrical, stanzaic, rhythmical, rhetorical. And the one line itself is part of the total structure of all the lines in the poem, and therefore a part of the total structure of rhythm, rhetoric, meanings, argument, progressive development, etc. So in the Eliot lines upon which I have just commented: these, though restricted in scope, are none the less a vital part of the total poem in which they occur, for the whole poem— like these two lines—is a groping for a pattern which grows more complicated at every stage of life. It is of course no accident that when I wanted an illustration of complex patterns Eliot sprang to mind, for it is characteristic of him to treat experience as offering a vast variety of patterns. Eliot's problem, even in *The Waste Land*, is never quite the problem of the man who finds life meaningless. The problem is rather that experience offers a vast variety of possible meanings or patterns, and the real misery is that all the patterns compete with one another. The individual as Eliot sees him is something like Zimri in Dryden's *Absalom and Achitophel*, who

> Was every thing by starts, and nothing long:
> But, in the course of one revolving Moon,
> Was Chymist, Fidler, States-Man, and Buffoon:
> Then all for Women, Painting, Rhiming, Drinking;
> Besides ten thousand freaks that dy'd in thinking.
> Blest Madman, who coud every hour employ,
> With something New to wish, or to enjoy!
>
> (1, 548–54)

All of us are to some extent like Dryden's Zimri; it is Eliot's peculiar insight, his characteristic bent as a poet, to have grasped this and expressed the longing for the master-pattern that will free us from the fret of a world in which there are too many equipollent patterns. It is therefore not surprising that in order to express this insight Eliot should have made himself a master of all the devices of language that make it possible to show various patterns competing for attention and to show the mind searching for the point of poise or of escape from partial patterns into the composure of the master-pattern. It is for this reason that *East Coker* is an immense system of shifting patterns. Consequently it affords endless examples of various formal structures interlocking below the magisterial surface of the diction.

I hope that I have done something to show that the imposition upon language of elaborate verbal patterning is not a 'study in a worn-out poetical fashion', that its function is not restricted to decorating and pleasing, that so far from having nothing to do with the meaning, it can organize and clarify it by giving prominence to syntactical relations, and is indeed capable of such powerful meanings that it can register or suggest intellectual relationships (such as sameness, opposition, continuity) which may even be so strong as to compete successfully with other meanings in a passage, or, if 'compete' be too emphatic a word, at least contribute decisively to their complexity. At one extreme, as in alliteration, patterning may be used for mere emphasis, but it can as well be pushed to that other extreme where an intellectual relation, articulated by schematizing the words, cuts across the abstractions of 'content' so successfully as to defeat the usual reductive processes we tend to apply in our usual procedures of getting at the meaning. At this extreme the poet's language may perhaps be said to have levitated above the sphere of normal language but, as I hope I have already shown, such a levitation depends not on anything radically abnormal in the schemes themselves, but on their potentiality, as meaningful forms, to interact with others in a finely articulated structure of language.

Patterned language may be used in ways less ostentatious, but no less decisive of our responses, than those I have discussed. When it is brought into alliance with poetic devices of another kind, it permits of very striking effects. In alliance with metaphor it may exercise a very close control over very complex responses in the reader. A passage may be so devised as to make the reader himself experience the kind of mental event the poet's language describes; the poet constructs a highly-organized structure of forms, which makes the

reader himself leap at the truth the poet sees. Such manipulation of
the reader, though startling, is no miracle. Poet and reader have in
common a vast number of mental habits: their habits of inferring
meaning from the forms of language; if we had no such array of
shared mental habits, communication in language would be impossible. I may illustrate this by examining two lines of Burns, from
a poem which is, except for these two lines, undistinguished:

> The wan moon is setting ayont the white wave,
> And time is setting with me, oh![1]

The difficulty one encounters in trying to account for the power of
these lines is that the individual constituents seem so simple. There
is nothing evidently novel in the phrase 'the wan moon' or in 'time is
setting with me'. And though the phrase 'ayont the white wave'[1] is
individual, this phrase itself seems an insufficient cause of the complex feelings excited by the lines. It seems at first sight a natural
enough conclusion, then, that what happens here is that our own
past experiences of scenes of sea and moonlight supply to the poem
the whole of the effect that the lines have. If this were true it would
be fair to say that the poem merely refers us back to common experience and depends on a universal or fairly general truth about
human nature; at most one might claim that the sinking moon is an
'objective correlative' for the poet's feeling of disastrous decline, and
that his art is to be praised (if at all) only for his choice of scene, plus
what he does to make that vivid, by the phrase 'ayont the white
wave'. This explanation, however, is unsatisfactory, since it does not
explain what is perhaps the most striking effect the lines have when
they are read. The effect is that of a great mental leap—from the
poet's own feelings within himself, out over the wave to the moon
beyond it, so that, distant and desolate as the moon is, it is recognized
as the perfect symbol of the feeling within the poet. It is not that the
moon makes him feel desolate but that he recognizes the identity
between its desolate decline and his own. This sense of identity with
a distant and alien object is, for me, very strong when I read the lines.

[1] *The Poetical Works of Robert Burns*, ed. J. Logie Robertson (London, 1904), p. 351.
'Ayont' is glossed as *beyond*.)

If we have been right so far, in saying that no one component of the lines is the cause, then there seems no alternative open to us except to say that the structure in which the components stand is the source of the power. Once this is said, it becomes easier to discern and to say why the lines are so effective. Whether by accident or design these two lines are a close-knit formal structure. A literal sentence is followed by a metaphorical sentence waveringly parallel to it and containing at one particular point—in the words 'is setting'—an exact verbal repetition; the very point at which the lines exactly coincide is also the very point at which the literal 'setting' of the one line becomes the figurative 'setting' of the other; it is this (a wording that suddenly identifies the literal and the figurative) which provokes that mental leap by which the reader instantaneously sees the setting of the moon as being in all its respects the model of the setting of life; thus all the attributes of the moonscape (specified and suggested) instantly become involved in the reader's concept of the setting of Time or life: the loneliness, desolation, imminent finality, the cold unnatural light whose source is disappearing (the wanness of the moon and the whiteness of the wave are bound together by natural causal relation, by colour, by alliteration), the sense of the darkening of the waves, which will follow—in short, all the attributes of the scene are apprehended as attributes of personal decline, in one instantaneous leap over the vastness of the waters to the wan moon beyond them. What makes that leap happen is the formal correspondence between the lines, which makes 'time is setting with me' the mirror-image of 'The wan moon is setting ayont the white wave'. The making of this leap of total recognition is what the lines are about, and it is the fact that the leap is instantaneous (the moment one takes in the word 'setting' at its second occurrence) that gives the passage its uncanny power; what matters is not only what is 'in' the words but, equally, what structure the words are in.

In this instance of a complex use of the potentialities of verbal repetition, interlocking with the potentialities of metaphor, we come by another route to the same observation as that made on Eliot's use of the schemes: that formal relations, though they provoke abstraction-processes, do not work so as to reduce or attenuate richness of sense. On the contrary: they may be used to defeat our natural tendency to abstract a much-simplified 'content' from a stream of words. In the passage quoted from *East Coker* this tendency is defeated by the multiplicity of abstractive models we are presented with. In the lines from Burns, verbal repetition of a conceptual word throws us back to a complex set of particulars and gives us the extraordinary experience of the instantaneous recognition of their symbolic character. However different in other respects these two passages may be, they have it in common that they use schematized language to circumvent the generalizing and abstractionist tendency of language and the tendency of the users of a language to reduce the particularity represented by words into the familiar conceptual schemata available for 'making sense' of them. 'I talk in general terms', says one of Eliot's dramatic characters, 'Because the particular has no language'.[1] If it be asked, 'Why is it that verbal schemes can be used to impede our tendency to reduce meaning to conceptual schemata?' the answer would seem to be one not peculiar to a question about verbal schemes but rather one proper to a question that might be asked of any complex literary device. I would suggest the answer that if the common procedures of conveying and interpreting meaning are complicated by some device that is formative of meaning in its own way, this 'interference' with our easy, automatic processes of getting the meaning out of words presents us, as it were, with the incentive to relate meanings to one another in a heightened state of mental activity. This 'interference' is not an obstacle to understanding but a challenge or an invitation to take a new route to understanding. As I. A. Richards says,

The mind is a connecting organ, it works only by connecting and it can connect any two things in an indefinitely large number of different ways. Which of these it chooses is settled by reference to some larger whole or aim. . . . The reader, I would say, will try out various connections, and this experimentation . . . is the movement which gives its meaning to all fluid language.[2]

The phrase 'fluid language' conveys something of the idea I am try-

---

[1] *The Family Reunion* (London, 1939), p. 30.
[2] *Philosophy of Rhetoric*, p. 125.

ing to suggest: the idea of a kind of language that sets our powers racing to compose the sliding wealth of meanings we are aware of into something we can take hold of and master.[1] Some such linguistic experience is given by Eliot's search for the master-pattern. In other cases, a more appropriate image might be 'lightning language'—that is in cases where the close-locking verbal form made by the poet is so compulsive of our mental processes that meanings seem to flash out of the words, as 'momentary and sight-outrunning' as the lightnings made by Ariel in the storm in which, as he says, 'I flamed amazement'.[2] What is important in both cases is the unusualness of the total linguistic experience, the necessity of leaving the hackneyed roads of everyday understanding. To be forced out of these may indeed force us to take real cognizance of the particulars about which 'Jove's lightnings' (the meanings) play, but I am of the opinion that particularity is not all-important in poetry, whereas an unusual wealth of meaning always is. For in heightening or increasing the wealth of meaning words can carry, poetry raises its medium to a new power. It is, after all, the essential business of language, that it should mean. Language itself rescues the particular from its own condition, which is that of having no meaning in itself. The great and amazing peculiarity of poetic language is its power to bridge or seem to bridge the gap between what has meaning but no particularity (that is, ordinary language) and what has particularity but no meaning (that is, the reality language is 'about').

It may be true that many readers, approaching poems with the expectation of a freshened response to appearances and experiences in the natural world, are already disposed to cash verbal counters into images, and the poet can facilitate this in many ways, of which perhaps the most obvious is to draw heavily on that area of our vocabulary which refers us to physical phenomena rather than to larger concepts of them (to 'yellow leaves' and 'bare boughs' rather

---

[1] Cf. R. N. Maud's comment on complexity of meaning in the work of Dylan Thomas: '. . . the indeterminacy supplying tensions which it is part of the excitement of reading to undergo. . . . The effort of the imagination involved in abstracting the concept . . . at the same time as we try to grasp the image . . . is perhaps the most rewarding experience in reading these poems'. ('Dylan Thomas's Poetry', *Essays in Criticism*, IV (1954), 416–17.)

[2] Shakespeare, *The Tempest*, I, ii, 198.

than to autumn; to the 'wan moon' and the 'white wave' rather than to merely the moon or the sea) but it still remains true that if he directs the reader to the physical universe and its minutiae, he will have to do something more than just that if he wants this detail to be suffused with meaning, importance, significance. There seems no reason why detail, as such, should make us catch our breath in surprise, or feel that meanings too rich for statement are flowering from the dead tree of the universe; there is something given by poems, which is not given by a walk in a wood or on the shore. If there is indeed some peculiarity in poetic language, as such, sufficient to bridge the gap between non-verbal particularity and significance, it cannot simply be that the poet obligingly sticks to the vocabulary indicative of concrete objects, and the reader obligingly visualizes them and sets himself in a suggestible posture of mind. Though these factors may very frequently be present, they cannot of themselves give us a sense of seeing significance in things or of receiving from poetry a more important meaning than ordinary language can give us. There seems to be no escape from the conclusion—however superlatively obvious it may be—that in order to be meaningful one must use apparatus that means, and that to 'see a meaning' in anything is always to make an abstraction from the thing itself. There is nothing odd or abnormal in verbal schemes; they are an extension of the kind of relations we perceive (as formative of the sense) in ordinary language, and when they are used to modify (by abstractions made at the level of form) abstractions made at the level of vocabulary and of what it refers to, their operation essentially is to increase the flow of meanings from language, or the speed with which meanings flow. Abstraction, a normal process of arriving at meaning, is 'dead' only when it has the 'deadness' of habit, of the automatic reduction of utterances to familiar signals to produce familiar behaviour, linguistic or otherwise. As Yvor Winters says, in discussing what he regards as the 'decay' of the short poem,

For the past two hundred and fifty years it has been common to assume that abstract language is dead language, that poetry must depict particular actions, or if it be 'lyric' that it must revery over remembered sensory impressions, according to the formula of the associationists. But these assumptions are false. . . . A race that has lost the capacity to handle abstractions with discretion and dignity may do well to confine itself to sensory impression, but our ancestors were more fortunate, and we ought to labour to regain what we have lost.[1]

The discerning reader will suspect that it is no very far cry from 'fluid meaning', or from the claim that poetry is interesting because it is more meaningful than ordinary language, to Fruitful Ambiguity, that popular *deus ex machina* of the contemporary critical scene. It is as well that I should say, here, that I am of the opinion that a concept of that kind (however unhappy the term 'ambiguity' may be) is useful, but only if it is used to push forward, rather than to bring to an end, critical discussion of the nature of poetic uses of language. But the full bitterness of the engagement with this concept is reserved for the next chapter.

[1] *The Function of Criticism*, p. 61.

VII

Ambiguity

REASON, according to Sir Francis Bacon, 'doth buckle and bow the mind unto the nature of things', but poetry 'doth raise and erect the mind, by submitting the shews of things to the desires of the mind'.[1] Conceding the truth of this, one must ask how language will bear the strain of presenting *The Universe*, *As You Like It*. According to some modern critics, the poet has an answer: sweet are the uses of ambiguity,

> Which, like the toad, ugly and venomous,
> Wears yet a precious jewel in his head;
> And this our life exempt from public haunt
> Finds tongues in trees, books in the running brooks,
> Sermons in stones and good in every thing.[2]

The term 'ambiguity' now has wide currency as a means of referring to diverse ways in which the language of poetry exhibits a charge of multiple implications and fits itself to contain within the form of discourse aspects of human experience whose difference or distance from one another might seem such as not easily to permit their coherent assembly in linguistic form. To offer such a definition is to attempt to incapsulate a number of critical trends. 'The term "ambiguity," as a general term for all kinds of secondary word- and sentence-meaning, was first installed in the critic's vocabulary by William Empson'[3] whose *Seven Types of Ambiguity* (London, 1930) 'brought home to a whole generation of readers the fact of the many-sidedness of language'[4] and because of the connection of this 'many-sidedness' with theoretical problems concerning the nature and

---

[1] *The Works of Francis Bacon*, ed. James Spedding, Robert Leslie Ellis, and Douglas Denon Heath (London, 1857–9), III, 343–4.

[2] Shakespeare, *As You Like It*, II, i, 13–17.

[3] Beardsley, *Aesthetics*, p. 151.

[4] William K. Wimsatt, Jr., and Cleanth Brooks, *Literary Criticism: A Short History* (New York, 1957), p. 638.

function of art it has come about that 'ambiguity' is now associated
with such concepts as ambivalence, tension, paradox and irony, and
with interest in metaphor and symbol as means by which the poet
can evade or transcend unequivocal assertion.[1] A contemporary
critic defines imagination itself as 'the power to envisage, or visualize,
ambivalence and ambiguity'[2] and holds that 'ambivalence, in the
sense of a copresence of contextually controllable and integrable
alternatives, is a prerequisite of great art'.[3] If as much as this can
seriously be claimed, it is evident that some consideration must be
given to the complex of problems that cluster about such terms in
their current uses.

The manysidedness of language has been the theme of this book
and it should by now be well enough established that every facet of
the language of a poem can be irradiated with meaningfulness; even
those facets whose potential for the display of meaning is, in the
everyday handling of words, least regarded, can take on polish and
give out light. Where meaning is many-faceted, language can become
prismatic as easily as it can become crystal-clear—the meanings pro-
jected by one and the same form of words can splay into a spectrum
of colour without loss of definition. If the poet wants to devise a form
of words that distinctly means more than one thing at the same time,
even though the things meant have some kind of resistance to becoming linguistically compatible, he can draw equally on what in
ordinary discourse is the central area of meaning and on what is
marginal or ignored. The first question, then, would seem to be, not
whether the poet can bring about a prismatic splay of distinct
meanings, but why he does it and why we like it.

I suppose there may be an array of reasons. Some have been
touched on in earlier chapters. In Chapter IV, where some intricate
poetic structures were considered, the examples chosen all contained

---

[1] Ullmann, discussing some forms of ambiguity in his *Style in the French Novel*, sums
up (p. 15): 'In all these cases, there is a strong tension between the two terms of the pun
as they belong to widely different spheres of experience. There is a fundamental similarity here between the structure of ambiguity and that of imagery'.

[2] Andrew Paul Ushenko, *Dynamics of Art*, Indiana University Publications, Humanities Series, No. 28 (Bloomington, Indiana, 1953), p. 82.

[3] ibid., p. 87.

some element of contradictoriness. The ordinary language we use in order to think and talk about human experience is in many ways alien to our experience. We often want to say, 'Yes, but . . .' in reply to any ordinary description of what we are in a particular situation, because ordinary language petrifies into lexicological 'opposites' what in experience is undivided. To go deeper into experience, to make language deal less unjustly with all that inheres in the situations it purports to describe, is very difficult. Poetry often finds a voice for our sense that things are not known except through experiences of what it was like, or would or will be like, not to have them.

Anybody will have to admit that there could never be any drama or story, either comic or tragic, without tension, without conflict, without evil. It may not be at first glance so obvious, but it is nevertheless true, that without some shade of these same elements there could never be any pastoral or idyllic retreat, any didactic or satiric warning, any lyric complaint—or, for that matter, any lyric rejoicing, so far are the springs of human rejoicing buried in the possibility, the threat, the memory of sorrow, so far is human life an experience of mutation, of struggle, of stasis only momentarily and dynamically attained.[1]

If this is true there will be little enough that is disreputable in the fact that poetry so often provides a kind of consolation, another kind of 'Yes, but . . .' to offset the intractability of hard facts, and devises forms of language capable of giving 'some shadow of satisfaction to the mind of man in those points wherein the nature of things doth deny it'.[2] And if the reverse is also true—if, as Tennyson said in *Locksley Hall*, 'a sorrow's crown of sorrow is remembering happier things'—the poet who finds words for this affords us another kind of consolation: that of recognizing our own experience in the poet's formulation of it. To enquire further into the nature of this recognition returns us from the flowering rod of experience to the cunning of the serpent, language. The 'recognition' that is part of our satisfaction with the poet's words may in fact be a clarification of our own inchoate feelings by the discovery of a form (the poet's words) into which they can flow. It would be foolhardy to attempt in such a book

---

[1] Wimsatt and Brooks, op. cit., pp. 743-4.
[2] Bacon, op. cit., p. 343.

as this to speak precisely of the process by which this sort of clarification comes about, or of what this sense of clarification means to the reader who has it. As Peter Munz remarks,

It is very difficult to give a precise description of the relationship that exists between a symbol and the feeling-state meant by the symbol. In a way, one ought not to speak of a relationship at all, because, as I have tried to explain, a feeling-state without a symbol is so opaque that it cannot really be said to have a separate existence at all.[1]

None the less, the experiencing of what Munz calls 'an enlarged state of lucidity'[2] is real enough. Our inability to translate the experience into analytical terms does not invalidate the experience. (One recalls I. A. Richards's remark that 'one of the worst snares' of the study of metaphor is 'the assumption that if we cannot see how a metaphor works, it does not work'.[3]) In Dr Johnson's comments on Gray's *Elegy in a Country Churchyard* there is an excellent passage of appraisal of such an experience:

The *Church-yard* abounds with images which find a mirrour in every mind, and with sentiments to which every bosom returns an echo. The four stanzas beginning 'Yet even these bones' are to me original: I have never seen the notions in any other place; yet he that reads them here persuades himself that he has always felt them. Had Gray written often thus it had been vain to blame, and useless to praise him.[4]

If then the richness or manysidedness of language can be so successfully pressed into the service of poetry that it enables the poet to declare our own inchoate and complex experience in a verbal form to which 'every bosom returns an echo', we shall have to regard 'ambiguity' in this sense not as an esoteric way of conveying esoteric attitudes, but as a familiar feature of poems dealing with recognizably common concerns.

---

[1] Peter Munz, *Problems of Religious Knowledge* (London, 1959), p. 56.

[2] ibid., p. 55. 'The first result of designating an event or an action as a symbol is ... an enlarged state of lucidity. After such designation we know exactly how we feel, how we feel ourselves to be.'

[3] *Philosophy of Rhetoric*, p. 118.

[4] *Lives of the English Poets*, ed. George Birkbeck Hill (Oxford, 1905), III, 441–2. This edition quotes (p. 445) Tennyson's comment on the *Elegy*: 'These divine truisms make me weep'.

But if 'ambiguity' has so many applications, it might seem unprofitable to enter upon a discussion of it at so advanced a stage in the argument of this book. My reason for discussing it here is that it gets in the way when one begins to approach the kind of language with which this chapter is to be concerned. Because the term 'ambiguity' is often used to refer to the manysidedness of language (and both 'ambiguity' and 'ambivalence' are used to characterize some effects derived from manysidedness) one is left with no distinct term to apply to language ambiguous in a narrower sense. It is my purpose in this chapter to consider ambiguity of this narrower kind, which is useful to the poet when the things he has to say will not go into straightforward unequivocal language. In considering it I shall not need to enclose the term in quotation marks, since ambiguity of this kind would be recognized as ambiguity by the ordinary (or pre-Empsonian) man.

In ordinary usage we say that a locution is ambiguous if it strikes us that there are more ways than one of fitting it into the context with which we are concerned. Ordinarily ambiguity is an accident and a nuisance. There are, however, forms of utterance in which it is deliberately contrived—oracular pronouncements, polite equivocation—and forms in which it is used for entertainment, as in a joke depending on a *double entendre*. In cases of merely inept ambiguity and in deliberately deceptive ambiguity, the addressee is intended to see only one meaning (though another construction could be put upon the actual words used); in the case of the *double entendre* the addressee is meant to realize that two meanings are present, despite the difference between them. To put the contrast otherwise: in inept and deceptive ambiguity the connection of the locution with its context is unclear or half-veiled; in the joke, two different connections are clear simultaneously. Already ambiguity (even in this restricted sense of the equivocal relation between a given expression and its context) begins to fan out into effects of very different kinds. The temptation to set about constructing a typology of ambiguity and a terminology for the different types, is strong. The deterrents, however, are stronger still. In the first place, there seems no good reason to accord to ambiguity a treatment different from that given to other features of language treated of in this book. It has been the argument throughout that no one feature of the kind of language with which we are concerned is capable of assessment except in relation to other features of the whole tissue of the particular piece of language under inspection. In the second place, ambiguity has a peculiarity of its own that makes it even less susceptible of an atomistic approach. For if we are right in positing that ambiguity lies in the relations of a locution to its context, it will follow that a group of words in itself and by itself has no existence as an ambiguity; the question of ambiguity will not even arise until the relation of the words to some context or contexts is brought into question. Karl Britton, discussing the scientist's use of language, remarks, 'He must . . . try to use words that *in their context* indicate one and only one sort of object—ambiguity is fatal'. To this he adds the footnote, 'It must not be forgotten that the spoken language may be highly accurate in the context of utterance and understanding, although it would be highly ambiguous if it were written down and read at another time and place'.[1] The existence of an ambiguity depends on a relation between some peculiarity in a context and something in the state of the language at large which makes it possible for a particular word or group of words to enter the particular context without reducing the context's complexity by its entry. If, then, ambiguity is non-existent except in such a relation, a typology of ambiguity would have to concern itself with peculiar contexts at one end and at the other with the structure of language in general, considered as a source of potentially ambiguous relations. No doubt a book, or many books, could be written on a subject as complex as this; a chapter cannot attempt to cover it. The purpose of this chapter is limited: it attempts to state something of the complexity of the problem and by so doing to make it easier to see why poetic uses of ambiguity may be considered without nagging interruptions from the 'common-sense' view that a writer or speaker 'ought to say what he means'.

The difficulty about this common-sense view is that to argue against it lands one in the intricacies of the problem of what meaning

[1] Karl Britton, *Communication: A Philosophical Study of Language* (London, 1939), p. 253.

is and how it gets into utterances. The common-sense view is that one knows what meaning is, sufficiently to be able to survive without defining it, and that the way it gets into an utterance is that the utterer chooses the word that puts it there. In what follows in this chapter the view taken is that it is more realistic (*vis-à-vis* the nature of vocabulary and syntax) to hold that the meaning of a locution is what is left in, what is not excluded, by the context of the locution. This is more easily argued, of course, when the context can be simply declared. In a real-life situation such as that of a group of children with two Marys in it, it is obvious enough that if the teacher calls out 'Mary!' two Marys may present themselves, and if the teacher wants to exclude one of them, this can only be done by additional specification. If the call is 'Mary Jones!' Mary Smith knows she isn't meant. There is no wilful paradox involved, nor anything exclusively applicable to poetic language at issue, when one says that in order to convey meaning, a speaker or writer must show successfully what he does not mean, and that more words (usually) are needed for a narrow meaning than for a wide one, as in the familiar domestic situation 'Where's my new tie?'—'In the drawer.'—'It's not in the drawer.'—'Not that drawer. The dressing-table drawer.'— 'Which drawer in the dressing-table?' and so on until someone settles it by personally fetching the tie; the rational method of labelling drawers 'A', 'B', 'C', etc. is not, oddly enough, regarded as a common-sense way out of the difficulties of language and drawers. More often than not we remain unaware of the extent to which the meaning we ascribe to remarks depends on what Gombrich calls our 'application of situational clues to "make sense" of what is being said'. This, as he points out, is done

not by any conscious process of inference but through that faculty which was given us for understanding our fellow creatures, the faculty of empathy or identification. We first grope for the intention behind the communication, and the key to this intention lies largely in the way we would react.[1]

Where, however, language has to dispense with the support of a particular context, its potential ambiguity becomes apparent. In many of the situations where legal language is used, it might be

[1] *Art and Illusion*, p. 232.

said that the usual process of meaning is reversed: instead of interpreting an utterance by reference to the context of situation, an emergent situation has to be interpreted with reference to an antecedent utterance by a legislator. Here the potential in language for leaving open a number of possible readings of the actual words would wreck the machinery of the law if it were not for the elaborate procedures used, in legal affairs, to control it, and it is instructive to consider that it is in trying to avoid ambiguity that legal language takes forms apparently very far removed from a common-sense use of language, and is held to have meanings against which common-sense may revolt. Legal language of certain kinds evinces highly developed techniques of 'expressly stipulating the relevant'[1] and is subject to rules of interpretation designed to meet the situation summed up by Cairns in his remark that 'the courts themselves are now generally in agreement with the linguistic position that every linguistic expression is ambiguous'.[2] Cairns points out (pp. 249–50) that

by formulating in advance the rules that will be applied in particular instances meaning can be attributed to hopelessly obscure or contradictory sentences. The application of rules *may not yield the meaning that was intended* [italics mine]; but it arrives at an intelligibility which notice was duly given would be the case, assuming the occurrence of the sentences in the legally defined realms of discourse. Thus a man who makes a will is on notice that if he uses technical terms they are liable to be construed in their technical sense, and a legislator is on notice that where general words follow the naming of particular classes of persons or objects, the general words will be held to be applicable only to persons or objects of the same general nature or class as those named.

If the common-sense view of meaning is that one 'puts the meaning in' by choosing words that expressly stipulate it, then it would appear that the language of legislators is the language of common-sense and that a common-sense interpretation of the language of testators depends on what they specifically said, even though this is not in fact what they meant. But of course legal language is notorious for its impenetrability. I have cited some observations on legal language

[1] Huntington Cairns, 'Language of Jurisprudence', in *Language*, ed. Anshen, p. 260.
[2] ibid., p. 255.

because they indicate what the consequences would really be, if we habitually conveyed meaning by 'putting it in'. The language of law, which, *par excellence*, needs to avoid ambiguity, shows how extremely difficult it is to determine meaning when the context of one particular situation does not of itself limit the potential meaning-spread of words by inducing us automatically to exclude meanings irrelevant to the situation in hand. A poem is like a law at least in this: that it is not embedded in a real context of situation which determines the meanings of the words used in that situation. But, unlike a law, a poem is under no necessity of using words unambiguously (or as unambiguously as possible). As Britton says, contrasting the language of the poet with the language of the scientist:

in poetry there is no such obligation to be definite; a sign that indicates ambiguously either A or B, may be a better word to use than a sign that indicates A alone or a sign that indicates B alone. For (i) poetry has its own obligation to be brief, pointed, condensed. . . . And (ii) the poet may wish to evoke emotions associated with both A and B and to produce a tension between these two feelings.[1]

There is no actual context of situation to limit what the poet's words may mean, and no 'obligation to be definite', and in these respects it is proper to hold that poetry is language that 'means all it says'[2] or, in other words, means all that the poem itself does not exclude.[3]

In discussing the poet's use of the potential ambiguity of language at large, we need some term likely to act as a corrective of the tendency to associate ambiguity with a censurable ineptitude in the use of words. A term suggestive of success rather than failure might help

[1] *Communication*, p. 253.

[2] Beardsley, *Aesthetics*, p. 152, summarizing an article by Dorothy Walsh, 'The Poetic Use of Language', *The Journal of Philosophy*, XXXV (1938), 73–81.

[3] Cf. Britton, *Communication*, p. 250: 'Now the referents *suggested* by any word may be very numerous indeed, and altogether heterogeneous; it is the poet's business to see that his poem (taken in its entirety, or all that precedes the given word in the poem) suggests only one of them, or only some of them, and excludes the unwanted others'. Cf. also Beardsley's discussion in *Aesthetics* (p. 144) of 'O frail steel tissues of the sun': ' "frail" prepares us to respond in a variety of possible ways; "steel" can only accept some of the connotations of "frail"; "tissue" further rejects and limits; and when the metaphor completes itself in "sun" only certain of the originally possible meanings of the separate words still survive—except that some of them, too, may be pushed out by the larger context'.

as out of some critical difficulties that follow from the entertaining of unreal notions of the processes by which meaning is established. For however true it may be, in theory, that the Empsonian approach to ambiguity 'permits a fresh and searching examination of literary works',[1] this or any comparable approach is likely to excite misunderstanding and even irritation if it appears merely to advocate as a virtue what many of us have been taught to regard as a vice. In a contemporary handbook of literary terms it is observed, under the heading 'Style':

Young writers are often told that they must avoid certain so-called style faults (*see* AMBIGUITY, ANACOLUTHON, BARBARISM, BOMBAST, CIRCUMLOCUTION, IMPROPRIETY, PLEONASM, SOLECISM, TAUTOLOGY, VERBOSITY), and cultivate the virtues of accuracy, simplicity, economy and clarity.[2]

The problem of a new terminology here is this: we need a term with which to refer to cases where it cannot be said that one certain thing or one certain kind of thing is meant, to the effective exclusion of all other things. These are cases of the absence from the context of directives such as would reduce to one simple meaning the meaning-potential of the locutions occurring in the context; alternatively we could say (talking about the context positively instead of negatively) that these are cases where there are implicit in the context more than one set of relationships into which the locution can enter or which it can precipitate into meaningfulness, its entry into one set of relationships not precluding its entry into another. In poems, as in jokes, the point of using such a locution in such a context may well lie not so much in the separate interest of each set of relationships, but in the very fact that two spheres of interest are brought together or superimposed; the superimposition itself may be said to have a meaning. If we are determined to have one meaning from a piece of language, we may be struck chiefly by the absence of directives for extracting it. If we have no objection to having two (or more) meanings, we may be struck chiefly by the presence in the context of equipollent sets of relationships. A tolerable term for these cases might be the term

---

[1] *Dictionary of World Literary Terms*, ed. Joseph T. Shipley (London, 1955), p. 15.
[2] *A Handbook of Literary Terms*, compiled by H. L. Yelland, S. C. J. Jones and K. S. W. Easton (Sydney, 1950), p. 199.

'extraloquial', if one might suppose that it would suggest *having extra meaning* or *leaving extra meaning in*. People could please themselves whether they approved or disapproved of the extra load, but whether they approved or disapproved, the term itself would be a reminder (as the term 'ambiguity' is not) that the extraloquial context, or the extralocution in it, is under discussion because it has more in it, not less in it, than we usually look to find. Moreover, the prefix 'extra-' is often used to mean *outside* or *apart from*, and this usage is not irrelevant to the kind of concept with which we are now concerned. Having more meanings than one is the result of not entering into the full commitment of unequivocal assertion; to use an extralocution, to permit a context to remain extraloquial, is to decline citizenship in that kingdom of single-eyed men to which language (as ordinarily used) aspires. It has been said that poetry aspires to the condition of muteness[1] and this is a useful paradox if it helps us to realize that one way of transcending the limitations of ordinary language, of appearing to get out of them, is simply to avoid ever getting fully into them. Extralocution is a stopping short of complete specification, of the maximal exclusion of alternatives; the poet, in order to bring it about successfully, has to provide a context capable of determination in more than one way, and preserve its extraloquial quality (wherever this is threatened) by using in that context a locution that does not decisively give judgment for one rather than another of these possible determinations, but does bring into prominence the fact that they are waiting to be realized; to use a word or phrase extraloquially is to refrain from limiting the potential of the context, whilst at the same time drawing attention to the potential.[2]

---

[1] '[Keats's *Ode to Autumn*] does no more than describe a scene, and is wholly poetical; there is no gloss of prose or philosophy in it; and the poem achieves, as I may say, the muteness to which poetry, in its essence, always aspires. Something is held up for us to behold; but nothing is said.'—D. G. James, in *Metaphor and Symbol*, ed. L. C. Knights and Basil Cottle, Proceedings of the Twelfth Symposium of the Colston Research Society [Colston Papers, XII] (London, 1960), p. 101.

[2] Cf. Susanne K. Langer, *Feeling and Form: A Theory of Art* (London, 1953), p. 226: 'A true artistic symbol always seems to point to other concrete phenomena, actual or virtual, and to be impoverished by the assignment of any one import—that is to say, by the logical consummation of the meaning-relation'.

I would suggest, then, that we should regard the humdrum potential ambiguities of language at large as raw material which the poet can process, if he so wishes, in such a way as to make it clear to the reader that there are more ways than one of thinking about the situation with which his poem deals, and, further, that when the raw material is so processed we should describe the poem not as 'an ambiguous poem' (because this tends to suggest muzziness of meaning, or defective meaning) but as 'an extraloquial poem' (because this will help to remind us that we are dealing with a poem that brings together in a simultaneous display a larger number of possible readings of a situation than we usually find provided for us in ordinary statements). A further advantage to be derived from adopting some new term that will free us from the embarrassment of talking about 'ambiguous poems' is that we shall not be constantly pushed into thinking that the only important thing about such poems is that they take up a Yes/No attitude to whatever they present. The expression of a Yes/No attitude, i.e. of ambivalence, is not the only use for extraloquialism. Moreover, though the language of poetry is often used to express or come to terms with ambivalence, and though in articulating ambivalence it may exploit the potential ambiguity of the common tongue, it is also true that ambivalence can be articulated without any such exploitation. To illustrate: Marvell in his poem *Mourning*, which questions the sincerity of Chlora's tears for her dead lover Strephon, devises as the climax of the poem two quatrains in each of which the words of the fourth line can be taken in either of two opposed ways: having told us that some people say that Chlora is weeping for joy, he goes on:

> How wide they dream! The *Indian* Slaves
> That sink for Pearl through Seas profound,
> Would find her Tears yet deeper Waves
> And not of one the bottom sound.

> I yet my silent Judgment keep,
> Disputing not what they believe:
> But sure as oft as Women weep,
> It is to be suppos'd they grieve.

If 'sound' is taken as a verb, the quatrain says that the waters of Chlora's tears are so deep that even the Indian pearl-divers could not sound their depths; if however it is taken as an adjective, then the quatrain says that if one were to procure divers experienced enough to get to the bottom of these waves it would be found that none had any solid ground beneath. Similarly with 'It is to be suppos'd they grieve'; this may be taken to mean either that when women weep, the obvious explanation is that they are really grieving —or that when women weep, everybody is expected to make a polite pretence of believing that they have properly demonstrated a proper amount of concern. Here the poet's ironical insistence on keeping silent about his own judgment of the case is maintained by using ambiguous syntax and idiom. But when Catullus writes (*Carmen* LXXXV),

> Odi et amo. quare id faciam, fortasse requiris
> nescio, sed fieri sentio et excrucior

the ambivalence of his feelings is expressed not through ambiguity but through the contradictory assertions that he hates and he loves.

It will be helpful, then, to be able to avail oneself of a term that stands clear of the contemporary practice of using 'ambivalent' and 'ambiguous' in ways that suggest that they are interchangeable terms. Indeed it would seem that the contemporary tendency to couple these terms has had the result that too little attention has been given to poems in which linguistic ambiguity is used for purposes other than the expression of ambivalence of feeling; recent criticism, making play with the concept of ambiguity as a means of traversing the antithetical categories registered in common vocabulary, has perhaps persuaded us to think too much in terms of the reconciling of oppositions (as between hate and love, sorrow and joy, gain and loss, good and evil). Perhaps, naturally enough, the prefix 'ambi-' has led us to think in terms of 'Not Either-Or, But Both'. The prefix 'extra-' is not likely to have this tendency.

Having done what one can to disentangle the idea of the extra-loquial poem from notions that it will necessarily be unclear or ambivalent, one may then ask what such poems are good for beyond the articulation of ambivalence. It seems obvious that the simplest approach to the question will be by way of the history of the language, since it is this that has provided the poet with the raw material from which he can make an extraloquial poem. The history of the language has brought it about that many words can be used in a large number of different ways, so that the 'same' word, used in different contexts, has different meanings; the meaning (or meanings) we ascribe to it will depend on the context in which we find it. As Fries points out,

the actual number of clearly separable senses covered by most of the commonly used words in English is enormous. Very few words have only one meaning; usually they have from fifteen to twenty. . . . The native speaker of a language uses the "words" in this great range of meaning without any consciousness of the diversity of the senses in the various contexts unless some friction appears in the communication which focuses his attention upon the differing uses.

. . . . .

On the whole the number and variety of meanings which the commonly used "words" have, far exceeds our belief even after our attention has been called to the facts. Without a great deal of painstaking analysis of the quotations we just don't believe that the Oxford Dictionary can be right in recording 69 numbered meanings for the verb *come*, 94 for *go*, 97 for *make*, 91 for *take*, and 126 for the verb *set*, in addition to 47 for the noun *set*. With only a little consideration, however, we are driven to the conclusion that we must not assume that any "word" is a single meaning-unit.[1]

Fries also points out that the study of the history of the language shows that the assumption 'that there is a "real" or basic meaning for each word and that all other meanings or uses are either figurative or illegitimate' (p. 41) is false; one may properly speak (at any given stage of the language) of 'the most frequent' meaning(s), but not of the 'basic' meaning: the use nowadays most frequent is not always the earliest use, nor is it always true that abstract meanings are derived from preceding concrete meanings (see Fries's example, *key*, p. 42), nor can appeal be made to the 'authority' of the dictionary, since dictionary 'definitions' are 'simply summary statements identifying and describing the important features of the

[1] Charles C. Fries, *Teaching and Learning English as a Foreign Language*, University of Michigan, Publications of the English Language Institute, No. 1, 4th printing (Ann Arbor, 1948), pp. 40, 41.

situations in which the "words" have been used' (p. 43). It is there-fore completely open to the poet who so wishes, to construct a poem of such a kind that the situation treated in the poem is given double or multiple aspects and the words used in the poem then have the double or multiple meanings appropriate to the context. No 'trickery' with meanings can be said to be involved.

The interesting aspect, then, of the poet's use of the potential ambiguity of the common tongue, is the art that goes to the con-structing of a context (the situation as represented in the poem) with a double or multiple aspect. This art is linguistic in the sense that it is by the verbal expressions in the poem that we are provoked to view the situation from any aspect whatever, but the art breaks out of the linguistic circle in the sense that verbal expressions call into play attitudes and considerations bound up with our whole cultural experience. As Britton says in discussing the power of words to move us (not only to refer us to objects designated by the words),

If we now ask: How is it that references are themselves signs for certain emotions, . . . the answer must tell us of the causal relationships between our organisms and surrounding nature. It is no accident (of course) that so much poetry is 'nature poetry', for the earth, the seasons, the sea, the sowing and the reaping, human society and human passion, are the con-ditions of the existence and persistence of the race. The poet uses words which are conventional signs for referents that are of *vital* importance to mankind.[1]

What Britton says here of our natural environment could as well be said of our cultural environment; the words of the poem refer us out to, and bring into play, elements and attitudes of the culture we share with the poet. But if one breaks out of the 'linguistic circle' in the sense that the poem brings into play attitudes, considerations and values lodged in our experience and not explicitly given in the poem itself, there is a deeper and truer sense (which makes this talk of the 'linguistic circle' absurd) in which it may be said that reality untinged by language is unthinkable. In one sense it is true that it is the nature of language to be 'about' non-linguistic reality but in

[1] *Communication*, pp. 248-9.

another sense it is true that what we apprehend as non-linguistic is formed for us by the forms of language itself:

We cut nature up, organize it into concepts, and ascribe significance as we do, largely because we are parties to an agreement to organize it in this way—an agreement that holds throughout our speech community and is codified in the patterns of our language. The agreement is, of course, an implicit and unstated one, *but its terms are absolutely obligatory*; we cannot talk at all except by subscribing to the organization and classification of data which the agreement decrees.[1]

The 'linguistic circle' runs, not through the words of a particular poem, but through nature and culture as we know them. When this has been conceded as the background of any statement one makes about poems and their language, one may then say, with less likelihood of being misconstrued, that in order to discuss what is done in extraloquial poems one has to bear in mind both the ambiguity-potential of words as such, and the peculiar structuring of the poem (as context) so as to activate in the mind of the reader more than one pattern into which the words of the poem may be fitted; the poem does not itself give these patterns in their entirety—it triggers them off, or cues them in, and by so doing it establishes the mental context according to which its own words have their meanings.

The vast meaning-spread of common items of vocabulary presents the poet with vast possibilities of double 'cueing-in' of mental attitudes. Among these many possibilities there is one which, as it appears to me, is of outstanding importance: that is, the possibility of cueing the reader to take a word as a referent both for some quality of a physical phenomenon and for some mental attitude towards it. The material for this double cueing is abundantly given by the state of our common language. Sturtevant writes in his account of linguistic change, 'There is a strong tendency to use concrete sensuous terms for abstract suprasensuous ideas. Some purely intellectual processes are denoted by words which primarily refer to physical action'.[2] Stern writes, 'Most adjectives denoting qualities of concrete

[1] Benjamin L. Whorf, 'Science and Linguistics' in *The Technology Review* (Massachusetts Institute of Technology), XLII (1939–40), p. 231; quoted by Fries, p. 47.

[2] E. H. Sturtevant, *Linguistic Change: An Introduction to the Historical Study of Language* (Chicago, 1917), p. 91.

objects can be used metaphorically of abstract things. The instances are innumerable . . .'.[1] It seems, then, obvious enough that if the language affords innumerable instances of words capable not only of referring to or describing concrete phenomena but also of relating them to some system of values, the way is wide open for the poet to describe or refer to objects in words which at the same time imbue the object with significance.

Since the concern of this book is with language as the poet's instrument, it is no part of my purpose to raise theoretical questions as to whether the significance the artist sees in something is or is not 'really there'; it is enough simply to observe that the fact that what we call the 'same word' is not a single meaning-unit, but rather a vast potential of meanings, allows the poet to write in a way that makes it appear that though he has in no way falsified the phenomena of the actual world, none the less he has 'revealed' a significance not evident in the actual objects we see about us. This 'revelatory' element is a characteristic of art; it has, indeed, been said that art is 'the meeting-point of phenomenon and significance'.[2] If this is so it would seem that there is a real connection between art and ambiguity, in that the ambiguity inherent in the medium itself serves as a bridgehead between 'things as they are' and the significance that may be imputed to them. The ambiguity of the medium enables the poet to meet that double demand we make of the language of poetry, that it should deal both with the phenomenal world and with the world of values. Wallace Stevens, in the opening section of *The Man with the Blue Guitar*, puts the complexity of this demand very clearly:

> The man bent over his guitar,
> A shearsman of sorts. The day was green.
>
> They said, "You have a blue guitar,
> You do not play things as they are."
>
> The man replied, "Things as they are
> Are changed upon the blue guitar."

[1] Gustaf Stern, *Meaning and Change of Meaning, With Special Reference to the English Language*, Göteborgs Högskolas Årsskrift, XXXVIII, 1932 (Göteberg, 1931), p. 325.

[2] Knight, *Pope and the Heroic Tradition*, p. 109.

> And they said then, "But play, you must,
> A tune beyond us, yet ourselves,
>
> A tune upon the blue guitar
> Of things exactly as they are."[1]

The use of ambiguity for such a purpose is seen in the following example:

> Magnolia, Philomel,
> Whose candid flowers
> Clasp each a ravished tongue
> In blunt, still hands,
> Who made you speechless,
> Gestureless?[2]

Here the striking features of the magnolia tree are recorded: the whiteness of the petals ('candid' bearing its Latin sense) presented simply and openly to the view ('candid' in a sense nearer to the modern use), the reddening streaks cupped or clasped in the almost unnatural stillness of these thick, heavy flowers—all this is closely observed from life. So is the element of the slightly unnatural, almost the grotesque, in the appearance of the magnolia—it looks too large, too white, too lavish to be quite credible, and the word 'speechless' suggests something of this element in the appearance of the tree loaded with these great flowers. 'Clasp each a ravished tongue In blunt, still hands' furthers the impression of the grotesque. All this is related to the visual appearance presented by the real magnolia. But there is more to it than this: this is not merely any magnolia at Kew, for it is associated with the myth of Philomel, ravished by Tereus and mutilated to prevent her from telling her tale. The myth is connected with the magnolia by a series of suggestions from its actual appearance, figuratively expressed: the red streaks, like red trickles, suggest the bleeding tongue, and the still, half-grotesque flower as a whole suggests the clasp of blunt hands. These suggestions are given prominence by the overt references to the myth in 'Philomel', 'ravished tongue', 'blunt, still hands',

---

[1] *Collected Poems*, p. 165.
[2] *No Impulse from the Vernal Wood* (anon.), *New Phineas* [Magazine of University College, London], Summer, 1945, p. 23.

'speechless', 'Gestureless'. We are made to think of the real tree as being somehow unnatural, mutilated, unable to communicate, despite its beauty. This suggestion, dominant in the language describing the visual appearance of the tree, is brought out in the ambiguous question, 'Who made you speechless, Gestureless?' where it is left indeterminate whether we are to take the question as implying that the tree was in the first place created like this (in which case the tone of the question would be similar to that in A. E. Housman's poem, 'The chestnut casts his flambeaux', where the speaker curses 'whatever brute and blackguard made the world')[1] or as implying that at some former time, in some ideal state of affairs, the tree would have been able to give some message about itself or about the beauty of the world (it would have been like Philomel before the rape) and its muteness now is the result of some catastrophic intervention. In the ambiguity of this final question (where 'made' can mean *created*, or *brought it about that*), the poem in effect asks, 'What are we to make of the startling, silent beauty of the world? Why does it tell us nothing of the nature of reality?' For the beauty that startles us most makes us look for the significance of its existence and makes us ask this kind of question.

The means by which these lines both remain faithful to the actual appearance of the magnolia and yet at the same time inject this significance into it, can be very simply described. They open with a line divided evenly into fact ('Magnolia') and significance ('Philomel'), thus making it clear under what aspects we are to see what follows. What follows is a series of observations couched in words whose range of meaning includes both factual description and evaluation. 'Candid' relates both to fact (to whiteness and openness) and to significance (the tree should, but doesn't, speak candidly); 'ravished tongue' relates to fact (the red streaks, the tongue-like shape of the bud) and to significance (the tree should tell something, but is mutilated); 'blunt' both describes the petals and implies that the tree should tell us something bluntly, but is unable to do so because its hands are blunted and cannot gesture expressively. As the lines gather momentum, the significance becomes more intricate. In 'still',

[1] *The Collected Poems of A. E. Housman* (London, 1939), p. 107.

the climax of the factual description, the implications are multiple: 'still' can mean *unmoving, stilled, calm*—the mystery of the tree and of how it is to be interpreted is deepest here. In order to relate fact to significance, play has been made with the multiple senses of common words. It is because ordinary language is such a shifty and unreliable means of communication that poetic language can say more than one thing at a time. If common language did not afford words with such multiplicity of meanings, this poem could not have been written. The fruitful ambiguity of poetry is rooted in the humdrum ambiguity of our common vocabulary. Indeed in this poem one may observe the writer eking out the supply of ambiguity by resorting to a Latinate sense of the word 'candid' to supplement its more familiar senses.

One may observe too that the working out of the poem's dual concern—with phenomenon and with its interpretation—has made it necessary to innovate. The compound 'gestureless' is brought in, in order to have a word as close as possible in form and function to the word 'speechless'. The analogical machinery of ordinary language makes this possible; the poem itself makes it necessary. The poem's need for the word 'gestureless' is not simply that it is necessary to say, 'The tree can no more gesture than it can speak'. It is also necessary that the word should convey the sense of being struck gestureless, as one is struck speechless. No word in our language conveys this sense of being deprived of the power to gesture, as 'speechless' conveys the sense of being deprived of the power of speech. It is only because 'gestureless' is put in the context of 'speechless' that 'gestureless' clearly has this meaning; the context in which it occurs determines, out of all the possible meanings it might have, the meaning it does have when it occurs here. (If it had been produced for the purposes of a different poem, it might have meant *not waving one's arms about in an excitable manner*, or *not fussing*.) A word newly invented, or one long fallen out of common use, comes into a poem innocent or almost innocent of coloration from usage. It is neutral; in so far as the components out of which it is made allow scope for nuance of meaning, the nuance of the word can be exactly what the poet determines by his shaping of the context in which it occurs. The fact that in this context one ascribes to 'gestureless' a meaning modelled on the relevance of 'speechless' to the context, may give some substance to the concept of 'contextual meaning', and suggest, too, something of the power the poet has to control the meaning-potential of the words he uses. The ambiguity of language as such would destroy the usefulness of language altogether if it were not that the particular context brings out the relevant meaning and causes the irrelevant to be excluded. This means, in effect, that the whole art of exploiting common ambiguities lies in the art with which a particular context is shaped to bring out a selection from the many potential meanings our vocabulary affords. The art does not entirely consist in the management of language as such; it is clear, from the poem just discussed, that the poem rests on a myth of Philomel antecedent to the poem, a myth not created by the poem's verbal manœuvres but only brought in by those manœuvres, and brought in to provide one aspect from which the topic of the poem can be viewed. Its presence makes us select, from all the meanings the words might have, some of the meanings they do have and must have in the poem and for the purposes of the poem. This means, of course, that the criticism of poems cannot be merely a study of verbalities, since the management of meaning is ultimately the management of the stock of our culture.

In poems set on communicating a strikingly new vision, the words in the dictionary and all the words one might make up are nothing without their relation to the structure designed by the poet as a whole, with the meaning residing in or emanating from the whole. This point may perhaps best be made by turning to another area of the ambiguity of ordinary language. So far the discussion has been concentrated upon the usefulness of ambiguity in vocabulary, but it is also possible to exploit ambiguity in syntax. Either, or both in conjunction, may serve to concentrate different interpretations of experience into a few words. Wallace Stevens's fable of Ozymandias, quoted above on pp. 104–5, achieves a vast ambiguity in the words, 'Then Ozymandias said the spouse, the bride Is never naked'; 'spouse' may be male or female and it is left uncertain where the omitted marks of direct speech should properly come and how the syntax should be taken; this concentration of devices of ambiguity makes the 'statement' of this stanza into a web of questions. Moreover, under cover of the poet's licence to depart from common forms of speech, ambiguities even more intricate than those already discussed can be successfully built up. To illustrate this, one might well choose an example from *East Coker*. It is clear enough that this poem sets out to say something new; to say, 'In my beginning is my end', is virtually to announce that the poem begins by throwing the dictionary away. And to say,

> In order to arrive there,
> To arrive where you are, to get from where you are not,

is virtually to announce that the rational categories in which the average man handles his experiences are not the categories appropriate to the understanding of this poem. Yet Eliot, whatever the difficulty of his vision, is not given to inventing for its communication a new vocabulary or to any conspicuous manipulation of the multiple meanings of the old; indeed, a great part of the magisterial effect of Eliot's performance is due to the very fact that he so successfully maintains the illusion that he speaks the common tongue, and is sparing of metaphorical language and of items of vocabulary conspicuously ambivalent.

In the passage of *East Coker* describing the dancers, the ambiguities that make it possible for the dance to seem to mean what the whole poem requires cannot be pinned down and explicated with one finger on an item of vocabulary and another finger running along the list of uses of it recorded in a dictionary, for, in addition to this form of source-material for ambiguity, Eliot uses—and to much more decisive effect—other forms, notably syntax and verbal patterning, whose potential for ambiguity develops with the development of the passage as a whole; we have here a structure of different kinds of ambiguity, which guides the 'meaning' of the dance to the necessary target, like a missile under unseen remote control. The passage runs:

> In that open field
> If you do not come too close, if you do not come too close,
> On a summer midnight, you can hear the music

Of the weak pipe and the little drum
And see them dancing around the bonfire
The association of man and woman
In daunsinge, signifying matrimonie—
A dignified and commodious sacrament.
Two and two, necessarye coniunction,
Holding eche other by the hand or the arm
Whiche betokeneth concorde. Round and round the fire
Leaping through the flames, or joined in circles,
Rustically solemn or in rustic laughter
Lifting heavy feet in clumsy shoes,
Earth feet, loam feet, lifted in country mirth
Mirth of those long since under earth
Nourishing the corn. Keeping time,
Keeping the rhythm in their dancing
As in their living in the living seasons
The time of the seasons and the constellations
The time of milking and the time of harvest
The time of the coupling of man and woman
And that of beasts. Feet rising and falling.
Eating and drinking. Dung and death.[1]

Here, the time of the dance is to become the time of the seasons, its rise and fall is to become living and dying, its round-and-round the cycle of nature—and all these 'equivalences' are to be inseparable from one another. The transition from [dance] time to Time is effected by sliding, into an intricate rhetorical pattern, a near-synonym of time, the word 'rhythm': 'Leaping . . . Lifting . . . Keeping time, Keeping the rhythm in their dancing As in their living'; then, by the immediate addition of 'in the living seasons', human living is verbally identified with the life of nature, and this in turn with the cycle of Time: 'The time of the seasons and the constellations'. Another combination of ambiguities (drawn variously from near-synonymity and from rhetorical repetitions involving syntactical similarity) can be observed in the chain of transitions that links the dance with death: 'Rustically solemn . . . Lifting heavy feet . . . Earth feet, loam feet', where the partial synonymities move towards the introduction of the phrase 'under earth', and this phrase in its turn prepares for 'Dung and death'. The absence from this

[1] *Four Quartets*, p. 16.

passage of normal syntactical articulation makes it easy to hark back across several lines and pick up at will any element in this long series of appositions and pseudo-appositions. For instance, the phrase 'Feet rising and falling' is made to hang on to the passage without full syntactical connection; the passage can assimilate it because the phrase, like the whole passage, rings the changes on -*ing* forms and antithesis. And just because the phrase hangs loosely, it is free to hark back to 'heavy feet' and to 'Keeping time', and yet simultaneously to look forward to a new development: that is, to the pattern $[x]$-*ing and* $[y]$-*ing* found also in 'Eating and drinking'. This pattern in turn is mutated into the pattern $[x]$ *and* $[y]$, in 'Dung and death'. The complicated back-tracking in sense and in pattern contrives the enactment of a circling movement, and the patterns of pairs ('Earth feet, loam feet'; 'Keeping time, Keeping the rhythm'; 'in their dancing As in their living'; 'rising and falling'; 'Eating and drinking'; 'Dung and death') contrive an enactment of the 'keeping time' of the rising and falling feet. The one enactment encompasses the other so that, though both the circling and the up-and-down are enacted, the enactments are involved with one another. Similarly, the concepts associated with these two patterns seem to flit in and out of the shifting 'synonyms' and rhetorical patterns set in such ambiguous relations. One can, as I have just done, analyse these mechanisms, but the effect of their co-working defies analysis because the mechanisms are, precisely, designed to make it impossible for sharp differentiations to be made at the level of vocabulary; the passage presents the dance in such a way as to make it seem to embody, in one object, concepts which in ordinary language could not be equated with one another.

Eliot's way of overcoming the resistance of an ordinary vocabulary to new ways of thinking is interesting because it shows that this may be done without recourse to metaphorical language. Eliot's method is to bear down hard on just those features of language that are themselves untrustworthy for the purposes of logical argument: he exploits the variety of metaphysical implications permitted by the range of meaning in prepositions, the treachery of near-synonyms which can slant meaning in a new direction, the indefiniteness of relationships permitted by appositional and interjectory syntax, and the ambiguity of much-used connectives ('and', for instance, can leave much in doubt, by alleging connection without precisely specifying what the connection is). Mere omission (of connectives, of verbs, sometimes of the subject of a sentence) can conceal decisive transitions of thought and permit the maintenance of patterned 'repetitions' which a fuller statement would expose as having only a pseudo-parallelism.

To analyse the means by which Eliot puts the language machine into reverse, achieving his own meaning by exploiting the weaknesses of language, raises very acutely the problem of what kind of truth (if any) may be said to reside in this peculiar compromise between vision and argument. Since this book is concerned with the nature of the language poetry employs rather than with relating poetry to other forms of knowing or creating, it would be irrelevant to my purposes, even if it were within my power, to do more than merely acknowledge the existence of this problem, and to admit that I intend to leave it alone. But it is, I think, within my brief to argue that such language, whether or not it conveys any truth, affords a kind of satisfaction that, so far, I have not attempted to describe, though I think it is probably of great importance both to the poet and to his readers. The satisfaction such language affords is that of a conviction of meaningfulness that cannot easily be analysed, an intimation that cannot instantly be identified as proceeding from a commonplace sender transmitting on one of the usual wavelengths and being received on a set whose circuit we think we understand. To be inexplicably haunted by or suddenly confronted with or obscurely convinced of meaningfulness, where no apparatus for its communication is visible, is an experience both remarkable and important—as it would be if we suddenly found we could fly, or live without air, or see with our eyes shut. Because it is a matter of intense importance to us to be able to encode and decode meaning, for this ability is the means of survival, of mastery, and of creativity, unusual experiences with meaning are arresting in measure as they are unusual, and this is one reason why poetry gives us the sense that something important is happening to us when we read it.

Unusual experiences with meaning can, of course, be provided without recourse to the kinds of ambiguity exemplified in this chapter. But to provide them will in that case involve recourse to 'ambiguity' in the wider contemporary sense of the manysidedness of language. Sometimes a meaning seems to flash on us irresistibly as though the lines had a radiance or ambience compulsively present to the inner eye, and this is often due to the poet's having set up a series of words or phrases each of which has an overtone that plays in with related overtones in the others, so that their mutual reinforcement amounts to a meaning nowhere explicitly stated in the lines. So, in the great description of the river Oxus at the end of *Sohrab and Rustum*, the lines

> Oxus, forgetting the bright speed he had
> In his high mountain-cradle in Pamere,
>
> (886–7)

flash upon the mind a meaning not to be accounted for by any one of their several components. But of these components there is hardly one that does not do something to project a sense that the old and sluggish river is continuous with, and in some sense the same as, its clear beginnings; 'forgetting' does a great deal to make this sense dominant; so does the shock–impact of the quasi–synaesthetic image, 'bright speed'; so does the permanence of the 'high mountain-cradle', and the persistent suggestion (in the personification, and even in the very name 'Oxus') that the river has identity as a human being has it, and a continuity, through time and change, like our own. The success with which these lines project a symbol, at once consolatory and elegiac, of human destiny, and at the same time conceal the sources of the conviction the symbol carries, is due to the diffusion, through several *loci* and various forms of suggestion, of an unstated but compulsive unifying sense. Sometimes (though I say this at a venture) it would almost seem that the poet contrives something like a blocking of the usual channels of meaning and a leap to some meaning conceptually unstatable. So in the third quatrain of Shakespeare's Sonnet 73, the mind baulks at the difficulty of youth as a death-bed ('on the ashes of his youth doth lie,/As the death-bed'), yet leaps at

171

the resolving image of ashes (the ashes of the fire's youth, the ashes into which the fire will die) and grasps for a concept of continuous process in which consuming and nourishing are one.

There is not, after all, so vast a difference between ambiguity in the narrow, ordinary sense of a distinct alternative between ways of relating a locution to its context (or even, as in the Eliot passage, an absence of overt directives for relating the part to the whole) and 'ambiguity' in its current critical sense of the manysidedness of language. Ambiguity and 'ambiguity' both depend for their existence on the fact that language, in order to work in all its manifold applications, must necessarily consist of a limited number of parts each with a range of possible uses and, therefore, with a whole spectrum of meaning concealed within what we call 'the same word'. When a particular context calls out meanings lying far apart on the spectrum (as in 'blunt' *in shape, in speech*) we may call this ambiguous because we feel that different meanings are involved; when a context calls out meanings lying closer together in the spectrum, we are not conscious of ambiguity because we are not conscious of what Fries calls 'friction in the communication'. None the less, meanings that a lexicographer would record as different meanings may be present in poems that we tend to think of as eloquent or moving, rather than as ambiguous. And the art that activates these meanings is, like the art of activating meanings in friction with one another, the art of creating a context capable of giving them prominence. Whether the significance we find in poems comes from the meeting of the phenomenon and the questioning of it, or from the meeting of situation and emotion, and however much or however little we are made conscious of the stratification of meaning within the words in which they meet, the ground for the meeting is the word or phrase that has this stratification, and the contriver of the meeting—the builder of the bridge between fact and significance—is the artist who gives the context a double or multiple character. The 'narrow' ambiguity I have discussed is only an extreme example of the condition of poetic language as a whole, a condition summed up by Susanne Langer's observations in *Feeling and Form*:

Illusory events have no core of actuality. . . . They have only such aspects as they are given in the telling; they are as terrible, as wonderful, as homely, or as moving as they "sound". (p. 214)

Everything in the poem has a double character: each item is at once a detail of a perfectly convincing virtual event, and an emotional factor. (p. 216)

The "facts" have no existence apart from values; their emotional import is part of their appearance. (p. 223)

In all the examples given in this chapter the common factor is their imputation of significance to the ordinarily mute phenomena of non-linguistic reality. If to impute meaning to the unmeaning involves some innovation upon normal ways of discoursing and an evasion of commitment to one meaning rather than to another, perhaps it can be claimed that the poet's refusal to 'say what he means' is worth while if it enables the universe to mean, or seem to mean, what he says.

VIII

Symbolism and Obscurity

AT an extreme point of differentiation from ordinary uses of language stands the language of what it has become customary to call 'symbolism'. '"That's the trouble with poems . . . they may be merely symbolic and mean nothing."'[1] The opposite view—that symbolism purveys a purer intuition of a higher or more important kind of reality and uses words not less but more meaningfully than is usual— may be represented by the words of Jean-Paul Sartre:

> The poet is outside of language. He sees words inside out as if he did not share the human condition, and as if he were first meeting the word as a barrier as he comes towards men. Instead of first knowing things by their name, it seems that first he has a silent contact with them, since, turning toward that other species of thing which for him is the word, touching them, testing them, palping them, he discovers in them a slight luminosity of their own and particular affinities with the earth, the sky, the water, and all created things.[2]

The claim that symbolism takes us (albeit by some means not clearly defined) to a sphere of knowledge above the ordinary is made by Helen Dunbar[3] in a different way when she says that a symbol 'is an expression of meaningful experience having basis in association' (p. 10), that it is 'unique in its power to give perspective of relationships' (p. 18), and that—in the words she quotes (p. 13) from J. H. van der Hoop's *Character and the Unconscious* [trans. Elizabeth Trevelyan (London, 1923), p. 119]—'symbols are the chief means by which the human mind expresses, not so much those ideas which it has outgrown, or wishes to conceal, but those which it has not yet mastered'. Even this handful of citations from various writers on

---

[1] Quoted from D. J. Enright's *Insufficient Poppy* (London, 1960) by John Coleman, in a review in *The Spectator*, 5 August 1960, p. 222.

[2] Quoted from Sartre's *What is Literature?* trans. Bernard Frechtman (New York, 1949), pp. 13–14, by Wimsatt and Brooks, *Literary Criticism*, pp. 606–7.

[3] Helen Flanders Dunbar, *Symbolism in Medieval Thought* (New Haven, 1929).

various aspects of symbolism should make evident the truth of Wimsatt and Brooks's comment (made *à propos* of the doctrines of the French symbolists, but applicable to many attempts to describe symbolism generally):

Any attempt to summarize symbolist doctrine exposes the vagueness of the pronouncements of the various symbolists and critics, not to mention their frequent contradictions. One might be forgiven for coming to doubt whether the term "symbolism" has any specific meaning at all, and to conclude that it is, like the term "romanticism", simply the name for a bundle of tendencies, not all of them very closely related.[1]

But this chapter can hardly get under way without some sort of description of what it sets out to discuss. A straightforward description is given in Monroe C. Beardsley's *Aesthetics* (p. 408):

What makes an object symbolic in a literary work is its being fixed as the focus of unusual attention either for the speaker or for another character in the world of the work. What it symbolizes is a set of characteristics that it embodies or causes and that are pointed up by the action or the verbal texture.

The description, it will be noted, relates to what makes *objects* symbolic. A similar emphasis is seen in the comment of Stephen J. Brown: 'Symbolism is in the sphere of things what metaphor is in the sphere of speech'.[2] With metaphor, the poet talks about object X as though it were a Y; he uses Y-terminology to refer to X. With symbolism, he presents an object, X, and without his necessarily mentioning a further object, his way of presenting X makes us think that it is not only X, but also is or stands for something more than itself—some Y or other, or a number of 'Y's; X acts as a symbol for Y, or for 'Y's. It is as though, in doing this, the poet were trying to leap out of the medium of language altogether and to make his meaning speak through objects instead of through words. Even though he does not tell us what the object X stands for, or even that it does stand for anything, he makes us believe that it means, to him at least, something beyond itself.

[1] *Literary Criticism*, p. 596. Chapter 26, 'Symbolism', from which this quotation is taken, is a most useful account of the 'bundle of tendencies' associated with the French symbolists and of continuing importance in relation to modern poetry and criticism.

[2] *The World of Imagery: Metaphor and Kindred Imagery* (London, 1927), p. 2.

What kind of language will make us believe this? What, in such cases, gives us the impression that we are invited to see into or to see beyond the object occupying the foreground of the poem? Something special about the language of the poem must in fact be the cause of our giving the object this 'unusual attention', of our deeming that it has depth or some kind of eloquence (or whatever other metaphor we may choose to express our sense that there is something particularly important about it).

It is of course true that in some cases we reject the merely literal reference of words, deeming them allusive to something not literally named, because we are familiar with comparable uses already frequent in the cultural background against which we read the poem. Familiar images tend, as R. A. Foakes observes,

to gather richer associations with repeated use, and come to embody a complex of relationships which do not need to be stated in the poem. Our familiarity with this complex of relationships enables us at once to interpret Herrick's 'Gather ye Rose-buds while ye may . . .' as something more than advice to pick flowers, and to recognize as far more profound than a lament for a dying rose Blake's poem *O rose, thou art sick!*[1]

This point is very strikingly made in Rosemond Tuve's comment on the cultural wealth in Milton's figure of 'the hungry sheep' in *Lycidas*:

The gradual figurative amplification of the Good Shepherd in scores of pastoral figures throughout the Old and New Testament, the constant liturgical emphasis in all centuries and all churches, the accretions and interpretations through centuries of use, Petrarch, Mantuan, Spenser's powerful satirical use in May of the *Shepheardes Calendar* . . .—these are what have given its allegorical power to Milton's figure. . . . the figure is 'dark'; this results from one term being left open, its meaningfulness left to the experience and wit of the reader.[2]

But we must be in some way cued to reject the literal reference of words. One might say that if in a poem a rose or a lamb is referred to, our experience of poems and our familiarity with these symbols

[1] R. A. Foakes, *The Romantic Assertion: A Study in the Language of Nineteenth Century Poetry* (London, 1958), p. 36.

[2] Rosemond Tuve, *Images and Themes in Five Poems by Milton* (Cambridge, Mass., 1957), pp. 80–1.

makes us think it on the whole more likely that the rose or the lamb is not to be taken literally. It is, however, possible to write a poem about a rose as such. Nothing except the language of the poem (and possibly the title of the poem, or the nature of companion poems if it has any companions—as many of Blake's *Songs of Innocence* and *Songs of Experience* have) can determine for us the question of how to take the poem.[1]

We may perhaps come closer to seeing what is special about symbolic language if we take some instances of it and try to set down tentatively any observable peculiarities of the symbols and of the settings in which they occur.

In Shakespeare's *King Lear* a number of particularly moving speeches and episodes involve mention of dress, and the question of whether or not this recurring feature has symbolic import has become almost a *locus classicus* of controversy.[2] The most immediately striking thing about dress in this play is that what it is discussed in connection with, or what it is used to show, varies from place to place as the play develops. It is related to contexts concerned with need, display, concealment of guilt or shame, protection, sophistication of the natural man, disguise, and the adornment of majesty. These contexts suggest a variety of meanings; variety is possible because clothes as such are neutral and do not 'mean' any one of these things, nor is clothing as such either morally good or morally bad. Here an object with no built-in, generally-agreed symbolism (unlike the lamb or the rose), an object having the advantage of moral neutrality and of a variety of uses in the ordinary world, is put in successive contexts that indicate a series of meanings in tension with one another. It is made evident enough what clothes stand for at any given point and it is clear that the characters attach importance to what they stand for; what we are not told is why clothes matter so variously and so much. One might suggest that here we have a typical situation for the building up of symbolic force: the situation that an object evidently matters and evidently does not have a simple single

---

[1] Cf. Beardsley on 'Logical Absurdity' and 'Metaphorical Attributions' (*Aesthetics*, pp. 138–44), and on 'Symbolism' (ibid., pp. 288–93).

[2] See Beardsley, op. cit., p. 439.

meaning. Would it be going too far to say that it is because it holds together different meanings, that the object matters? Or that in this tragedy clothes matter because the tensions between the various meanings they have come to have, are of tragic importance? What we can safely say is that the means by which in *King Lear* clothes acquire both their importance and their conflicting meanings, is by their being set in a succession of contexts that confer these on the object and promote it into a symbol.

We may now consider another symbol in a different kind of work: Eliot's dancers circling the fire in *East Coker*. It has already been remarked that in this passage a conviction of the 'sameness' of round-and-round and up-and-down is the product of a structure of patterned, ambiguous language, which 'enacts' the sameness. It is particularly striking, when one reflects on these patterns and ambiguities, that the object—the dance, or the movements of the dancers—is only nominally one object; if analysed, the movement of the dancers turns out to contain two different movements, the circling of the dance and the rising and falling of the dancers' feet. The poet sets himself to blur the distinction, insisting by all means at his disposal that these two movements are inextricable from one another and that each is the same as something further and that all the movements executed in the poem evince the circular pattern, 'In my end is my beginning . . . In my beginning is my end' and that this ratifies the vision that all experience and all history point to God, and that the dance is an exemplar of the pattern that runs through the whole of life. What makes it possible for the dance to act as the centre of these widening circles of meaning is that the poet has used pattern and ambiguity to overcome the difficulties which a logical statement of such a point of view would present. In the dance passage it becomes particularly clear that the poet in his writing can make use of the difference (which, in reading, we do not consider) between a real object and a merely verbal object. A dance, as a real object in the real world, may indeed include something like up-and-down and round-and-round, but it is only in Eliot's selective, contrived and ambiguous presentation in words that these two movements are apprehended as being the same as one another. In short, Eliot's success with this symbol is possible because the dance in the poem is a verbal objective selectively treated—not an object existing in the world outside the poem or in our perception of that world, nor even in what we might think of as a sort of mental register of word-meanings in which we can turn up the word 'dance'. No more do 'lendings', as such, exist when Lear says, 'Off, off, you lendings!' (III, iv, 113). It is true that the actor who plays the rôle of Lear on the stage is wearing portions of the theatre's wardrobe and that those bits and pieces can be seen by the audience, but if Lear were not calling them 'lendings' we might ourselves think of them as borrowings (from the wardrobe), or as cloth or fur; the descriptions we might be able to think up for ourselves would almost certainly not include 'lendings'. 'Lendings' is what the clothes verbally are when Lear says that is what they are, and what he says about them is what matters. The writer, presenting objects verbally, has the advantage that at any given point he can specify only those aspects he chooses to have specified, for, as Susanne Langer remarks, 'illusory events have ... only such aspects as they are given in the telling;[1] moreover he can give different names and varied contextual meanings to what a reader might vaguely describe as 'the same thing' or 'the same sort of thing'. An object in verbal presentation can become the centre of an accretion of different meanings because the writer is able to manipulate the aspects under which objects are seen and the relations between them.

'Literary symbolism' is perhaps a less repellent formula than the one we seem to be moving towards: that is, 'contextual manipulation of verbal objects so as to suggest importance in these objects and to bring about an accretion of different meanings for them by exploiting the indeterminacy of their status', but such a formula has its uses. At least it indicates the scope the symbolist writer has, to make us think we see something important and meaningful 'in' his symbols, without our noticing that it was he who put that something into the setting of the symbol and into the language by which it is presented. (Perhaps too it may suggest several points at which those who believe that symbols are revelatory of truth and those who do not are likely to be

[1] *Feeling and Form*, p. 214.

talking at cross-purposes.) It would be interesting to try to find out whether the formula would apply to a sufficient number and variety of symbolic works to suggest that symbolic works are effective because of the kind of language in which they present objects; if this were so, there would be no need, when passing from literary works in general to those specially labelled 'symbolic', to abandon forms of criticism generally applicable, and to look for quite different forms of criticism, or despair. At the very lowest estimate, such a formula will certainly serve to direct attention to some characteristics of symbolic language—though whether or not these characteristics are the most important ones is hardly for the proponent of the formula to say.

So far, not much has been said to show the extent to which exploitation of the ambiguity of language is characteristic of symbolic language. If we turn to Blake's poem *A Poison Tree* we find there in a striking form a kind of linguistic ambiguity that seems frequently to occur in poems bent on symbol-making: that is, indeterminacy as to whether the language is to be taken literally or figuratively.

> I was angry with my friend:
> I told my wrath, my wrath did end.
> I was angry with my foe:
> I told it not, my wrath did grow.
>
> And I water'd it in fears,
> Night & morning with my tears;
> And I sunned it with smiles,
> And with soft deceitful wiles.
>
> And it grew both day and night,
> Till it bore an apple bright;
> And my foe beheld it shine,
> And he knew that it was mine,
>
> And into my garden stole
> When the night had veil'd the pole:
> In the morning glad I see
> My foe outstretch'd beneath the tree.

What Blake does in this poem is to show that a feeling that is repressed does, none the less (or rather, all the more, because it is repressed), get out into the world so effectively that it can actually kill. Nowadays there is a much wider understanding of the processes by which repressed emotions become destructive, but Blake in his time was putting an unfamiliar point of view, and for the purpose he devised a symbolic poem, which presents the growth of repressed hatred into a real poisonous tree. Even if we leave out of account any implicit reference of Blake's fable to the apple on the tree in Eden, and confine ourselves to asking how it is that in this poem wrath turns into a tree, we find that we cannot account for this transformation except by giving an account of the verbal devices in the poem.

One device is that of leaving it indeterminate whether some important locutions are to be taken literally or figuratively. A related device is that of sustained syntactical ambiguity in the use of the word 'it': that is, ambiguity as to what 'it' stands for at any given moment in the poem. The word itself remains constant in line after line, but the reference of the word changes. 'It' is at first 'my wrath'; then 'it' is something growing; then a tree; by the end of the poem, 'it' refers to the poisonous apple on the tree.

The studied ambiguity of 'it' is supported by studied evasiveness as to how we are supposed to take the description of the ways in which the wrath/growth/tree/apple was made to grow. Are these literal or figurative processes of growth? The word 'grow' is in common literal use (as of plants); it is also in common figurative use. By beginning with a common word so well-poised between the literal and the figurative, Blake opens the way for the ambiguity in his use of 'it'; we do not know whether 'it' refers to 'wrath' or to a natural growing thing when we are told, 'I water'd it'. The phrase 'water'd it in fears, . . . with my tears' is not necessarily metaphorical, nor necessarily literal. Even if 'it' refers to the literal 'wrath', the 'wrath' can be 'water'd', without metaphor; there is Biblical precedent for using 'water . . . with tears' merely in exaggeration of literal fact (as in Psalm vi, verse 6: 'I am weary with my groaning; all the night make I my bed to swim; I water my couch with my tears') and Blake himself, elsewhere, uses the phrase to mean *produced a copious flow of* (as in *The Tyger*: 'When the stars threw down their spears, And water'd heaven with their tears'). But on the other hand, if 'it' refers to something that 'did grow', with the implied *growth* operating as a metaphor for wrath, then 'water'd' is part of the metaphor and, within the metaphor, can be taken to mean the process of giving water to a plant so as to make it grow. By these connected ambiguities Blake has achieved a form of language whose merit for his poetic purpose is that what is truly said of wrath [*I wept copiously and aggravated it*] can also be convincingly and naturally said of a real growth [*I gave the plant water*]. In this way he makes it impossible to determine where metaphor or reality begins and ends. This technique continues in 'I sunned it with smiles', a sentence which draws strength from the familiar metaphor of 'a sunny smile'—one so familiar and in normal use so faded as virtually to have a merely referential sense. Though at this point in the poem the emphasis is shifting away from wrath, towards a thing growing, it cannot yet be said that there is an overt metaphor; 'sunned' may still be taken as only an extension of the normal usage, 'sunny smile', and the 'it' is not yet exclusively a plant or sapling since the word 'it' goes back in unbroken syntactical connection to the 'wrath' of line 4. (The unbroken syntactical connection is one of the advantages Blake derives from the 'And . . . And . . . And' framework of the narrative.) As the poem proceeds, 'it', having been so long and so assiduously watered and sunned, is felt to be going on growing (it is this very continuity of process that ultimately, though without syntactical break or overt transition into metaphor, swings the emphasis from wrath to growth) and so it becomes full size and bears fruit: 'it bore an apple bright; And my foe beheld it shine, . . . In the morning glad I see My foe outstretch'd beneath the tree'. Let us try to imagine ourselves making, in rational prose, the statement symbolically made in this poem, or trying to recount, as a connected prose story, the action the poem verbally brings to pass. The statement or story would run something like this: 'I was angry and said nothing and grew more angry. I wept incessantly, smiled hypocritically at my enemy and deceived him. My enemy stole something from me, consumed it, and died. I was glad' (or, 'In the joyous morning I saw him lying dead'). One cannot, of course, make a rational story out of this poem unless one repeats Blake's linguistic trick of making wrath turn, verbally, into a tree that bears visible, living, lethal fruit. In effect, the basis of the linguistic manœuvre is to reanimate the 'dead' metaphor in 'grow' and to make it feed on other dead or doubtful metaphors, and on the syntactical ambiguity of 'it', and on the continuity of the 'And', until, like an enormous parasitical growth, the symbolic tree engulfs its own beginnings, takes on identity in its own right, becomes a 'real' tree and kills a man, just as, in Blake's view, a repressed emotion does, within and without the human psyche. And, we may note, wrath becomes a 'real' tree because it is a verbal tree. When we say that an object in a poem is a verbal object, it is misleading to say it is *merely* a verbal object; it would be better to say that what can be done with verbal objects is much more remarkable than what can be done with objects that are merely real.

Studied erosion of the boundary between figurative and literal is a common device in symbolic language. And, since it is usually the common word that has the long history and the great range of uses, this kind of symbolic language can use vocabulary that is apparently very simple and innocuous, but conceals a tracery of fly-overs from literal to metaphorical terrain. Another instance of 'simple' vocabulary put to symbolic purposes can be seen in the climax of Yeats's poem *The Circus Animals' Desertion*:

> Now that my ladder's gone,
> I must lie down where all the ladders start,
> In the foul rag-and-bone shop of the heart.[1]

'Lie down' has a range of uses, some figurative, some literal, and Yeats brings both figurative and literal uses to life by means of other words in the sentence. The word 'ladders' brings to life the senses in which 'lie down' refers figuratively to mental attitudes such as *contenting oneself with, reconciling oneself to*, etc., whilst 'rag-and-bone shop' activates the literal sense of *lying down* (in a certain place, on something). But the language sets up an intricate criss-crossing between what is figurative and what is literal, and between what is physically real and what is spiritually real, for the ladder (which activates figurative senses having to do with spiritual states) has its

[1] *Collected Poems*, p. 392.

foot—like Jacob's ladder—on solid ground, whilst the rag-and-bone shop (which activates the literal sense of lying down) is itself a metaphor for the sordid nature of the heart. Yet while all this intricacy of reference and implication is going on, the vocabulary still remains simple in appearance.

Symbolic language using apparently simple vocabulary and syntax is again found in some parts of *King Lear*, as in 'Give me an ounce of civet, good apothecary, to sweeten my imagination' (IV, vi, 132–3). The word 'sweeten' has a double status: it looks back in its literal sense to 'civet' and forward in its figurative sense to 'imagination'. Its double function is facilitated by its medial position between 'apothecary' and 'imagination'. The medial position is again given to the double-edged word 'cut' in the sentence (IV, vi, 196–7), 'Let me have surgeons; I am cut to the brains'. Again in the episode where Gloucester tries to kiss Lear's hand and Lear says, 'Let me wipe it first; it smells of mortality' (IV, vi, 136), we do not know where the distinction comes between reference to a real smell of decay and a figurative expression for the whole human condition, since two terms in the sentence are ambiguous: 'smell of' and 'mortality'. Language of this kind, poised between the figurative and the real, is what makes Lear in his old age symbolic of something beyond his personal nature and predicament.

Another way in which poetic language can indicate the larger meaning that is to be seen in or attached to objects, is by way of persistent analogies, which operate, as it were, to argue: 'A does this, B does this, C does this; the common factors point to the meaning of what is done'. This device is found in Blake's *London*; one stanza will illustrate its working:

> How the Chimney-sweeper's cry
> Every black'ning Church appalls;
> And the hapless Soldier's sigh
> Runs in blood down Palace walls.

Here there is a strong repetitive structure:

Chimney-sweeper—	cry	— Church
Soldier —	sigh	— Palace
[helpless person] —	*[sound he utters]* —	*[building]*

and in both cases the sound of human suffering has some horrifying effect on the building, despite the apparent helplessness of the sufferer; moreover in both cases the sufferer has some moral claim on what the building is representative of, for each building has an understood symbolism in ordinary life, the church representing organized religion and the palace standing for government or power; the child has a claim on the pity of the church, the soldier a claim to the care of the government he serves and upholds; in both cases the poem explains or draws attention to the setting of the building in the social and political scene, for the church is a 'black'ning' church, set in the industrial scene (and, in Blake's view, the industrialization of England was accompanied by the atrophy of compassion and by exploitation of the helpless), and the palace walls are bloody because, in Blake's view, war and tyrannical government are corollaries of one another. So each parallel comments on the meaning of that which it parallels: the child's predicament illuminates the soldier's and the soldier's the child's, when both indicate the same moral evil. The analogous position of the soldier and the child is brought out by the parallel syntactical constructions. But it should be noted that there are some respects in which the diction varies, though the construction is repeated. The cry of the child gains in force from the stronger language of 'runs in blood'; the soldier gains in pathos from the figure of the child. It would be difficult to exhaust the meaning of such a structure of language; the analogical relations make it possible to put a powerful symbolic charge into the apparently simple human beings spoken of in the poem.

There are yet further observations to be made on the kind of language in which these analogies are expressed. It is not literally true that the soldier's sigh runs in blood down palace walls. The poem however claims that this is true, for it emphatically begins in actuality, by using phrases asserting observation ('I . . . mark', 'I hear') and it repeatedly stresses the universality of what is marked and heard: 'I wander thro' each charter'd street, . . . And mark in every face I meet . . . In every cry of every Man, In every Infant's cry of fear, In every voice, in every ban . . .'. The claim to literal and universal truth could hardly be more strongly made. The poem emphatically states as true something that is not literally true and by so doing it makes us construct or divine the point of view from which the statement can be seen to be true. We are forced to read the poem as meaning whatever-it-is-that-will-make-such-language-true-in-some-sense. The sense in which such language is true is a moral sense, and also a prophetic sense. The poem itself provides the pointers both to the moral and the prophetic point of view, for one stanza tells us that the poet 'hears' in all these cries the moral ill at their root:

> In every voice, in every ban,
> The mind-forg'd manacles I hear.

Another stanza tells us that the victims will punish the society that wrongs them—that indeed even now the suffering of the victims is the beginning of their revenge on society:

> But most thro' midnight streets I hear
> How the youthful Harlot's curse
> Blasts the new born Infant's tear,
> And blights with plagues the Marriage hearse.

One is led to infer that a revenge for the soldier and for the child will come about as inevitably as the harlot's. My main point, however, in commenting on this poem is not to explain its social philosophy but rather to study the kind of language used. This very remarkable language demands that we should supply to it the kind of meaning that will make sense of the words. The language, claiming to be truth, will only become true, or be seen to be true, if we attribute to it a particular kind of meaning (which, of course, the poem itself directs us how to provide). To characterize this kind of symbolic language I cannot do better than repeat the excellent phrase used by Ramsey: he describes religious symbolic language as 'language in search of a situation'.[1] That is to say, when one attaches the language to the right sort of situation, or constructs the situation such language demands as its explanation, the language will ring true. The peculiarity and violence of the language forces us to look for or imagine a situation capable of calling such language into being. Language of

[1] Ian T. Ramsey, *Religious Language: An Empirical Placing of Theological Phrases* (London, 1957), p. 119.

this kind offers advantages to poets who want to say something outside the experience of their audience and outside the range of more ordinary language. But since part of its strategy is to flaunt that peculiarity for which we have to construct the explanation, language of this kind—however simple the individual items of its vocabulary may be—stands at the peak of the ascent of difficulty in the language of poetry, and at the extreme point of differentiation from the linguistic stereotypes used in common life.

In order to illustrate more fully what is meant by describing symbolic language in poems as 'language in search of a situation', I propose to make some study of Dylan Thomas's *There Was a Saviour*,[1] in the hope of showing how the peculiarity of the language compels us to set about constructing a meaning for it, and how it is that the poem contrives to direct us towards the particular kind of meaning that must be apprehended in order to make sense of the language of the poem.

THERE WAS A SAVIOUR

> There was a saviour
> Rarer than radium,
> Commoner than water, crueller than truth;
> Children kept from the sun
> Assembled at his tongue
> To hear the golden note turn in a groove,
> Prisoners of wishes locked their eyes
> In the jails and studies of his keyless smiles.
>
> The voice of children says
> From a lost wilderness
> There was calm to be done in his safe unrest,
> When hindering man hurt
> Man, animal, or bird
> We hid our fears in that murdering breath,
> Silence, silence to do, when earth grew loud,
> In lairs and asylums of the tremendous shout.
>
> There was glory to hear
> In the churches of his tears,

Under his downy arm you sighed as he struck,
    O you who could not cry
      On to the ground when a man died
Put a tear for joy in the unearthly flood
And laid your cheek against a cloud-formed shell:
Now in the dark there is only yourself and myself.

    Two proud, blacked brothers cry,
    Winter-locked side by side,
To this inhospitable hollow year,
    O we who could not stir
    One lean sigh when we heard
Greed on man beating near and fire neighbour
    But wailed and nested in the sky-blue wall
Now break a giant tear for the little known fall,

    For the drooping of homes
    That did not nurse our bones,
Brave deaths of only ones but never found,
    Now see, alone in us,
    Our own true strangers' dust
Ride through the doors of our unentered house.
Exiled in us we arouse the soft,
Unclenched, armless, silk and rough love that breaks all
    rocks.

Dylan Thomas himself in a broadcast reading of some of his poems
described this poem as being among those of his 'that do move a little
way towards the state and destination I imagine I intended to be
theirs when, in small rooms in Wales, arrogantly and devotedly I
began them'.[1] There is then, to sustain us through the difficulties of
understanding the poem, some warrant that the poet himself thought
that it had been worth while to write it.

The poem does indeed present considerable difficulty. Even the
syntax is difficult. The immediately striking thing about the syntax is
the peculiarity of the tenses and pronouns.[2] In reading the poem it is

---

[1] *Quite Early One Morning : Broadcasts by Dylan Thomas*, 4th printing (London, 1954),
p. 130.

[2] Readers apprehensive of seeing the poem reduced to a grammatical exercise may
perhaps feel less suspicious if they note that there is reason to suppose that Dylan
Thomas himself thought that tense has some importance to poetry. Speaking of three
poems of his which, he said, 'will, one day, form separate parts of a long poem which is in

difficult to make out, at first, what point in time we are supposed to be looking at or looking from. It begins in an unplaced past: 'There was'. In stz. 2 this unplaced past becomes even less easy to locate, since it becomes part of something told by 'The voice of children . . . From a lost wilderness'. Now that T. S. Eliot's work is so prominent a part of the modern reader's experience of poetry, we are all rather cautious about the voices of children coming from such places as rose gardens or wildernesses; we know by now that these are unlikely to be embodied voices, and are more likely to be figments or haunters or intimations of something lost, buried in the past, or unattainable. In the course of stz. 3 the poem moves into the present: 'Now . . . there is only yourself and myself'. The fourth stanza, from the vantage-point of the present, speaks again about the past. The fifth stanza speaks in a kind of eternal Now, even a prophetic Now: 'we arouse the . . . love that breaks all rocks'.

The pronouns shift too. The change in the pronouns is very striking at the words [stz. 3], 'O you who could not cry' (this is the first appearance of 'you') and again [stz. 4] when this form of words is almost repeated but the pronoun changes back to 'we': 'O we who could not stir'. It would be a reasonable inference from this series of changes that 'we' and 'you' are somehow the same and yet somehow different. If, struck by these changes, we ask what exactly is done with the pronouns from first to last, we find that stz. 1 speaks of 'saviour' and 'children' and uses the pronouns 'his' and 'their', in stz. 2 the situation is that 'we' did this and that in 'his . . . unrest', in stz. 3 'his' persists but 'we' is replaced by 'you'—in three different uses at that, as may be seen by considering them one by one. The first use of 'you' is in 'you sighed as he struck' [stz. 3]. It is most natural to take this as the generalizing use, equivalent to *everybody*, a use implying *anybody in the same situation would feel the same*; 'you' is

preparation', he remarked, 'The remembered tellings, which are the components of the poem, are not all told as though they are remembered; the poem will not be a series of poems in the past tense. The memory, in all tenses, can look towards the future, can caution and admonish. The rememberer may live himself back into active participation in the remembered scene, adventure, or spiritual condition'. (See *Quite Early One Morning*, pp. 155, 157.)

often used in this way to introduce a description of a common and familiar reaction. The same stanza's second use of 'you' is in 'O you who could not'. Here the pronoun is the opposite of universalizing. To say 'O you . . .' to anyone is normally to mean *you as distinct from me, you who are different from me*. The stanza's third use is in 'only yourself and myself'. The poet doesn't say *only us*, or *only you and I*; he says something radically ambiguous, for 'only yourself and myself' could be intimate [*only the two of us, together*] or it could be separative [distinguishing *your self* from *my self*]. The people referred to in this phrase may be very intimately together or on the other hand it may be (or may at the same time be) that their confrontation is startling. It may even be that each one of them is, as we sometimes say, alone with himself. This obscure situation becomes even more puzzling when we realize that the syntax of the lines containing these changes is continuous: from 'O you' to 'yourself and myself' there is no break. (Moreover the 'yourself and myself' become in the ensuing stanzas 'we' again—looking back to the 'We' of stz. 2, which itself looks back to 'children' in stz. 1.) It would seem, then, that it is being forced upon our notice that this is a poem about continuous identities with a changing outlook, taken at various points in a continuum running through the poem. The poem starts with a number of children who all feel or are taught to feel the same about a saviour; then in stz. 2 the children recede into the past, where only their voice remains, telling—as from a distance—more about experiences of the saviour and of attitudes to him and to the world; in stz. 3 a speaker (un-identified) generalizes about everybody's attitude to the saviour, then makes a distinction between that attitude and some other; then speaks suddenly from the darkness of 'Now' in which there is 'only yourself and myself'; if only these, then presumably no saviour. Of course, what brings about the change of pronouns in stz. 3 is the vanishing of the saviour out of the picture: whereas formerly there was a collective attitude to him, now two identities detach themselves from this shared attitude and have a real encounter, in which—as stzs. 4 and 5 show—they feel really one with each other and talk of themselves in a new sense as 'we': we who now have compassion. As this new 'we', these 'two brothers' now have the attributes of the saviour. (Perhaps one should, more precisely, say that they have attributes commonly associated with the concept *saviour*.) Now they look back at the living and address them with a message that takes the form of a revaluation of their own lives on earth and a proclamation of the power of love.

Thus the tenses and pronouns carry the most important thing in the structure of the poem: that is, the fundamental process of the poem, its beginning with children taught about a saviour and its moving on through their lives to death and the redefinition of salvation. All the contrasts in the diction of the poem hang upon, or are related to, the process expressed through the changing pronouns and tenses.

But the contrasts in the diction are far from simple. Even a cursory look at the diction of stzs. 1–3 is enough to make one realize that the question of what those old values were, which the brothers' values replace, can have no simple, immediate answer. The diction of stzs. 1–3 is violently difficult in its repeated use of oxymoron (e.g., 'locked their eyes In . . . keyless smiles', 'safe unrest'), in its indeterminacy as to whether the saviour and his devotees are good or bad, and above all in its strangeness, of a kind R. N. Maud describes well when he says, 'Reading Dylan Thomas, we rarely find uncommon words; yet all the words seem tantalizingly unfamiliar, pressed by the poet into strange image-combinations'.[1] Since the diction is so baffling, it may be as well to find out first whether there are any clear patterns in the ground-plan of the poem or in its verbal devices; the poem does not adhere to the idiom of common life, so there is no way open to us but to find out whether it has an expressiveness of its own, in its own terms.

Looking at the general plan of the poem, one observes first that the poem seems to turn on a hinge in the line, 'Now in the dark there is only yourself and myself'. The word 'Now', with which this hinge-line begins, is also used to begin two other lines in the poem, which may suggest to us that these lines, like that, act as nodal points in the system of contrasts or series of developments running through the poem and underlying the peculiarities of the diction. And so in fact it

[1] *Essays in Criticism*, IV (1954), 416.

proves. In the line 'Now see, alone in us, . . .' [stz. 5] the word 'see' looks back through the poem to 'in the dark', and 'alone in us' looks back to 'only yourself and myself'. The other 'Now . . .' line, 'Now break a giant tear for the little known fall', goes back to 'O you who could not cry' and to 'Put a tear for joy' in stz. 3 and to 'O you who could not stir One lean sigh' and 'wailed' in its own stanza [4]. Moreover this 'Now . . .' of stz. 4 is very emphatically signalled as some kind of new departure by a change in the rhyme-scheme and the lineation: it is here that the only full rhyme in the poem ['wall'/ 'fall'] occurs, and this is the only line to occupy the end-position in a stanza and yet not to stand aligned with the one before (all the other stanzas end with a pair of lines printed as one prints a couplet, but stz. 4's penultimate line is indented as a 'short' line). Everything possible is done, to emphasize that at the word 'Now' a new development takes place and a new stage in the argument of the poem gets under way.

If 'Now'-lines introduce changes, we must ask ourselves what marked change occurs along with the third of these, 'Now see, alone in us' [stz. 5]: that is, we must ask what is new about the last five lines of the poem, what aspect of the world of the poem they set in a new light. The most obvious answer to such a question would seem to be that in this part of the poem the brothers' attitude or message ceases to be merely, or generally, something to do with compassion; the poem now moves on instead into the terminology and imagery of sexual love between man and woman. The problem for the reader is to know what to make of this, since it is far from being made immediately evident what relation obtains between the triumphant sexuality ['Ride through the doors of our unentered house'] and universal liberation ['breaks all rocks'] of these lines, and the concerns of the preceding stanzas. We can, however, say that the ground-plan of the poem has the outstanding characteristic that there are three hinges or turns in the argument, and that the first turn has to do with the vanishing of the saviour, the second turn has to do with expression of human compassion, and the third has to do with the entry of sexual love. We may then suppose that these themes, if we may call them so, must be related to the peculiarities of the diction.

To make this supposition does not instantly result in a clarification of the peculiar expressions the poet uses; the diction does not so easily declare the logic of its mysteries. It is almost as though the poet had gone out of his way to write a kind of language that is 'symbolist' in the sense Wallace Stevens expresses so well when he writes in the opening lines of his poem *Man Carrying Thing*:

> The poem must resist the intelligence
> Almost successfully. Illustration:
>
> A brune figure in winter evening resists
> Identity. The thing he carries resists
>
> The most necessitous sense . . .[1]

If we ask what the point is in writing of this kind, perhaps the answer is at hand in the conclusion of this same poem by Stevens:

> We must endure our thoughts all night, until
> The bright obvious stands motionless in cold.

If there is indeed a 'bright obvious' to be reached for, through the struggle to understand why the poet has chosen just these (baffling) expressions, it seems likely that we shall not get at it unless we look for what the diction can tell us about itself through characteristics that recur with sufficient frequency and emphasis to suggest that some pressure of meaning has extruded these curious forms; we must look, that is to say, for striking formal relations at the level of the diction.

To readers who are familiar with the symbolism of William Blake, one aspect of the imagery of the poem will stand out very sharply: its preoccupation with buildings and rocks. In the symbolism of Blake, rock or stone, and buildings made of these, are associated with evil, as being manifestations of the forces that produce the dark Satanic mills, the modern industrial hell, the obscurantism of institutionalized religion, tyranny and war. Dylan Thomas's poem too uses images of rock and of building ('jails and studies', 'churches', 'wall', 'rocks'). But even without knowledge of Blake, one might grasp (since it is

---

[1] *Collected Poems*, p. 350.

prominent both by its peculiarity and by its repetition) the importance of the formal relationship between

> In the jails and studies of his keyless smiles
> In   lairs and asylums of the tremendous shout
> In the churches   of his tears

where the sense of the poem declares itself through a persistent verbal pattern suggesting persistent analogy. The constant elements in
the pattern are:

> In the *buildings* of   [*some expression of*] *human feeling*

and if we go back to what precedes the 'In', and ask *what* is 'in' these
buildings, we find another constant element, for what is in them is
again something to do with human beings:

> locked their eyes/In
> silence to do, . . ./In
> glory to hear/In

The abstractable common pattern is:

> *something human   in the buildings of   something human.*

The term that sticks out as not belonging is always the building-
term. The 'we' of the poem and the 'saviour' of the poem are presented in human terms but between them there intervene buildings.
This is a very peculiar pattern, but its very peculiarity and its
repetitiveness give it a prominence that attracts our attention, and,
moreover, we are not left without the necessary directive for interpreting it. The directive is most sustainedly given in the first stanza.
There, on the first appearance of the pattern, in 'Prisoners of wishes
locked their eyes In the jails and studies of his keyless smiles', the
'smiles' are explicitly described as 'keyless', and we are explicitly
told that those who contrive to lock eyes in the jails and studies of
these smiles are themselves the prisoners not of the smiles but of
wishes; that is to say, it is because they are prisoners *of wishes* that
they *transform* the smiles of the saviour into jails.

R. N. Maud has said of Dylan Thomas's 'strange image-combinations' that 'the first step in overcoming the strangeness is to

insist to ourselves that the poem means literally what it says'.[1] No doubt it is true that people who are familiar with the idiom of Dylan Thomas tend to use the word 'literally' in a sense peculiar to the context of their experience of getting at Thomas's meaning. Elder Olson puts the difficulty clearly: 'What did a poet, so obviously given to metaphor and symbol in his poetry, mean by saying that he wanted to be read literally?'[2] It is true that Dylan Thomas himself said he wanted his words to be taken 'literally', and indeed, *à propos* of a phrase in the very poem with which we are now concerned, he wrote to Vernon Watkins,

I'm so glad you liked my lyrical poem, that you thought it was one of my best. I'll think of 'stupid kindred', which is right, of course, in meaning and which prevents any ambiguity, but kindred seems a little pompous a word: it hasn't the literal simplicity of hindering man.[3]

This passage shows that whatever 'literal simplicity' meant exactly, it certainly meant something opposed to being 'a little pompous'. This would seem to suggest that 'literal', for Thomas, is not opposed to 'figurative' or to 'metaphorical' but rather to techniques of expressing meaning by depending on the meanings words acquire from the sort of situation in which they are usually chosen (in preference to other words having reference to the same thing, but not having the same overtone of attitude to that thing). It seems to me that if we are to take Dylan Thomas 'literally', what we are required to do is to interpret his language (in this respect) rather as one interprets the language of a child. The child uses the phrase that seems to him to be the most direct and accurate description of what he is talking about, but because adult conventions of meaning demand that we say what we mean in the way other people would say it, the child's description strikes us, not as factual, but as quaint or even incomprehensible. It is, I think, because of some such

[1] op. cit., p. 416.

[2] Elder Olson, *The Poetry of Dylan Thomas* (Chicago, 1954), p. 61.

[3] *Dylan Thomas: Letters to Vernon Watkins*, ed. Vernon Watkins (London, 1957), p. 81. From another passage, in a postscript to the same letter ['To avoid ambiguity, and also the use of the word "kindred" I've turned "his": in line 6 of verse 2 into "that." '] it is clear that the ambiguity to be avoided was the possibility of relating 'his breath' to 'hindering man'.

characteristic of the style, that though Dylan Thomas means exactly what he says, it is still difficult to identify what is being described—if we persist in expecting to have things described according to common stereotypes of description. I take it, then, that in the phrase 'prisoners of wishes' what is meant is that 'wishes' are prisons to the people who cannot break free of them and who, therefore, are 'kept from the sun' (or, since stz. 1 allows of this construction, keep children from the sun). The obverse side of Thomas's 'literal' technique is that though he uses words with almost childish directness, and 'innocence' of the proprieties of usage, their 'factual' reference is often to the 'facts' that only the sophisticated adult would know about. It is at this point that, in order to understand Thomas's language, one has to look before one leaps. The necessary leap, here, is to the Freudian interpretation of the psyche. (That is also, in a sense sufficiently approximate, Blake's view of the psyche.) In that interpretation, people who have repressed their desires are always so busy repressing them that they cut themselves off from life as it might naturally be (cf. 'kept from the sun'). The 'prisoners of wishes' then are people suffering from repressions, who connect this process (arbitrarily) with the smiles of the saviour; there is no real connection between the repressions and the saviour's smiles; it is the repressed them-selves who set up the connection and make the saviour's smiles into jails. 'Keyless,' again, is 'literal' in this peculiar double sense. In the direct way of the child, it observes that smiles have no keys. But there is also a leap to be made to a situation in which a saviour would, to the knowledgeable mind, have a connection with keys. The neces-sary leap is to St Peter, to whom Christ said (Matthew, xvi, 18–19), 'Thou art Peter, and upon this rock I will build my church; and the gates of hell shall not prevail against it. And I will give unto thee the keys of the kingdom of heaven'. (The problem of how one is to know which way to jump, to arrive at the right area of knowledge and associations and so to see a 'literal' or 'factual' meaning in these imagistic descriptions, is one that will recur in a much more acute form, when some literary allusions are discussed, later on in this commentary. Here it is perhaps sufficient to observe that St Peter's connection with rock, and the prevalence of rock-references in the poem, and its concern with 'churches', together make this as good a guess as any.)[1] I think it should also be observed that there is also a certain difficulty in relating Thomas's 'literal' technique (even if we allow for its reliance on sophisticated 'facts') to his other and sometimes concurrent practice of expecting us to catch the reverberations of an expression against the minutely-differentiated various usages of stereotypes analogously related to it; 'keyless', for instance, may very well share in that Joycean technique (dear to Thomas) of making one expression a palimpsest of references and travestied usages; it does seem to me that 'keyless' gives us an echo-bounce to *clueless*, and if so there is nothing one could call even remotely 'literal' about this indirect meaning. Again, this interpretation of what 'literal' means at the stylistic level does not exclude the further possibility that the style permits also of specific reference to a particular identifiable situation. An interpretation 'literal' in this sense would say that the children of stz. 1 are not vaguely in any imprisoning jail or study but are in Sunday-school (as, in stz. 3, somebody is in a church and, later on, in a grave). We are then in the very thorny position that this diction means what it says (though it does not say what it means in the ways other people would do) but it also asks us to make leaps to particular areas of knowledge and terminology, and sometimes it may mean what it doesn't *quite* say (as in 'keyless'/ [*clueless*]) and it probably also has reference to a specific situation ultimately identifiable if we can grasp the complicated idiom of the poem.

[1] For the thorniness of the problem, cf. Beardsley's discussion, in his *Aesthetics*, p. 158, of Olson's treatment (p. 74) of Sonnet V of *Altarwise by owl-light*: 'It is hard to see what plausible principles would justify the method of explication used by Elder Olson [*sic*] . . . for example, he says that "And from the windy West came two-gunned Gabriel" refers to the constellation Perseus, for Perseus had two weapons, his sword and the Medusa's head; two guns recall the Wild West, the West recalls poker, poker is a game of cards, cards suggest trumps, and trumps suggest the Last Trump, hence Gabriel. . . . Is there any limit to explication by this method? See Theodore Spencer, "How to Criticize a Poem", *New Republic*, CIX (6 December 1943): 816-17; but it is a nice question at what point his attack becomes unjust'. But cf. also Beardsley, op. cit., p. 145: 'A proposed explication may be regarded as a hypothesis that is tested by its capacity to account for the greatest quantity of data in the words of the poem—including their potential connotations—and in most poems for which alternative hypotheses can be offered it will turn out in the end that one is superior to the other'.

Despite the difficulties outlined above I think it is fair enough to say that the first stanza does succeed in making it so difficult to get any sense out of it *unless* one takes a leap to the assumptions of modern psychiatric theory, that we can hardly read the poem at all without being conscious that it is going to relate its concerns to what any reasonably sophisticated reader might be expected to know about Freud. (Whether the poet 'has a right' to take this knowledge for granted is not my business to argue; I would argue only that the poet does take it for granted.)

In subsequent stanzas the reader is not so explicitly told what stage of psychological development the words refer to. The explicitness of 'children' and 'Prisoners of wishes' is not kept up in what follows; we are left more to our own devices of placing the speakers of subsequent stanzas in the appropriate position on the Freudian graph. But we are given clues at least adequate to enable us to do this. (If it be complained that the poet is asking rather a lot of us, it might be retorted that he has rather a lot to get in anyway, since—as it now appears—he is concerned not only with the relation of people to a saviour, and to other people, but also with the psychological drives within the people.)

Stanza 2 speaks of 'the tremendous shout'. In so far as this relates to the saviour, it would seem to mean the cry from the Cross. But what can it mean, on the Freudian graph, to say that the speakers of the poem hid their fears in lairs and asylums of the tremendous shout? It seems reasonable to suppose that this line, following the language-pattern of the last line of the first stanza, must, like that, have a psychological as well as a religious reference in the pattern of its ideas. We may take it, at least, that the psychological phase referred to is one that follows childhood, since in this stanza the children have receded into the past; the presumption, therefore, that this is the phase of adolescence is warranted by the phrase 'safe unrest'—which one might say was a factual description of normal adolescence—and by the fact that the stanza makes sense if we refer its language to that stage of development of the psyche in which the dominant concern is a complex relation with the father-figure, the symbol of Authority towards whom the rebellious adolescent has feelings of hate, guilt, fear, and an unconscious expectation, even desire, of punishment. Correspondingly, in religious terms, the saviour becomes the scapegoat (the religious attitude mirroring the emotional attitude). Stanza 3's relation to this train of ideas must be dealt with later, lest in treating it we should at this point have to make its diction bear all the weight of a reading whose corroboration is to be found in aspects of the poem not yet discussed.

Thus in stzs. 1 and 2 something human about the saviour becomes (metaphorically) for his devotees something built of rock or stone and devoted to purposes associated with imprisonment ['jails'], with education or indoctrination ['studies'], and then with fear and ferocity and concealment ['lairs'] and madness and refuge ['asylums']. As to these 'fears' that were 'hid' in 'lairs and asylums', we may ask, is the beast in the lair fearful or fearsome? Is the asylum a madhouse or a sanctuary? The metaphor, it would seem, is becoming both ambiguous and ambivalent. It is now much nastier (implying lurking beast and madman) and yet at the same time more pitiful (if we look at the matter from the side of the hunted beast or the insane). The saviour too changes; his progress is from smiles to the tremendous cry from the Cross. What is happening is that the saviour and his devotees are changing together.

In stz. 3 the increasing interpenetration of saviour and believers goes a stage further again: whereas in stz. 2 the believers had recourse to the saviour in fear and mental confusion, in stz. 3 the fear and confusion are replaced by a complacent (and evidently perverted) enjoyment:

> There was glory to hear
> In the churches of his tears,
> Under his downy arm you sighed as he struck,

and here the strained linguistic connection which was so striking in 'hid . . . fears in . . . shout' gives place to the less strained connection 'glory to hear In the churches'. Now the devotees are 'Under his downy arm'. Now the devotees rejoice—in suffering, it would seem; they 'Put a tear for joy in the . . . flood'. The people concerned appear to be churchgoers, presumably adults, and the 'glory' they are enjoying, if the word has a simply factual, specific ground, may equally well be elaborate church music, a martial hymn, or the 'music' of tears; the language is permissive of all these interpretations—they glory in whatever it is that they hear in churches. It is notable, too, that 'the churches of his tears' may be taken in one way that is not (if we relate it to other usages) metaphorical at all; one may speak without a metaphor of 'the Church of St Michael and All Angels' this being an accepted way of naming churches and giving them a special dedication. By analogy with that, 'churches of his tears' means something like churches *dedicated to* tears; as a metaphor analogous to other members of this metaphor-pattern in the poem, it means that the tears of the saviour have been metamorphosed into an institutionalized church whose members glory in suffering and in whatever else 'glory' stands for in the context. Translated into the Freudian scheme, this stanza presumably is a comment on the alleged element of sado-masochism in some religious attitudes and on the alleged element of perversion in the personal emotions of those who find these religious attitudes congenial.

To sum up what we have so far: with the aid of this little language-pattern involving images of buildings, we have found that the cult of the saviour, as presented in the poem, is radically unlike the nature of the saviour himself; man remakes the saviour in his own image by distorting him to correspond with the distorted views and institutions that dominate society; in stz. 1 education is indicted; in stz. 3 the organized church is indicted. What then is indicted in stz. 2? That is to say, what institution or what aspect of organized society is referred to in 'lairs and asylums'? I do not see any easy way of answering this question satisfactorily at this point, but it may prove, later on, that other aspects of the poem suggest an acceptable answer. The fourth and fifth stanzas look forward to the cure, the new salvation, described at the end of the poem as breaking 'all rocks'. This cure is not merely brotherly compassion, as in stz. 4, for in stz. 5 it is suggested that the cure ultimately resides at a much deeper level, in the release of sexual love, for it is a sexual love that the brothers see, in the concluding lines, as a liberated and liberating force. This liberation concludes the Freudian pattern in the poem.

The difficulty about discussing, in full detail, the management of the Freudian level of the poem, is that it is conveyed partly by means of literary allusions. I have tried to keep the literary allusions out of my commentary as long as I possibly could because this is tricky material to deal with, but by now they almost shriek for admittance. Before I embark, reluctantly, on these, I should first point to another unexplored strain in the poem: its half-explicit, half-implicit use of a diffused image of birds, clearest in 'wailed and nested in the sky-blue wall', but tinging the diction at a number of other places as well. Yet another concern of the poem is with war and the bombs dropping, clearest perhaps in 'Greed on man beating near and fire neighbour', 'drooping of homes' and 'Brave deaths of . . . ones . . . never found', but also, like the bird-image, implicating the diction at other places too. The date of the poem—published in May 1940—should be borne in mind. If one asks why the speakers of the poem should be imaged as birds, two reasons at least present themselves: the bird is a not unfamiliar symbol for the soul, and in 1940 the bombs were falling from aeroplanes. If this seems to my reader a completely arbitrary concatenation of facts (though, for all I know, my reader by now may have jumped ahead of me and be waiting impatiently for commentary to come to the point) I must ask him to wait until I have plodded my way through the literary allusions, placating himself the while with the ancillary information that in a letter of 1940 Thomas wrote to Watkins:

A 'plane brought down in Tottenham Court Road. . . . Are you frightened these nights? When I wake up out of burning birdman dreams—they were frying aviators one night in a huge frying pan: it sounds whimsical now, it was appalling then—and hear the sound of bombs & gunfire only a little way away, I'm so relieved I could laugh or cry. What *is* so frightening, I think, is the idea of greyclothed, grey-faced, blackarmletted troops marching, one morning, without a sound up a village street. Boots on the cobbles, of course, but no Heil-shouting, grenading, goose-stepping. Just silence.[1]

Anyone who brings literary allusions into a commentary on a poem must be hag-ridden by uncertainties. How is allusiveness to be established? Even if it is established, what does it mean? Is allusiveness

[1] *Letters to Vernon Watkins*, pp. 98–9.

distinguishable from unconscious plagiarism? Even if it can be shown that an allusion is deliberate as well as verifiable, what limits are to be set to the relevance of the allusion (and its context) to the concerns of the poem in which it is included? There are no critical rubrics or Queensberry rules about this game, despite the fact that James Joyce and T. S. Eliot (to go no further) have made the game necessary, interesting and respectable.

The first problem can be illustrated in connection with 'a saviour Rarer than radium'. I entertained the opinion that this was an allusion to the opening lines of the fourth part of *East Coker* ('The wounded surgeon plies the steel That questions the distempered part'), where Christ is the 'surgeon', until I realized that though Thomas's poem was published [*Horizon*, 1, May 1940] after *East Coker*'s appearance in the Supplement of the *New English Weekly* of 21 March 1940, it was sent to Vernon Watkins before 6 March.[1] So much, then, for the reliability of an unsupported judgment on the phrase 'a saviour Rarer than radium'.

What then of the possibility that 'The voice of children says From a lost wilderness' is a deliberate allusion to the children in the rose-garden in *Burnt Norton* ('Quick, said the bird, find them, find them' [1, 21], 'Go, said the bird, for the leaves were full of children, Hidden . . .' [1, 42–3]) and that the 'hollow year' and the 'lean sigh' together are a deliberate recall of 'We are the hollow men . . . Leaning to-

[1] In a letter dated 6 March 1940 [*Letters to Watkins*, pp. 81–3], Thomas replies to Watkins's comments on the poem, and though in a postscript to the letter he says, 'Since this—I lost the post—I've been reading the (my) poem very carefully, and have made these slight but, I think, important (relatively) alterations: [a list follows]', the fact that he was at that date making 'slight but . . . important' alterations is neatly offset by the fact that the alterations he lists have nothing to do with the 'Rarer than radium' line. And in this letter of 6 March he says he is now writing a 'satirical poem. . . . I had to have a change after my austere poem in Milton measure' (p. 82). This all makes it extremely improbable that *There Was a Saviour* could have been in any way affected by the appearance of *East Coker* on 21 March, and to clinch the matter Mr Watkins in private correspondence assures me that he has no recollection whatever of there having ever been any changes made in the second line of the poem, apart from the changes discussed in the letter of 6 March; to the best of his knowledge the text of the poem as he received it from Dylan Thomas, well before the appearance of *East Coker*, was the same as the text printed in *Horizon* in May 1940. (The *Horizon* text varies in a few slight details from the text as printed in the *Collected Poems* but, again, line 2 is not involved.)

gether' [*The Hollow Men: A penny for the Old Guy*, ll. 1, 3]? 'Key-less', similarly, may allude to the end of *The Waste Land* ([v], ll. 411–14):

> ... I have heard the key
> Turn in the door once and turn once only
> We think of the key, each in his prison
> Thinking of the key

and 'Now in the dark there is only yourself and myself' may be another allusion to *The Waste Land*: to

> Who is the third who walks always beside you?
> When I count, there are only you and I together
> . . . .
> I do not know whether a man or a woman.

([v] ll. 359–60, 364)

If any of these echoes, or the cumulation of possible echoes, evinces an intention to allude openly to Eliot, what might any or all of the allusions be taken to mean? And, if we could settle the first question and the second to our satisfaction, how much of the allusion's own context may it be said also to bring to bear on the meaning of *There Was a Saviour*? That is, does the allusion consist only of the lines that enable us to identify it, or is the immediate context of the allusion relevant? Is the main purport of *The Waste Land* as a whole relevant? Is what we know about the symbolism of *The Waste Land* relevant?[1]

---

[1] The last question might be—embarrassingly—restated in this form: Did Dylan Thomas know, and expect his average reader to know and recall as relevant, what Grover Smith tells us in a commentary on Eliot's use of *London Bridge is Falling Down*:

The song "London Bridge" and the game dramatising it, are said to be folk survivals of the primitive rite of the foundation sacrifice—of the slaughter of a victim to avert evil from a newly built bridge or other structure. The scapegoat is represented in the song by the prisoner behind the stones:

> Take the key and lock him up, lock him up, lock him up,
> Take the key and lock him up, my fair lady.

Belladonna, the fair lady ['a symbol of loveliness', p. 79], has locked Tiresias up in a tower of morbid enslavement'.—Grover Smith, Jr., *T. S. Eliot's Poetry and Plays: A Study in Sources and Meaning* (Chicago, 1956), pp. 96-7.

Problems of meaning and intent are raised by Grover Smith—'There is danger lest multiplied allusions, adventitious or not, should defeat meaning' (p. 79)—but in the present state of criticism no answers to these problems are available.

The problem of what an allusion 'means' seems to me to be vitally affected by the answer we would give to the question, 'Was the poet aware of it?' For clearness we might say 'allusion' only when we would give the answer 'Yes' and 'origin' or 'part-origin' when we would give the answer 'No'. And if for any reason it should seem probable that the poet was aware of it but would hardly expect his reader to register the fact that a literary echo was present, such a case would rank as an origin, not as an allusion. For if the works drawn upon by a poet have only the status of compost on which his own work was nourished, it would be absurd to talk about the 'meaning' of the compost; to study the compost is to study the genetics of the poem, not the meaning of the poem. But if the echoes are deliberate and the reader is deliberately cued to catch them, the fact that they are cued into the poem is an aspect of the meaning of the poem. (This will not settle the question of what they mean, but it will settle the question of whether they are meaningful.)

The problem, 'Compost or Cue?' comes up in a very sharp form in connection with the peculiar phrase 'hindering man' [stz. 2]. Alongside this phrase we may put one of Blake's comments on Lavater's *Aphorisms on Man*:

But as I understand Vice it is a Negative. It does not signify what the laws of Kings & Priests have call'd Vice. . . . Every man's leading propensity ought to be call'd his leading Virtue & his good Angel. . . .

Accident is the omission of act in self & the hindering of act in another; This is Vice, but all Act [from Individual propensity *inserted and del.*] is Virtue. To hinder another is not an act; it is the contrary; it is a restraint on action both in ourselves & in the person hinder'd, for he who hinders another omits his own duty at the same time.

Murder is Hindering Another.

Theft is Hindering Another.

Backbiting, Undermining, Circumventing, & whatever is Negative is Vice. But the origin of this mistake in Lavater & his cotemporaries [*sic*] is, They suppose that Woman's Love is Sin; in consequence all the Loves & Graces with them are Sins.[1]

In this passage 'Hindering' means something more appropriate to Dylan Thomas's meaning in stz. 2 than the normal use of it (in which

---

[1] *Complete Writings*, ed. Keynes (1957), p. 88.

it means *preventing* or *getting in the way*), since, in the poem, the context shows that 'hindering man' is cruel and injurious and frightening. Moreover the reference to 'the origin of this mistake . . . They suppose that Woman's Love is Sin' is highly relevant to the theme of repression in stz. 1 and to the release of love in stz. 5. I do not think there can be any doubt that Thomas knew this passage and consciously or unconsciously recalled it when he wrote 'hindering man'. But Thomas would have had little reason to hope that his reader would recognize the echo; how many people read Blake's marginalia? Moreover, in writing to Vernon Watkins, he does not, in defending the phrase, refer to Blake's use of the word.

Immediately after his defence of 'hindering man' in this letter, Thomas goes on to discuss the lines that finally took the form

> Our own true strangers' dust
> Ride through the doors of our unentered house.

It appears that for 'ride', he first had 'fly', and that 'seep' had been suggested as an alternative:

No, I can't 'seep' with dust, & unless a better word can be made will remain true to 'fly'. (pp. 81–2)

. . . .

[in postscript:] For 'fly' in the last line but 2 of last verse I have now 'ride'. I'm sure of that: it's mysteriously militant, which is what I wanted. (p. 83)

Here again, though he gives an explanation of his choice, he does not make any reference to the famous lines from Marvell's *Coy Mistress* that seem to flicker just under the surface of the diction of his last five lines:

> then Worms shall try
> That long preserv'd Virginity:
> And your quaint Honour turn to dust;
> And into ashes all my Lust.
> The Grave's a fine and private place,
> But none I think do there embrace.
>
> . . . .
>
> Now let us sport us while we may;
> And now, like am'rous birds of prey,
>
> . . . .

> Let us roll all our Strength, and all
> Our sweetness, up into one Ball:
> And tear our Pleasures with rough strife,
> Thorough the Iron gates of Life.

The reader of poetry who knows these lines (as who does not?) can hardly fail to have from their sexual imagery, and from the 'dust', the 'rough', the 'Iron gates' and the 'preserv'd Virginity' a recall strong enough to make him fully aware of the sexuality of Thomas's concluding lines—even if it does not make those lines shout 'Marvell' at him, and make him ask what Thomas meant by this recall of Marvell's manner.

If only because Marvell has made this kind of sexual imagery an open book to the modern reader of poetry, nothing strikes us as odd in the imagery of dust riding through the doors of an unentered house. But when Thomas speaks of 'silk and rough love' one is brought up short. It can be read as a metonymy for *female and male*, and left at that, but it is hard to exclude from one's mind those lines from Brooke's *The Great Lover*:

> Then, the cool kindliness of sheets, that soon
> Smooth away trouble; and the rough male kiss
> Of blankets;

and one begins to wonder whether Thomas relied on this recall to make 'rough male kiss' so nearly part of the meaning of his own line that it would be impossible for a reader to miss the point that the two brothers' message is a message not only of human compassion but also—as being at the root of all outgoing human feeling—of fearless sexuality. To consult the context of which the allusion (if allusion it be) is a part, will not settle the question of whether Thomas recalled the 'rough male kiss' consciously, and expected his reader to do so, but it will certainly settle the question of whether or not *The Great Lover* is at least a source, for the conclusion of that poem has many points of contact with Thomas's theme and diction, and at the same time with Marvell's. The conclusion of *The Great Lover* runs:

> Nor all my passion, all my prayers, have power
> To hold them with me through the gate of Death.
> They'll play deserter, turn with the traitor breath,

Break the high bond we made, and sell Love's trust
And sacramented covenant to the dust.
—Oh, never a doubt but, somewhere, I shall wake,
And give what's left of love again, and make
New friends, now strangers . . .

. . . .

O dear my loves, O faithless, once again
This one last gift I give: that after men
Shall know, and later lovers, far-removed,
Praise you, 'All these were lovely'; say, 'He loved.'[1]

This, it seems to me, brings the problem of 'Compost or Cue?' to
a head. On the one hand, there is a sufficient number of sporadic verbal links between the Thomas, Brooke, and Marvell passages to
suggest an 'associative cluster' in the pre-artistic mind, which would
account satisfactorily for the verbal resemblances between the three
poems without bringing in any theory of deliberate allusion. On the
other hand, one does not expect of an associative cluster that what
gets into it will have such a high degree of congruence as these passages have if, going beyond mere verbal links, one considers the
character of the whole context in which each passage occurs: the
poems drawn upon for verbal detail have the further very striking
characteristic that *as wholes* they are relevant to Thomas's theme.
Brooke's poem is a poetic testament, coming to its climax in a message to be given: 'say, "He loved." '; Marvell's poem advocates a certain attitude to living and loving; Thomas's 'brothers' cry a message
of love. In all three poems the message is given, as it were, in the
teeth of the grave. The kind of love, in all three, is assertively human
and physical. So far as the 'meaning' of the allusion is concerned, the
position is that the poem alluded to deals with a concern of the same
kind as Thomas's concern, and deals with it in such a way as to
advocate a point of view close to his. Other allusions in Thomas's
poem share this striking feature. The line, 'And laid your cheek
against a cloud-formed shell' (another phrase that seems to cry out
for an explanation) suggests the visual and tactile image in the sestet
of Keats's 'Bright star' sonnet:

[1] For the complete poem, see *The Collected Poems of Rupert Brooke* (London, 1918),
pp. 18–20.

207

Pillow'd upon my fair love's ripening breast,
To feel for ever its soft fall and swell,
Awake for ever in a sweet unrest,

and here—almost as if to make up for the delicacy of the allusion, so fragile in its merely verbal contacts that one wonders if one is 'seeing things' when it floats before the mental eye—the relevance of the allusion's context is extraordinarily complex. The sonnet itself puts this symbol of steadfastness over against the symbol of 'The moving waters at their priestlike task Of pure ablution round earth's human shores', and rejects the purity of the 'new-fall'n snow' and the 'priest-like' waters, in favour of human love. This is also the sonnet that was for a long time called 'Keats's last sonnet', and even though it is known now that this was not so, it is inextricably associated with the death of Keats. (In Thomas's poem the line reminiscent of Keats comes just before 'Now in the dark . . .'.) If this is indeed an allusion its context is not only the whole of the sonnet, but also the circumstances connected with it, which Colvin recounts as follows:

On board ship the same night Keats borrowed the copy of Shakespeare's poems which he had given Severn a few days before, and wrote out fair and neatly for him, on the blank page opposite the heading *A Lover's Complaint*, the beautiful sonnet which every lover of English knows so well:—
Bright star, would I were stedfast as thou art,

. . . .

Severn in later life clearly cherished the impression that the sonnet had been actually composed for him on the day of the Dorsetshire landing. Lord Houghton in his *Life and Literary Remains* distinctly asserts as much, and it had seemed to us all a beautiful and consolatory circumstance, in the tragedy of Keats's closing days, that his last inspiration in poetry should have come in a strain of such unfevered beauty. . . . But in point of fact the sonnet was work of an earlier date.[1]

On pages 493 and 494 Colvin quotes the earlier form of the sonnet, and it is perhaps worth noting that in the earlier version the line with which we are concerned ran: 'Cheek-pillow'd on my Love's white ripening breast'.

There can of course be no dogmatizing about what the human memory is capable of at the pre-conscious level, but it seems much to

[1] Sidney Colvin, *John Keats*, 3rd edn. (London, 1920), pp. 492–3.

suppose that Thomas, unaware of what he was doing, should dredge up (whenever he drew on other poems) contexts so inevitably and complicatedly relevant. When, in addition to being relevant, the context is also one that 'every lover of English knows', and when it has to be called in to shed light on the fitness of an expression otherwise inexplicably peculiar, it seems a reasonable conclusion that Thomas knew what he was doing and expected his reader to see that he was doing it and to grasp the implications—especially if, in a large number of allusions, these features are steadily repeated.

Because the poem has a 'before' and 'after' in its design, it is not to be expected that all the allusions will bring in contexts where physicality is finally advocated as a positive value. Earlier in the poem the other side of the debate is more relevant. In stz. 1, where 'Children . . . Assembled . . . To hear the golden note turn in a groove', it is possible to see an allusion to Yeats's *Sailing to Byzantium*, if 'turn in a groove' recalls 'perne in a gyre'—

> O sages standing in God's holy fire
> As in the gold mosaic of a wall,
> Come from the holy fire, perne in a gyre,
> And be the singing-masters of my soul

—and the 'golden voice' recalls the bird 'set upon a golden bough to sing . . . Of what is past, or passing, or to come'; Yeats's theme, the escape from human sexuality into 'the artifice of eternity',[1] is relevant here, and it may also be that the peculiarity of 'In the jails and studies' has something to do with its being designed to accommodate an allusion to Yeats's *The Tower*—

> Now shall I make my soul,
> Compelling it to study
> In a learned school
> Till the wreck of body,
> Slow decay of blood,
>
> .   .   .   .
>
> Seem but the clouds of the sky
> When the horizon fades;
> Or a bird's sleepy cry
> Among the deepening shades.

[1] See *Collected Poems*, pp. 217-18.

It will not have escaped notice how often, in the context of these allusions, there is some reference to a bird. The fact that this is so may possibly add credence to the suggestion that a passage from Wordsworth's *Prelude* (1850 version, v, 372–9) has some relevance to the 'tremendous shout' in stz. 2 (though this, like the reminiscence of Swinburne in 'murdering breath', has—if any relevance—relevance to some of the problems connected with stz. 2 that so far I have left to one side) and to the suggestion that 'Under his downy arm you sighed as he struck', already reminiscent of the Biblical 'under the shadow of thy wings', is also reminiscent of *The Wreck of the Deutschland* ('O Father, not under thy feathers . . .' [stz. 12]) where the theme of suffering and sacrifice and of 'The dense and the driven Passion' would explain the reminiscence. The recurrence of the bird image suggests not merely deliberateness, but even calculation. Bird-imagery becomes overt in the latter part of Thomas's poem, and these contexts do something to prepare the way for it; they may also signalize the fact that the allusion is admissible, and they may be meant to provoke the question of what birds and the heritage of English literature have to do with one another. It seems at least possible that 'bird' is a symbol for *poet* (as well as for *soul*, and for *combatants in air-war*), since the situation now begins to look not like one of sporadic allusion to other poems but of a sustained placing of emotional, religious and social attitudes in relation to comparable poetic postures. To complete the tally of phrases in the first three stanzas which have a peculiarity that (if my suggestions are valid) accommodates a literary allusion involving bird-imagery, one must note the extremely odd phrase 'could not cry On to the ground'. (It may be pertinent to mention that 'On to' is a revision of the text as it appeared in *Horizon*, where the reading is 'On'. 'On to' makes it clear that those who could not cry were *above* the ground, or, at least, that their tears fall down from above, and it may be supposed that the change was made to bring this out.) Gertrude Stein is not a writer familiar to many, but one quotation from her work, at least, is: it appears in Bartlett's *Familiar Quotations* (11th edn., rev. and enlarged, 1937). The quotation is from St. Ignatius's aria in *Four Saints in Three Acts*—an opera, words by Gertrude

Stein, music by Virgil Thomson. I quote from Van Vechten's text:

[He had heard of a third and he asked about it it was a magpie in the sky.] If a magpie in the sky on the sky can not cry if the pigeon on the grass alas can alas[1]

Such is the obscurity of Gertrude Stein that one is tempted to disregard the context of this passage, and confine oneself to the observation that St Ignatius's aria is headed in the score, *Vision of the Holy Ghost*. But Maurice Grosser's scenario, which describes the original production, has many curious points of interest. 'Saint Teresa, for reasons of musical convenience, is represented by two singers dressed exactly alike' (col. 1); 'The two Saint Teresas were costumed as cardinals' (col. 2); 'The use of Negro artists in the original production was a result of the composer's admiration . . . for the naturalness of their approach to religious themes' (cols. 2–3); Act I . . . represents a pageant, or Sunday School entertainment. . . . Saint Teresa enacts for the instruction of saints and visitors scenes from her own saintly life' (col. 3); 'Saint Teresa II. . . . converses with Saint Teresa I' (col. 3) [cf. 'Can two saints be one', score, 48]; 'she rises and asks, "Can women have wishes?"' (col. 3); 'the Compère and Commère, in front of the house curtain, discuss whether there is to be a fourth act' (col. 6)—this is presumably related to the Last Judgment, prepared for at the end of Act III. These and other features of the action make one wonder whether they were 'compost' for Thomas's poem, though one can hardly suppose that the phrase 'could not cry On to the ground' actually 'cues' anything beyond the passage from St. Ignatius's aria. There would be nothing odder in

---

[1] *Last Operas and Plays by Gertrude Stein*, ed. Carl Van Vechten (New York, 1949), p. 468. In the Introduction (pp. ix–x), Van Vechten writes, '*Four Saints in Three Acts* . . . was originally produced . . . at Hartford, Connecticut, February 8, 1934 and subsequently has been performed in New York and Chicago. It has been sung in concert, over the radio, and it has been recorded. This opera was first published in America in 1934. . . . the complete original text may be examined in *transition*, No. 16 (June 17, 1929) or in *Operas and Plays*, published in Paris in 1932, but these are no longer generally available'. The complete vocal score (New York, [1948]), has prefixed to it a Scenario by Maurice Grosser, who writes (Scenario, col. 1): 'The present scenario was written after both the text and the music had been completed; and although it was done with the help of suggestions from both the poet and the composer, it is to a large extent my invention'.

his deriving hints for the action of his poem from the action of a work by Gertrude Stein than there is in his showing the influence of Eliot's allusive technique and of the verbal technique (of simultaneous reference at different levels) of James Joyce. It seems at least possible that the oddity of the two Saint Teresas who are one Saint Teresa seemed to him to have an imaginative congruence with Eliot's treatment of Tiresias ('Just as the one-eyed merchant . . . melts into the Phoenician Sailor, and the latter is not wholly distinct from Ferdinand Prince of Naples, so all the women are one woman, and the two sexes meet in Tiresias' [*The Waste Land*: note on l. 218]) and with Joyce's method in *Finnegan's Wake*, where the Fall in Eden and Humpty-Dumpty's fall are the same fall, and any two brothers are any other pair of brothers, and (to exaggerate only a little) everything is the same as everything else that can in any way be connected with it. Certainly we have to suppose 'layering' of references to make sense of the poem's diction.[1]

I have laboured over the question of whether the recall of other literary works entitles them to be regarded as cues, and, if they are regarded as cues, how far the relevance of the cued-in work may properly be said to extend, because the poem has so many layers of meaning that it is sometimes difficult when one has shown the presence of some to argue convincingly for yet more without recourse to the allusions. And when one of the layered meanings is of a particularly shocking originality, commentary needs all the help it can get. This kind of interpretative difficulty occurs in stz. 2, where one level of reference, now that twenty years have elapsed since the poem was written, is perhaps not so quickly evident to the reader as it would be in 1940. I have already interpreted this stanza as having, at one level, reference to the stage of adolescence where guilt and the father-figure are important, and, correspondingly, at the religious level a scapegoat is sought. In 1940 comparable features of Hitler's Germany were evident to many and it was a commonplace that Hitler's success in Germany was a classic example in political life of identification with a father-figure, that the Jews were the scapegoat, and that in the release of psychopathic violence and sadism that

[1] I am indebted to Charles H. Peake for help on Thomas's relation to Eliot and Joyce.

accompanied his régime there was a hideous projection of the distur-
bances of adolescence. The 'Fascist beast' was a symbol only too
horribly familiar, and the Fascist shout likewise. 'Lairs', 'asylums'
and 'tremendous shout', occurring in a stanza concerned with
cruelty, the scapegoat, and the father-figure, make an almost compulsive combination for anyone who lived through Hitler's rise to
power, and the war. These circumstances are now at a distance, as
are the patterns of talk and of newspaper writing familiar at that time.
But the verification of such a parallel is written into the allusions. If
we ask for an explanation of the phrase 'that murdering breath', it is
to hand in Swinburne's famous line from the *Hymn to Proserpine*
(*After the Proclamation in Rome of the Christian Faith*), which begins
with the motto '*Vicisti, Galilaee*':

> Thou hast conquer'd, O pale Galilean; the world has grown grey
> from thy breath;

in the word 'grey' (which I think there can be no doubt Thomas recalled) though Swinburne himself was alluding to the suppression by
Christianity of the colourful gods of earth, there is the further
relevance that the uniform of the German army, which in 1940 was
overrunning Europe, was grey; 'grey from thy breath' also alludes to
the devastation of Europe at the command of Hitler. It may come as
a shock to have to accept that an allusion to Hitler is brought in by
way of a line about Christ, but it is part of the argument of the poem
that an ethos of suffering may become involved with a displacement
of aggression that finds its release in militarism, and that the wor-
shippers of the Father, travestying His image into a mirror of their
own conflicts, execute the same psychological manœuvre as those
who identified themselves with the strength of Hitler. The 'tremendous shout', in which 'We hid our fears', allows of reference both to
the cry from the Cross and to the Fascist shout; 'we' in this
stanza are not only Christians and Germans but also, simply, boys—
and, I suspect, at the same time the Wordsworthian boy in *The
Prelude* (with, I take it, the further relevance that some might hold
that Wordsworth's involvement with the father-figure is betrayed by
some of the famous passages on feelings of guilt and supernatural

menace). These almost Joycean 'correspondences' may be involved
if there is indeed any parallel between the 'tremendous shout' and
that passage in *The Prelude* where a boy halloos through his cupped
hands and

> as through an instrument,
> Blew mimic hootings to the silent owls,
> That they might answer him; and they would shout
> Across the watery vale, and shout again,
> Responsive to his call, with quivering peals,
> And long halloos and screams, and echoes loud,
> Redoubled and redoubled, concourse wild
> Of jocund din.

(1850 version, v, 372–9)

It may however be that the stanza is Wordsworthian because it deals
(on the poem's graph of growing up) with the boy, and (on the graph
of the developing religious life) with the stage of a religion involving
Nature as well as God, and because the subject of *The Prelude* is
'The Growth of a Poet's Mind'. The tissue of allusion, however, is
precariously thin here. In the third stanza, where we are concerned
with young men and (it would appear) with a ritualistic, church-
going, devotional stage of religion, the appropriate literary parallel
with Hopkins and the metaphysical poets is much more clearly indicated: 'churches of his tears' is a metaphysical conceit; 'Under his
downy arm you sighed as he struck' is applicable to devotional attitudes in Donne and Crashaw (as well as in Hopkins, to whom this
line most openly alludes); 'Put a tear for joy in the unearthly flood',
in its awkwardness no less than in its emotions and in the epithet
'unearthly', suggests Vaughan. The inclusion of Keats in this stanza
is not random; he comes as the climax of this stanza's review of poets
who have in some way attempted approximation between the artistic
and the religious sense—and rightly as the climax since Keats's
attitude to the human and natural world is closer to Thomas's own
than that of any other poet in the register he has called. Even here the
allusion is shrewdly critical in that it touches upon the languorous
and death-loving element in Keats. There is, indeed, nothing random
in the couplings between certain religious attitudes and certain poets;

the allusions also function as critique. Perhaps the harrowing parallel between the early death of Keats and of Dylan Thomas (which haunts the mind because of the nature of the Keats allusion and of the position in which it is placed) is no more than an accident, but we are told by Caitlin Thomas that he 'kept saying he would die before me: would never reach forty'.[1] In the placing of the allusion to Keats's 'last sonnet' at the point where the poem itself is suddenly abrupted by the death of the poet, I think one must recognize a testimony to the importance of the function—a more than illustrative function—of the literary allusions throughout the poem. These establish the poem's *persona* as that of a poet who reviews the attitudes of other poets to the relation between nature and religious and cultural superimpositions, and represents their attitudes and his in a critique not only of religion but also of culture. It is this that warrants and indeed explains the prominence of allusions to Eliot and Blake, both confronting the waste land of the heart and mind of man in society, and explains too the influence of Wordsworth on the structure of the poem, in the continuity of the speakers and the review of past growth from the vantage-point of the present, in a retrospective and reflective narrative whose stages flow in and out of one another, for this is a poem of the growth of a poet's mind in its relation to nature, religion and man. The scope, depth and multiplicity of reference in *There Was a Saviour* is necessitated by the ambitiousness of its purport: the poet in a time of war examines the religious and cultural symbols that have themselves in great measure shaped the intelligence and feeling that turn to question the meaning of their world. He traces, within the sustained figure of the poem—that men are but children of a larger growth—three stages (child's; boy's; young man's) in religious consciousness (the stage of wonder and pleasure and being taught; the stage of experience of moral problems; the stage of established religion), in social and cultural relationships (children at school; the alternate solitudes and gang-activities of boys; the spiritual and human experiments of adults aware of ritual and beauty). In so doing it presents the growing boy in ways sharply distinct from the Wordsworthian, by the very

[1] Caitlin Thomas, *Leftover Life To Kill* (London, 1957), p. 35.

marked infusion of a Freudian evaluation. All three stanzas imply comment on the sexual, emotional and social dispositions analogous to the poetic *Weltanschauung* of the poets alluded to: the repressions of childhood, the patterns of fear, guilt and aggression in adolescence, the elements of *volupté* and masochism in a fervent devotional tradition. This, however, is critique, not indictment. The toys of tradition and intellectualized art are entrancing, even if alienated from the natural life; the boy is compassionate and moral until the pressures of fear and the father-figure erupt; the glorification of suffering and death in the poets recalled in the third stanza is the co-ordinate of their vital concern with eternity, with the numinous, with man's ecstasies and with the metaphysical status of man, of evil and of beauty. The antiphon (stzs. 4 and 5) is a statement of the concern of Dylan Thomas's own poetry: its metaphysics and its ethos. His poetic voice is Blake's as well as his own; to re-read the *Songs of Experience* alongside these stanzas is to realize that the poem is deeply indebted to the inspiration of Blake.

The background is Blake's compassion for 'Another', his deep religiousness, his indictment of inverted emotion, inverted religion, cruelty, war, and the 'mind-forg'd manacles' put by society on the natural and supernatural man, his grasp of the correspondences between all these evils, and the symbolism in which he deals with them. A specific allusion to the *Songs of Experience* is present in 'Brave deaths of only ones but never found'. In *Songs of Innocence* there is a poem *The Little Boy Lost* and another *The Little Boy Found*; in *Songs of Experience*, again, there is *A Little Boy Lost* but this time there is no companion 'Found' poem, and Wicksteed writes that the title Blake gave to this third poem is

intended to connect it with "*The* Little Boy lost" and "found" of "Innocence," and conveys the meaning that though a lost little boy *may* be found, *this* is an instance of one who was lost and not found. It is a fierce indictment of man's interference with the growing mind; the assumed authority of the priest . . . crushes the freedom which leads through experience to wisdom. . . . To rob the soul of its necessary experience is to destroy it, and this is what in our presumption we are always doing.[1]

[1] Wicksteed, *Blake's Innocence and Experience*, p. 178.

But it is hard to set a limit to the overtones of Blake, since Blake's *Songs* are so much interconnected. Wicksteed's commentary (p. 162), stresses the parallel with *A Little Girl Lost*:

it is closely related with "A Little BOY Lost," and the two are generally associated in "Experience." The basic theme of "A Little BOY Lost" is this: A child sets out to think for himself. . . . Unhappily, this is a country where the adventure is not tolerated, with the consequence that the soul of youth is systematically murdered. . . . Substitute "Love" for "Thought," and you have the basic theme of "A Little GIRL Lost," and Blake insists that youth *must* be allowed to find in the body a Paradise that perishes . . . if it is ever to know the imperishable Paradise of the Spirit.

The 'blacked brothers' too may be related to the *Chimney Sweeper* poems. The connection between religion, pity and the love of man and woman in Blake's poems is not unlike the connection Thomas makes between compassion and physical love at the end of his poem.

Though I have dwelt on the literary allusions, it should be pointed out that the poem can be read without them; without them, one layer of its reference vanishes, and with it some of the justification for the peculiarity of some of the phrases, but the other layers of the poem remain comprehensible enough. 'Brave deaths of only ones but never found', quite without Blake, refers clearly enough to deaths in the war, and I should suppose that, in view of the contention in the opening stanzas that men twist the saviour into something alien, it would also appear that another meaning of the line is that men never truly find the saviour who dies for them. Similarly in stz. 3 (at least in retrospect from 4 and 5, which evidently refer to the bombing raids) a reader might work it out that 'the churches of his tears' is a metaphysical conceit, and that the churches of tears are bomber aircraft if Christ's tears are bombs, and the 'glory' they hear is the explosion of the bombs they drop; they sigh with pleasure as God and the air-force strike and they do not weep for those who die. The 'cloud-formed shell' might be understood (without reference to Keats) as being the dead body of Christ—'cloud-formed' because of the manner of His conception[1] and 'shell' because it is empty of the Spirit—but in this case the contrast with the breathing humanity of

[1] Cf. 'cloud-made' at an earlier stage of composition, cited in *Letters to Watkins*, p. 83.

'my fair love's ripening breast' would be lost, and it is doubtful whether the idea of a contrast between the veneration of a dead body and the disregard for living people would be conveyed, and I think it must be said that the implication of the canalization of natural emotions into religious activities would drop out altogether and with it would go some of the relevance of this stanza to the psychological pattern unfolded in it. Though the poem can survive without its allusions, it would survive in a form less consecutive in pattern, and sometimes apparently arbitrary in diction.

And it is of great importance to the effect of the poem that the presence and main outline of the psychological pattern should be discerned, since the whole poem leads to the massive antithesis, at its climax, between the values attached to the figure of the saviour by a deformed society with deformed emotions, and the 'unclenched' love the two brothers assert. 'Unclenched' negates both the clenched fist and the twisting of sexual impulse, as 'armless' not only rejects armaments but at the same time associates this love with the image of the Venus de Milo. The cry of the two brothers in their exile is answered (as·in Thomas's *A Winter's Tale* prayer is answered) by a vision of the coming of Venus; her 'mysteriously militant' 'ride' is a powerful sexual image; the 'silk and rough' that is applicable to marble is applicable to, and indeed fully establishes the presence of, sexual love. This triumphant Venus is Venus in apotheosis, laying open all the springs of passion and life, re-creative of what man has petrified and destroyed, Venus as she might be in a man's dream of his liberation from all his conflicts.

The poem is not concerned simply to reject institutionalized religion in favour of one of the poet's own making. In it the poet re-lives his life, surveying at every stage the process by which it became distorted, enabling himself to understand and pity the child within the man even while he grieves for his perversion, so that in the last resort, finding pity for his own corruption and suffering, and forgiving himself his own guilt, he can release his love and assert it as a liberating power. What makes this an unforgettable poem is the continuity of the persons (the man and the poet, and they themselves are one) who move from 'saviour' to 'love'. And if one asks, 'What, as a poem, not as a message, does it all come to?' it might be replied that all of the poem comes to its own last, great statement, which, gathering into itself all that has gone before—the jails, the asylums, the churches, the frozen earth in which the dead are locked, the buildings blasted by bombs, the wailing wall, the rock of Christ's tomb and the rock from which breaks the goddess of Love as water broke from the rock struck by Moses—declares, in the formulation, 'that breaks all rocks', that anything that has been, is, or will be symbolized by rocks is subject to the love this poem defines, and so extends the triumph of Venus out of the poem into infinity.

In order to lead up to the shattering and endless reverberation at the end of the poem, the poet has had to devise a diction that does not so much say what it means, as allow all the range of meaning involved in the poem to fit into the peculiar phrasing used at any given point. The diction is polyvalent because it is bare; it is bare of those overtones of general usage which, in a less idiosyncratic diction, allow us to identify what the poet is talking about, not necessarily because he names it (one of the lessons on the nature of language, given by the 'symbolic' writer, is that a 'bird' may be any kind of bird, or any of the things for which 'bird' may be a metonymy), but because the tone of the language in which he talks about it will tell us where to look. A bare diction does nothing to narrow the number of possible areas in which the objects it names have a significance. One reason at least for the symbolist poet's quest for 'purity' of language is that a 'pure' (or bare) language—if he could invent it—would preserve the absolute freedom and undifferentiation of the symbolic object. This sort of freedom to multiply significant meanings is, however, bought at the price of sacrificing the illusion that one is using language as the common man uses it; just *because* the language is purified of colour, it seems to the reader to be opaque. Wallace Stevens—having absorbed the lessons of French symbolist poetry—observes, 'The poem must resist the intelligence Almost successfully', but in terms of diction this may very well come to the same as saying that the poem must resist the application of the reader's mental card-index of linguistic usage—so that instead of looking up what the poet means on this card-index, he has to resort to an intelligent response to all the directives for interpretation that the poet has built into his poem. This kind of procedure may lay the poet open to the charge that though he has written a poem of amazing meaningfulness, he has not written it in the English language. In a sense this is true. It is true in the sense that he has not written it in the English language as it was before he wrote the poem. But if the structure of the poem is strong enough to show the reader how to read the poem, it is none the less a meaningful use of the English language, and if the poem is read and understood by a sufficiently influential body of readers (especially by other poets) the English language will itself expand; the uses of language worked out in the poem will contribute to the range of the language as a whole. If the power of a language to endure through time and change depends on its power to convert old apparatus to new uses, we should regard the poet not only as a source of poems but also as one who does something of incalculable importance for the future of the language. The joke that tells of someone who came away from a performance of *Hamlet* saying that it was a good play but was too full of quotations, has a point for anyone who tries to understand the relation between poetic uses of language and the language as it is used for other purposes. For, as E. H. Sturtevant writes, in his book *Linguistic Change* (1917):

A literary language tends to become a common language, and a common language tends to become a literary language. . . . Chaucer chose the dialect of London because it was already beginning to be used as a common language, and Chaucer's example fixed that dialect as the common language of England. It has now become the common language of communities living in every one of the six continents and in countless islands. It may yet become the common language of the world. (pp. 156–7)

However, from the point of view of one who concerns himself with poems and is content to let the history of the language take care of itself, the final question must be the difficult one of why the infinitely diverse relations that may obtain in poems between the total meaning and the elements that carry it, should have the common factor of exciting in us a kind of interest that we recognize as specifically poetic experience, since reflections on the history of the language will not themselves provide a reason why he should welcome difficult poems, or undertake the struggle to understand them. It cannot be maintained that there is a necessary connection between difficulty of diction and profundity of thought; this chapter has furnished examples enough of poems whose diction is hardly more baffling than that of a nursery-rhyme, but whose over-all meaning has as much claim to profundity as a poem full of verbal puzzles. If there is any measurable difference in the profundity of the thought evinced in the poems with which this chapter has been concerned, I should not like to be the one who set about taking the measurements; it is far from my intention to suggest that the fashioning of expressions which are difficult or even obscure at the first onset, is to be defended by reference to the weight of philosophy, or the like, which the poet has attached to his subject. I have tried in this book to pass no judgment on any difference there may be between a poet who would modify an attitude for the sake of a cadence, and the poet who would remake the English language if it stood in the way of articulating a vision of life; I have talked of poems simply from the point of view of the linguistic excitement they afford. But I hope it has become clear that this linguistic excitement is an excitement about encounters between relationships, and that these can be set up among any of the elements present in poems. If this is indeed true, poetic form may as readily depend upon a cadence as upon the intricacies of intellectualized relations, and it may do without the appeal of an immediately eloquent diction as well as it may do without the *cachet* of tackling the mysteries of life. All that can reasonably be demanded of a poem, difficult or not, is that it should prove to have brought language to the condition of poetic form; what the poet has done, or not done, should be referred to that end.

If finally I had to commit myself to a statement of what I understand by the phrase 'poetic form', I should say that it consists in the stasis achieved in the poem between all the interests it activates. I do not know how to think of 'form' except under the image of the 'swift, circular line' described before the mental eye when an impulsion to go in one direction (intellectually, emotionally, or pattern-wise) encounters another impulsion that deflects it. Why this should excite and satisfy us I do not know, unless it is that poems give what life does not: that all the impulsions allowed into the poem have sufficient relevance to one another to exercise a reciprocal control and to determine the status of one in terms of its function towards another. I have borrowed my image of the 'swift, circular line' from Wallace Stevens's *Earthy Anecdote*, with which the volume of his *Collected Poems*, so much concerned with exploring the nature of poetry, begins, and with which this book—whose medium does not share the privileges of poetry—may fittingly end:

> Every time the bucks went clattering
> Over Oklahoma
> A firecat bristled in the way.
>
> Wherever they went,
> They went clattering,
> Until they swerved
> In a swift, circular line
> To the right,
> Because of the firecat.
>
> Or until they swerved
> In a swift, circular line
> To the left,
> Because of the firecat.
>
> The bucks clattered.
> The firecat went leaping,
> To the right, to the left,
> And
> Bristled in the way.
>
> Later, the firecat closed his bright eyes
> And slept.

Index

INDEX

Fries, C. C., 159–60, 161n, 172
Frye, N., 2n

Ghiselin, B. (ed.), 51n, 58n
Goethe, J. W. von, *Wanderers Nachtlied*, 21–2
Gombrich, E. H., 103, 152
Goodman, P., 13
Gray, T., *Elegy*, 149, 149n
Groom, B., 28–9
Grosser, M., Scenario for *Four Saints*, 211, 211n

Hatzfeld, H. A., 1
Henle, P. (ed.), 20n
    (contributor), 52, 56
Hill, G. B. (ed.), 149n
Hobbes, T., 26
Holloway, J., 21
Homer: Arnold on, 15, 32; Hobbes on, 26; Pope's *Iliad*, 3–4, 17
Hoop, J. H. van der, 174
Hopkins, G. M., 214
    Blessed Virgin, 50
    Deutschland, 210
Horizon text (Thomas), 202, 202n, 210
Hospers, J., 106
Housman, A. E., [164]
Hunt, J. H. Leigh, 7–8, 8n

James, D. G., 156n
Johnson, Dr, 49n, 149
Joseph, Miriam, Sr, 127n, 128n, 131
Joyce, J., 197, 202, 212
    Finnegan's Wake, 212

Keats, J., [96], [116], 214–15, 217–18
    Bright star . . ., 207–8
    To Autumn, 116, 156n
    To a Nightingale, 47–8
Kipling, R., *Recessional*, 35
Knight, D., 3, 162n
Knights, L. C. and Cottle, B. (ed.), 156n

Langer, S. K., 156n, 172–3, 179
Lavater, *Aphorisms*, 204–5
Lever, J. W., 103n
London bridge is falling down, 203n
Lord's Prayer, 22

Magnolia, Philomel, 163–6
McFarlane, J., 30n

Mallarmé, S., *Le vierge, le vivace . . .*, **104**
Marston, J., 101
Marvell, A.,
    Coy Mistress, 205–6, 207
    Gallery, 87, 92–6
    Mourning, 157–8
Massinger, P., 20–1
Maud, R. N., 143n, 191, 194–5
Milton, J., 125, 126, 176, 202n
    Paradise Lost, 22–4, 102
    Samson Agonistes, 17, 33–4, 36, 37, 134n
Miriam Joseph, Sr. *See* Joseph
Moore, M., *. . . All external marks . . .*, **121**
Munz, P., 149, 149n

'New Critics', 19, 19nn
New English Weekly text (Eliot), 202, 202n
Newman, F. W., 15, 32

Olson, E., 195, 197n
Oxford English Dictionary, 26–7, 159

Pascal, B., *Pensées*, 37
Peacham, H., 128
Pope, A., 9, 12n, 13
    Dunciad, 45
    Epilogue to Satires, 41
    Iliad, 3–4, 17
    Pastorals, 11–12, 13, 125
    Rape of the Lock, 7–9
Pound, E., 57

Raine, K., *Water*, 32–3
Ramsey, I. T., 186
Reed, H., *Lessons of the War*, 37–8
Richards, I. A., ix, 49n, 50n, 142, 149
Richardson, J., 103
Rowley, B. A., 50n

Sartre, J.-P., 174
Sayce, R. A., 1
Schlauch, M., 20n, 22n
Shakespeare, W., [73], [84], [97], [102], [108], [143], [146], 13, 20–1, 29, 63, 66, 127–8
    Antony and Cleopatra, 51, 64–6, 101, 102
    Hamlet, 220
    Henry V, 5
    John, 49
    Lear, 48, 49, 177–8, 179, 184
    Love's Labour's Lost, 6

224